SECTIO

THE TRIAL LAWYER

What It Takes To Win

■

David Berg

AMERICAN BAR ASSOCIATION
Defending Liberty
Pursuing Justice

Cover design by ABA Publishing

Library of Congress Cataloging-in-Publication Data

Berg, David, 1942–
    The trial lawyer : what it takes to win / by David Berg.—2nd ed.
       p.   cm.
    Includes bibliographical references and index.
    ISBN–13: 978-1-59031-589-7 (paperback)
    ISBN–10: 1-59031-589-8 (paperback)
    ISBN–10: 1-59031-232-5 (hard cover)
    1. Trial practice—United States. 2. Lawyers—United States. I. Title.

    KF8915.B448 2006
    347.75'75—dc22

                                                        2006019741

Discounts are available for books ordered in bulk. Special consideration is given to state bars, CLE programs, and other bar-related organizations. Inquire at Book Publishing, ABA Publishing, American Bar Association, 321 North Clark Street, Chicago, Illinois 60610.

www.ababooks.org

For Kathryn, Caitlin, Geoff, and Gabe

Contents

Foreword

by *Morris Dees*

In 1981 I introduced David Berg to the Texas Knights of the Ku Klux Klan. Neither would ever be the same.

Refugees from the Vietnam War had been moving to the shrimping town of Seabrook on the Texas Gulf Coast. The locals who had fished those waters for decades were not pleased at the prospect of added competition for scarce shrimp. Eventually, one of those locals turned to the Grand Dragon of the Texas Knights of the Ku Klux Klan for help. Always happy to accommodate, the Klan cruised Galveston Bay, burning some of the Vietnamese boats and threatening the owners of other boats. The paramilitary wing of that particular chapter of the Klan, known as the Texas Emergency Reserve, did its part by training about 60 of the local fishermen in "self-defense" at the group's camp in the swampy flatlands northwest of Galveston Bay.

My organization, the Southern Poverty Law Center, decided to get involved as part of our Klanwatch Project to help these hardworking Vietnamese Americans who had every right to fish in the waters off Seabrook. We also hoped to put this dangerous Klan group out of business.

I asked David to be my co-counsel in what would become an historic case. Already one of the best criminal defense attorneys in Texas, David, I knew, was no stranger to cases with the potential for real danger and violence. Even so, when he agreed to help me sue the Klan, he was really stepping out of the box.

On the morning after we filed our complaint, David discovered a Klan calling card taped to his office door. The business-size card with a fiery cross symbol read that this friendly "social visit" could easily be followed up with a "business call." Two nights later, he found a similar greeting waiting for him at home. On the first day of the deposition of the Grand Dragon himself—who attended in his white robe and carried a concealed revolver—David was followed home by a red and white pickup truck. Fortunately, nothing happened, but several weeks earlier, a person seated in that same truck had pulled a gun on the Vietnamese owner of a seafood café in Seabrook. David reacted to these threats with his characteristic humor, joking that the Klan was facing its own worst nightmare in the case: an Alabama Bubba, a Jewish lawyer, and a black judge.

David proved to be an invaluable addition to the trial team, brain-storming on how to best tell the fishermen's story, putting on a ton of good evidence, and working tirelessly to overcome local resistance to our cause. With his help, we won an injunction barring the Klan from committing acts of violence and intimidation against the Vietnamese fishermen. A second injunction followed. It effectively shut down the Texas Emergency Reserve and its paramilitary activities.

Along the way, David and I became close personal and professional friends. I think of him now as a people's trial lawyer in the Clarence Dar-row tradition. David practices the kind of law young people dream about when they go to law school. He has tried almost every type of criminal and civil case, from murder to patent infringement. He has an ability to per-suade juries that is the equal of any practitioner I know. He is deeply respected by opposing counsel because he isn't afraid to go to trial, whether in a civil or criminal matter. Juries trust him because he empowers them to do justice. Clients retain him because he knows how to win.

In 1970, less than two years after opening his law office, David won a case in the United States Supreme Court, reversing his client's conviction for taking part in an antiwar demonstration, and establishing "guerilla the-ater" as a recognized form of protest. In 1978, using the battered wife defense for the first time in Texas, he won an acquittal for a woman accused of murdering her husband and transporting his dismembered body across the country in the trunk of a car.

I always urged David to combine civil work with his criminal practice. In his first personal injury case in 1991 he won a record $12.5 million verdict for the survivors of a young woman killed in a collision with a Missouri-Pacific train. That same year, he won a unanimous verdict for Robert Sakowitz, Houston's "merchant prince," who had been accused by family members of fraud and mismanagement of his father's estate. Later that decade, he won a verdict in a fraud case for Robert Bass's investment group, Acadia Ltd. Partners, worth $52 million.

In 1994, he negotiated a $4.25 million settlement for the survivors and estate of a young mother, a Mexican national, who came to El Paso to give birth to her second child. In this astonishing case, the young mother was shot and killed in a hotel room in front of her husband and first child by an employee of E-Systems, Inc., a CIA-funded defense contractor. The employee, who was staying in an adjacent room, had decided to test-fire his semiautomatic weapon by pointing it at an internal wall and pulling the trigger. In 2000, he obtained a $425 million settlement from Marriott Corporation for thousands of investors who alleged that they had been defrauded when they invested in several limited partnerships.

Notwithstanding these noteworthy settlements, David is no settlement lawyer. Big-firm attorneys could learn a lot from David in this area. He doesn't run up fees during discovery, only to settle before trial because the alternative is "too risky." He doesn't just rubber-stamp management decisions like most boards of directors. He has a conscience, he has backbone, and he is perfectly willing to hold the bad guy's feet to the fire.

Nor is David afraid to subordinate personal advancement to "doing the right thing," which just happens to be one of his favorite trial themes. Case in point: When I first met him in 1976, David was a member of Jimmy Carter's Justice Department transition team. I was still serving as national finance director of Carter's presidential campaign. Among other things, David drafted a presidential pardon for Vietnam War draft resistors. As reported at the time on the front page of the *Washington Post,* David was a leading candidate for White House counsel. In Plains, however, he argued that service members who received less-than-honorable (but not dishonorable) discharges should get an upgrade. Otherwise, these men—poor and disenfranchised—would be ineligible for GI benefits and would start to fill the nation's jails. A falling-out with Carter ensued. At the end of the storm, David didn't get the counsel job, but he did remain true to himself and his convictions.

Texas Monthly puts him in the same league as Joe Jamail and Racehorse Haynes, and properly so. *The National Law Journal* has named David in its annual list of the nation's top ten civil trial lawyers. *Best Lawyers in America,* 2003–2004 Edition, recognizes him in three trial specialties: business litigation, personal injury and civil litigation, and criminal defense. He is driven by a sense of justice, a desire to win contests that he believes in, and a genuine passion for assisting clients who are powerless.

I also know David to be a great family man. He is committed to his wife, Kathryn, and their daughter, Caitlin, and to his two sons, Geoff and Gabe, both of whom are trial lawyers. Geoff has his own firm; Gabe practices with the old man.

I have read many "how to" books over the years. Just one or two good ideas usually make the purchase price worthwhile. *The Trial Lawyer* meets that standard on virtually every page, whether David is discussing how to uncover deadly evidence on cross-examination or the importance of investigating each case personally. His confident and seasoned voice comes through loud and clear. He is instructive, to the point, funny—even poignant.

Like other successful trial lawyers before him, David, I believe, is at a point in his life where he is starting to think about leaving more behind than just a winning record and a large bank account. With this book, he has achieved that goal by making a lasting contribution to the craft he practices with passion and love.

Morris Dees
Montgomery, Alabama

June, 2003

Acknowledgments

While I have written dozens of articles over the years, nothing in that experience prepared me for the commitment required to write a book. It has taken me a little over two years and thousands of hours to complete it. Each chapter was subjected to rigorous editing, and, without counting, at least 20 to 30 drafts each.

For editing help, I owe several people my deepest thanks, but especially my wife, Kathryn, once a trial lawyer, and now a full-time mother. Her honest opinions and graceful rewrites have added another dimension to this book. I was dazzled by her intellect when I first met her, and nothing of that has diminished as the years have rolled by. She and my daughter, Caitlin, have made extraordinary sacrifices these past two years, and I say thank you to both of them from the bottom of my heart.

Chris Lutz, the lead editor, has been, as my friend Mike Tigar puts it, the reader's advocate—insisting that I never telegraph a point, that I always explain clearly what I mean. A practicing lawyer with Steptoe, Johnson, and twice editor-in-chief of *Litigation Magazine,* Chris spent long hours doing the line edits on what I thought (mistakenly) were polished drafts.

Jeff Knight, a former Cravath associate, and now legal research professor at Hofstra, has offered insight into the minds of young trial lawyers, and what they need to know that their practices won't teach them. I am especially grateful for his suggestion to reorganize the first chapter ("I would never read anything that long") into three.

My friend and neighbor Le Melcher, a former trial lawyer, read each chapter as it came off my printer. His enthusiasm for the project meant as much as his considerable skills as a grammarian and editor.

Thanks also to my mother-in-law, Jenny Page. She read the earliest drafts, offering her thoughts and unwavering encouragement.

I frequently discussed ideas about the psychology and strategy of jury selection and argument with Dr. Bob Gordon and Robert Hirschhorn, both of them forensics experts whose advice I value greatly. Pam Radford, a graphics expert who works frequently with our firm, spent time discussing her discipline with me before I wrote a word about it.

Jim Quinn, who appears frequently in this book, is head of litigation at Weil Gotshal & Manges. A trusted friend and brilliant trial lawyer, he frequently helped me translate things we do instinctively in the courtroom to advice on the written page.

The final weeks of publishing a book, like the final moments of a trial, are among the most critical. The ABA's Executive Editor, Tim Brandhorst, shepherded *The Trial Lawyer* from final draft through galley proofs to finished product, not an easy task. Denise Eichhorn, Director of Marketing, earned her pay in many ways, too, but especially when she suggested the subtitle of the book: *What It Takes to Win.* Both are consummate professionals, and the ABA is lucky to have them on board.

My partners—Joel Androphy, the author of a multivolume work on white-collar crime, and my son Gabe—have picked up the slack I've created in our practice, and for that I am deeply grateful. Gabe also helped with this book, providing wise counsel and clear edits. I also want to compliment my other trial-lawyer son, Geoff, for having the foresight to leave our firm to form his own before I caused everyone's workload to double. One of the joys of my life is watching my two sons in court, possessed of skills well beyond my own at the same age.

I also want to thank my mentor and close friend, Richard "Racehorse" Haynes, one of the great trial lawyers of this or any other generation. No one in the law has had a greater influence on me than Richard. He taught me when he was unaware that was what he was doing—and not just about trying cases, but how to live, and how to treat others. Much of what is written on these pages I learned from him. What times we have had together— fit topic for yet another book.

Finally, I would be remiss if I didn't mention my friends at the Avalon Drug Store, who left me alone for hours on end to write, stoking the fires with endless rounds of coffee. To Sarah, Cassie, Brenda, Deborah, Lisa, Velma, Elvira, and Ronny, I say, thanks.

Introduction

Over the past 35 years, I have tried a wide variety of cases, everywhere from the austere courtrooms of South Texas to the imposing civil courthouse in New York City. In the 1960s, I defended young people arrested for flag-burning and for marijuana possession. During the 1970s, I successfully defended a woman who had killed her husband and dismembered his body with a chainsaw, employing the first battered-wife defense in Texas. In the 1980s, I tried white-collar cases, and once, with Morris Dees of the Southern Poverty Law Center, helped shut down the Ku Klux Klan's paramilitary training camps in Texas.

In the 1990s, my practice grew to include a wide range of civil cases, beginning with a wrongful-death verdict against a railroad line for killing a motorist at a train crossing. I was also retained as trial counsel by large corporations defending and prosecuting bet-the-ranch litigation. By the end of the decade, I did little else.

In those commercial cases, I worked frequently with lawyers from major firms. I witnessed firsthand what I instinctively knew to be true: that lawyers on both sides of the bar work very hard, often at great personal sacrifice, to give their clients their best. I also verified something else I believed to be true: that many litigators would love to try more cases, but can't. Trapped in a culture of settlement, they are prevented from fully practicing their craft. For them, discovery has become an economic model, and jury trials, a gamble to be avoided at all costs.

That is a shame. There should be more to a litigator's life than just taking depositions and arguing motions. Much of it should be spent in trial, and not just for professional development or personal satisfaction. Word gets out fairly quickly on lawyers who won't try cases. Their clients inevitably pay more and get less.

That is why I wrote this book. I want to motivate all trial lawyers, especially younger ones, to become more willing and able to try cases. While *The Trial Lawyer* teaches you how to improve your trial skills, it is meant to be more than just a "how-to" manual. I have attempted to pass on what I have learned about winning, whether by a decisive verdict or an excellent settlement. I also wrote this book out of the fear that the great war stories of the next generation of trial lawyers will begin, "And then, I looked that mediator in the eyes and I said. . . . "

The examples in the book, sometimes blurred for confidentiality, come from real trials, focus groups, summary jury trials, depositions, and a trial lawyer's memories. I have used a limited number of cases (and themes) to illustrate a wide variety of points, so that the reader is spared having to learn new facts in each chapter.

David Berg
E.H., New York

2003

The Constants of Persuasion

1

I. THE IMPORTANCE OF PERSUASION

The Atlantic is calm today. The beach, rearranged by a tropical storm, is incredibly wide and white. Before I cast, I use pliers to clamp down the barbs on my lure. At first, I thought that would make it easier on the fish, but it didn't. It just forced me to become a better fisherman.

So it is with my practice. Early on, I cross-examined everyone like they were ax murderers, including schoolteachers and old ladies: "Exactly what do you mean, you were tending your roses? And quit fiddling with your oxygen tank." Arguing much of the time at the threshold of pain, I feel certain many jurors concluded that I meant to do them physical harm.

Now, I clamp down the barbs during trial. The reason is simple. Jurors don't like constant confrontation. They don't like it in their private lives and they tire of it quickly in the courtroom. Don't misunderstand: The object of the exercise is still a very large, very dead fish. You still have to dominate the courtroom. You still have to crush your opponents. You can't prevail with tender sensibilities. But better to do it *sotto voce* than bellowing, better by *persuasion* than bludgeoning. That's the way to win a trial.

II. EVERY TRIAL LAWYER'S GOAL

On the day that I was sworn into the federal bar, John R. Brown, the great chief judge of the 5th circuit, said to our group, "You worry about winning. Let us worry about justice." No comment could have captured our role better.

Trial lawyers have a singular goal: to persuade juries. Once you learn to win jury trials, you can win any kind of trial at all—judge, jury, arbitration—whatever the forum might be. Of course, "winning" includes great settlements, especially in an age of alternative dispute resolution. But you can't get great settlements without the credible threat that you will go to trial.

A. The Constants of Persuasion

The techniques trial lawyers use to persuade jurors are no mystery. They can be reduced to a handful of rules, the collected wisdom of generations of lawyers, filtered through the prism of modern forensic science. Because they are the same no matter the type of case, I call them the constants of persuasion. Master them and you will have all the tools you need to persuade any jury in any case.

1. Think *inside* the box.

Trial lawyers should do virtually everything with persuading jurors in mind—from the initial meeting with the client to the final word of closing argument. Long before you empanel a jury, think *inside the box*, and of how to persuade the people who may one day be seated there.

As you develop your case, continuously ask yourself how you will use each significant piece of evidence and testimony to win the jurors over. Will this document make sense? Will this picture move them? Am I doing all I can to break down the barriers between the jurors and my clients? It just stands to reason: Even if the case is never tried, building a persuasive case greatly enhances your chances of getting an excellent result.

2. Tell a compelling story.

We all love a good story, and jurors are no exception. To hold their attention, you must present your case in the form of a story. Organize your facts as if they were a work of fiction. Put together a narrative that builds to a climax and features clearly defined characters. Construct your story around an overarching moral or theme. For inspiration, think about the great themes in literature—good v. evil, justice v. injustice, pride v. humility, greed v. generosity. They have held up for centuries because they tap into our common human experience.

The right theme also makes the legal issues more accessible. For example, fraud is a concept far removed from the daily lives of jurors. However, at the heart of every fraud case is a betrayal of trust. That is a concept everyone can understand and identify with, because we have all experienced it.

3. Humanize clients and key witnesses.

In every case, there are barriers that separate the jury from your client and key witnesses. Money, education, job status, and social standing are common ones. But it doesn't matter if you represent an injured worker or the largest corporation in America: You must tear down those barriers and reveal the humanity common to both sides.

Humanizing your clients and key witnesses turns litigants into real people. But they won't be real to jurors unless they are real to you first. In a single dinner, you can learn the kind of personal things that jurors identify with, such as frustration with a boss, or admire, like the scholarship that got your client through college. Those few hours away from the office talking about something other than the case can transform your relationship. You can't fake the comfort level that results. The jury will pick up on your good feelings toward your client and key witnesses, and will follow your lead. On the other hand, if you don't like your client or believe in her cause, the jury will sense it and your case will suffer. Singly, a juror may or may not be perceptive. Collectively, jurors pick up on everything.

4. Warm up the courtroom.

Don't forget to be human yourself. Transform the sterility of the courtroom with warmth, sincerity, and humor. Of course, not all trial lawyers are blessed with a great personality or the ability to easily connect with people. Those lawyers can compensate by being more knowledgeable about the case than anyone else in the courtroom. Jurors respect lawyers who have done their homework.

5. Earn the jurors' trust; trust the jury.

Jurors don't distinguish between lawyers and their clients. For that reason, you can't produce a good result for your client unless the jury trusts you. To earn that trust, you have to be candid about your case from the beginning—the lawyer jurors depend on to tell the whole story and set the record straight. If you inadvertently make a misstatement, as we all do during trial, admit the mistake, apologize if it's serious, clear it up, and move on. If jurors believe that you have consciously misled them about a single significant fact, their trust will be broken completely.

As important as it is for the jurors to trust you, it is equally important for you to trust them. Jurors can sense when you don't. Without being obsequious, jurors have to know that you believe they will understand your case and do the right thing in reaching their verdict. If you really don't believe that, they will know, and your client will pay a heavy price.

6. Set the agenda.

If you want a decisive verdict, jurors' hearts have to race when you talk about your case. By the time you sit down from opening, you want to leave jurors with an impression so vivid they won't forget it, and your opponent so overwhelmed he can't dislodge it. That sets the agenda for the entire trial.

7. Prove that standards have been violated or upheld.

It is an unwritten law of the governed and the enduring credo of juries: Everyone must play by the rules. A group of strangers can reach agreement on a verdict because we all react similarly to proof that standards have been violated or upheld. That means you need to educate the jurors on the standard of conduct that applies to your case, and then prove to them that your client lived up to it or that the other side violated it. Nothing is more important in motivating jurors.

8. Don't run from your weaknesses.

Your worst facts are generally your opponent's greatest strength—especially if you run from them. Whenever possible, bring them up first. Pull the teeth of your adversary's arguments and cross. If you admit, embrace, and explain your bad facts, you reduce their impact. If you can't go first, don't be defensive about them. Be ready with a powerful and direct response.

Ignoring bad facts is never an option. Moreover, openly discussing your weaknesses sends a signal of strength to the jury. If you are willing to admit your client's mistakes, jurors assume your case must be strong.

9. Undermine adversaries with impeachment and admissions.

Use impeachment and admissions to put the lie to your adversary's case. If you can capitalize on an opponent's evasion and deceit, the jury will conclude quickly that he can't be trusted. Impeachment alone isn't enough. You must show that the false testimony means something important to the case. Put it in context; demonstrate its consequences.

10. Make the jury mad (at the other side).

This is the unspoken constant of jury trials. Jurors give favorable verdicts to people they like, but they return great verdicts when they get mad at the other side.

The best way to arouse the jury will vary from case to case. If your opponent has been dishonest with them, use that. If a corporation has put profits ahead of safety or damaged the environment, drive the point home. When even a badly injured plaintiff has made an outrageous demand, don't flinch from telling the jurors how greedy that is. Examine the facts of each case for conduct that is deliberate and outrageous. When you find it, build it into your narrative and remind the jury of it periodically, but especially during closing. Whether you represent the plaintiff or defendant, inflame their passions and send them out mad. Inspire them to return a decisive verdict that reflects their indignation.

Finally, don't underestimate the power of your opponents to alienate the jury totally on their own. Jurors take dishonesty and deceit personally, turning instantly on lawyers and witnesses they perceive are misleading them. When something like that happens, don't pile on, or you'll risk creating sympathy. Stay patient and calm. Let the other side destroy itself.

B. Conclusion

Persuading jurors is the overarching goal of every trial. The constants of persuasion tell you how. For that reason, they are a subtext of every chapter in this book, whether they are identified by name or not.

No matter your level of skill, the constants will make you better. Use them to give unity and purpose to your pretrial preparations. Be guided by them at every stage of trial. That you are focused with near single-mindedness on persuading the jury will not be lost on your adversaries. Being "trial-ready" not only leads to decisive verdicts, it scares your opponents into great settlements.

Preparing to Win 2

I. THE IMPORTANCE OF PRETRIAL PREPARATION

For a moment, forget that you hate discovery. Everyone (normal) does. For defense lawyers in particular, the pretrial period is trial law's own sausage factory, a time to make something appealing of the mess they've inherited.

Instead of the tedium, remind yourself of discovery's ultimate value. Pretrial preparation doesn't exist in a vacuum. What you accomplish during the pretrial period determines the strength of your case and, if it gets that far, influences your performance at trial. The admissions you get in the first deposition can create a closing argument, the documents you discover, the four corners of direct and cross. The possibilities are almost endless.

The trial lawyer's maxim is true: Ninety percent of winning is preparation. The days are gone when a surprise witness dramatically waltzes into the courtroom to save the day for one side or the other. Long before trial begins, you should be able to discover the answers to the ultimate questions of representation: How good is my case? How strong is my opponent's? Should I try the case or settle it?

Regrettably for some lawyers, all the practice will ever be is discovery. For others willing to go to trial, it is an opportunity to build a solid case and to develop the skills that separate them from their peers. Most important, when you are truly prepared, the courtroom is no lawyer's special province, regardless of talent. If your case is triable, and you are ready, there is no trial lawyer you can't beat.

II. THE GOALS OF THE PRETRIAL PERIOD

The ultimate goal of pretrial preparation should be to win the case, not to pay the light bill. Nevertheless, some firms turn discovery into a profit center that builds fees but sacrifices common sense—and often, the ability to develop a strong case. Don't get me wrong: I understand the practice of law has to be profitable. In my experience, however, most of the great cases go to lawyers with a reputation for winning—not for abusive discovery tactics.

Admittedly, in some cases lawyers can grind down an underfunded opponent with overlong depositions and endless motions—but that is rare. Most often, those tactics backfire. Lawyers who can't afford to fight get mad and fight anyway, often with a passion that can generate great verdicts. Judges hate abusive tactics, too, evening the score not so much with sanctions, but with adverse decisions on critical motions and jury instructions that could have gone either way.

To the extent that you can, avoid going down that road. Conduct sharply focused discovery. Make developing the constants your goal. Mold that mountain of evidence into a compelling story. Get admissions. Impeach witnesses. Bear in mind each step of the way: The more persuasive your case, the more likely you are to get an excellent result—whether you try it or not.

III. INFORMAL DISCOVERY

A. Get to Know the Clients

There are some well-known problems with representing a friend or getting too close to a client. Most important, your judgment about the case can be clouded by personal considerations. At trial, you may play things too close to the vest, when risk taking may be necessary.

Nevertheless, getting to know the clients—and their key witnesses—is the place to start in every case. It is the most effective way to build the trust and cooperation critical to the relationship between a lawyer and client. Anyone who has ever represented a difficult client, that is, anyone who has practiced law, knows how important that is. You don't want a client doubting your judgment about producing documents, how to testify, or being in attendance every day of trial. You want them to follow your advice because they trust you to tell them the right thing.

Most important, juries don't give verdicts to people and companies they don't like. If you don't like your client, the jury won't, either.

1. The jury will pick up on your relationship.

In his work, *The Betrayed Profession*, former Xerox board chair Sol Linowitz, who was counsel to the company at its infancy, writes that "personal relations not only make legal services more pleasant but also more effective." He points to the relationship between Pennzoil's CEO, Hugh Liedtke, and its lead trial lawyer, the gifted plaintiff's lawyer Joe Jamail, as one of the main reasons the company won an $11.1-billion verdict in its case against Texaco. That Jamail was fighting for someone he cared about—instead of just a fee—was by all accounts apparent to everyone in the courtroom. The chemistry and comfortable banter between Liedtke and Jamail made Liedtke's testimony about Texaco's interference in Pennzoil's attempt to purchase Getty Oil that much easier to believe.

The same was not true on the other side of the case. As Linowitz points out, Texaco's lead counsel, Dick Miller, also a great trial lawyer, had never represented the company before. He had difficulty getting its witnesses to spend time with him prior to testifying. Several were arrogant—awful—on the stand. Miller apparently had to fight a rear guard action against in-house counsel, who wanted to run the show, violating the trial lawyer's "one riot, one ranger" rule—a shorthand way of saying that the lead lawyer must be in charge, in and out of the courtroom.

There has been a great deal of criticism of this case. Most of it says that Texaco got "home-towned." There is some truth to that. But Linowitz is also right: Pennzoil's runaway verdict was a tribute to the relationships on both sides of the aisle.

If your chemistry with the client is as good as Jamail's, your chances of winning will only be enhanced. The warm bond between the two of you and the easy exchange of questions and answers during direct send a powerful message to the jury.

On the other hand, bad blood follows you into the courtroom. Jurors sense even the slightest tension between lawyer and client. With corporate clients especially, an unpleasant relationship is a real danger. Some executives are hostile to trial lawyers as a matter of principle. They believe we produce nothing. When we show up to represent the company, they think, "There goes all the money for R&D down the drain." Under those circumstances, establishing a good relationship takes on even more urgency.

2. You'll learn something useful for trial.

From the start, experienced trial lawyers size up Exhibit A, the client. They ask themselves, "What will the jury think?" "How can I help him become a believable witness?" And, "Uh-oh. Is that a pinkie ring?"

Sizing up the client means taking a detailed history of his life—not just his involvement in the case. The same goes for key witnesses. Get to know them in their own element, away from your firm. Spend time with them at their office or plant. Go to dinner at their homes. Meet their spouses and children. Take them to a ball game. Pick up the phone just to stay in touch. Do anything but relegate them to a case number and file. Invariably, you will learn something that proves valuable at trial.

The virtue of knowing more about a client than just his legal problems was impressed on me one day in 1969, a year into my practice—and I never forgot it. I listened from the back bench of a Harris County courtroom as

Richard "Racehorse" Haynes, the famed Houston criminal lawyer, conducted voir dire in an attempted murder case. He represented the heir to a Texas cattle empire accused of beating a neighbor who had disputed the property line separating their ranches, and—I'm serious—said ugly things about his client's momma.

A panelist said she knew the defendant from church. Without hesitation, Haynes pounced. "Would you then be incapable of fairness to the prosecution because you are aware of my client's involvement at Second Baptist Church, teaching Bible class, taking the church's scout troop to Mexico, that sort of thing?" The panelist responded, "Well, sir, that's not the only reason I couldn't be fair. I also know how well he treats his momma, and I cannot believe a man that kind could hurt another soul—not without a reason."

The trial was all but over. Haynes had disclosed the defendant's church life to a Bible Belt jury, and the panelist had gone one better. After a three-week trial, the jury acquitted him in one hour. To get that verdict, all Haynes had done was go to dinner at his client's home, where he spent a few moments discussing a photograph on the living room wall of the man and his scout troop.

Until I could no longer afford the luxury of languid afternoons at the courthouse, I followed Haynes to trial frequently during the early years of my practice. His sonorous voice captured the jury and my imagination. As time goes by, I become even more convinced that what he did that day—interjecting something personal he knew about his client, humanizing him when the chance presented itself—is essential to winning any kind of case.

True, times have changed and jurors are far more sophisticated today. However, the lesson of that exchange will never change, nor is it limited to humanizing clients. Successful trial lawyers are like heat-seeking missiles carrying payloads of information prejudicial to their opponent's case, constantly looking for the chance to unload their cargo, right up until the final moments of trial.

3. Corporations are people, too.

The financial scandals of the early 2000s at Enron, Arthur Andersen, Tyco, WorldCom, and other companies did not make the already difficult task of humanizing corporations any easier. If anything, they make it even more essential. In my experience, however, with a little extra effort and insight, you can humanize any business you represent.

The first step is to unearth the corporate culture—the ethics and practices, or lack of them, that govern the everyday life of the company. Frequently, what you learn will explain the transaction at the heart of your case. However, you won't find the answers reading company directives or policy manuals. Corporate culture is about relationships: How does the company treat its employees? Are they well paid? Do they have good benefits? What is the rate of turnover? Are the employees proud of the products or services they provide? How do employees feel about their bosses? How do their bosses feel about them? Does the customer really come first? What kinds of business deals do the executives cut? Are they win-win? Or is business to them a zero-sum game where someone wins and someone loses? What is the company's litigation history? Does it have trouble staying out of court? Once in litigation does the company generally settle or try the case? In either event, do they usually win or lose? Most important: What does the corporation give back to the community?

If you have represented the company previously, you'll probably know what the corporate culture is. But if you don't know what makes the company tick, you can get blindsided during depositions and trial. As with any client, it's in the company's best interest that you find out the bad facts as soon as possible. However, that information is sometimes hard to ferret out from corporate executives and other employees. Often, they stonewall their own lawyers, telling them only what they think they need to know to shield themselves from blame for the incident that caused the company to get sued, or caused it to bring suit. Candor is the first casualty of arrogance, and arrogance is endemic in many American businesses. If you have to cross-examine your own clients in your office to get the truth, then do it.

After getting a good feel for the corporate culture, the next step is to find out what is best about the men and women who work there, the same information you need to humanize individual clients. How long have they been married? How many children? What are their activities outside of work? Are they active in their churches and synagogues? Are they involved in charitable work? How does any of that affect their work? How long have they been with the company?

The answers to those questions will allow you to put human faces on corporate logos—the kind of evidence that creates a soft landing for the often ugly transaction that brought the corporation to court in the first place. If you are successful in imbuing the corporation with the most admirable characteristics of the people who work for it, you can follow it up with evidence of the company's charitable endeavors and high-minded principles. On the other hand, don't overdo it. There is no need to make saints of employees and executives. You don't need to hide the fact that your client is in business to make a profit. Jurors expect that. But if you are able to leaven the profit motive with principled decisions, moneymaking will not look like greed.

Consider this example from a friend of mine, a former general counsel to a large manufacturing company. At a board of directors meeting, one of the executives reported that the company could save millions on an impending purchase of equipment. The seller was having serious financial problems, and the purchase contract wasn't yet signed. The founder of the company asked, "Did you say we agreed to the price?" When the executive said yes, the founder replied, "Then that's the price we'll pay." Later, when the company was sued on a different matter, that story came into evidence. It's the quintessential example of letting a businessman's good character help inform the defense of a case.

Sometimes you won't be able to find any motivation in the corporation's decision making other than to make a buck. Stories that tend to humanize the corporation through the humanity of its executives and employees won't be there. That is a difficult problem, one that is best handled head-on. If you are honest with the jury, perhaps conceding, "This company is not particularly involved in anything but the business," they may very well be forgiving. However, in the best of all worlds, companies not only have to earn their money fairly but also give back to the community. They must be "good corporate citizens." If they aren't, then they run a good chance of getting hit hard. The best example: Texaco, in the Pennzoil case. Lawyers involved in that trial have said that Texaco failed to introduce one good thing the company had done, and it has done plenty.

I am not suggesting that you can't successfully represent a company whose culture and conduct are reprehensible. Those are among the clients who need your talents the most. Their cases present the greatest challenges. What I do suggest is that you work hard to find something positive the company has done. Work even harder to uncover the ugliest facts. It may not be your role to judge, but it is your role to make informed judgments about the possible outcome of the case.

4. Choose corporate representatives carefully.

Because corporations represent a lot of things average people don't like, including indifference toward the suffering they sometimes cause, picking the best corporate representative is crucial. The right person can help dispel that preconception, especially if she was the one most intimately involved in the transaction being litigated—not some nonessential executive. If she attends the trial faithfully, testifies well, and is likeable, the verdict will reflect it. During deliberations, jurors will consider the effect of their verdict on her (and other employees who may have testified) instead of just a faceless corporation with a $20-billion market cap. If, however, the corporate rep arrives in a fancy car, frequently slips out of the courtroom to make cellular calls, or is absent from trial for days on end, the verdict will reflect that, too.

Actually, getting to choose the person who will be in the courtroom with you is one of the advantages of commercial litigation. Just make certain that you, and not the executives or general counsel, make that choice. If you leave it to them, you may get someone they can do without for an extended period of time, which ought to tell you something right there.

There's no magic to selecting the right corporate rep. Ideally that will be the person with the greatest knowledge of the facts. (See p. 249, "The Order of Witnesses.") But if he is going to be a bad witness, bury him in the middle of your case, no matter how much he knows, and choose someone else to tell the story first. Default to the employee who is the next most knowledgeable, or if it takes two of them to tell the story, and they can be spared from work, designate both of them as corporate reps. Somewhere on the list of possibilities is just the right executive or employee, but failing that, select someone with what we call at my firm an "affidavit face," an open look that conveys honesty to compensate for knowing little about the case.

5. Globalization and the neighborhood trial lawyer.

Some very smart lawyers figured out years ago that the world was getting smaller for big businesses. Companies were opening offices and plants around the globe, and law firms followed them. Transactional lawyers aren't the only ones who should be mindful of this development. Parties and witnesses increasingly include recent émigrés, foreign (non-U.S.) corporations, and foreign nationals. Jurors, too, represent a wide mix of recently naturalized citizens. That makes representation and jury selection even more complex.

In 1996, in anticipation of a trial on behalf of Samsung, I traveled to Seoul, South Korea, to meet with my clients and the various witnesses who were going to testify. Dr. Bob Gordon, a forensic psychologist who has worked on many of my cases, came with me to help prepare them for their testimony.

Our goal was to make them feel comfortable about getting on the stand, and to tell their story well, even through an interpreter. We also wanted to find ways in which American jurors could identify with the witnesses and the lives they led in Korea.

However, the first day went badly. We were unable to communicate to the witnesses our ideas about their testimony—and it wasn't the interpreter's fault. It was the wide cultural gap between us. They made no progress toward becoming good witnesses. Even more puzzling, given how important the case was to the company, they didn't appear to try.

That evening, Dr. Gordon consulted with an American-trained Korean psychologist from the local university. Then he stayed up all night reading a book about Korean culture the psychologist brought him. With a somewhat better understanding of Korea and Koreans, Dr. Gordon began our next meeting by explaining the ways Samsung would benefit if its witnesses did well on the stand—an important point in a culture that values institutions over individuals. As we both learned from the employees, when profits fell, it was terrible for the corporation, but not for the employees or executives. Because they had already benefited so much during the company's good years, they felt they had no right to complain in the lean ones.

We also got to the bottom of another issue. From some of their answers the day before, we knew the men were skeptical of American justice, and not just because they would be foreigners in our courts. They couldn't believe O. J. Simpson had been acquitted. Chairman Kim, the highest-ranking Samsung official who would testify at our trial, told us that Koreans were shocked by the verdict—and not just because the evidence of Simpson's guilt was so overwhelming. He said that they could not understand how, if the state brought criminal charges, a jury of 12 ordinary citizens could possibly disagree. We assured the Koreans that many Americans were also shocked and disappointed, and that the verdict was an aberration. They had not heard that before: You could feel their relief.

Their attitudes were, literally, foreign to us. While a healthy skepticism and outright distrust of government and corporations is endemic to our culture—something of our national pastime—Koreans are just the opposite: far more submissive to the state. We emphasized that juries were part of the U.S. government, that they were at the heart of our American tradition, and therefore deserving of respect. Dr. Gordon also spoke of creating unity between the witnesses and the jury—a show of respect for their Buddhist beliefs.

That made sense to them, but it really took with Chairman Kim. When he testified, his humility in the jurors' presence gave him great credibility. He also showed a real ability to connect with them. When asked on cross if he received a million-dollar bonus the year before, he frowned and said, "I don't know. Samsung sent it to our joint account, and then it disappeared. I could call my wife." The jury roared. Then, mindful of our instruction to be very direct, he added, "The answer is 'yes.'" If counsel was trying to give the jury a reason to dislike him—his wealth—it didn't work. When it was over, the jurors told us that what they liked about Mr. Kim was his dignity. They were also struck by the comment about his wife, relishing the fact that people really aren't all that different, no matter where they are from.

My experience with Mr. Kim was an important lesson to me. For jurors to be able to identify with a witness from another culture, the witness must first be able to identify with the jurors, and to understand their role.

If your client can't afford a forensic psychologist or a trip abroad, there are plenty of other ways to learn about other cultures on your own. You'll probably do just as well researching the subject yourself, and knowing lawyers, you'll probably enjoy it. So get online or into the library. Some of my best memories from the early years of my practice include all-nighters in the office library, watching the sun come up and sipping coffee.

B. Investigate the Case Personally

If there is one striking difference between criminal and civil lawyers, it is the willingness of the former to investigate cases personally, and the inclination of the latter to rely on formal discovery. Like Blanche DuBois in *A Streetcar Named Desire*, civil lawyers often "rely on the kindness of strangers," that is, opposing counsel, for relevant information. They ignore the fact that some lawyers won't produce anything meaningful until you beat it out of them with a crowbar—and sometimes, not even then.

Generally—but not always—it is the defense that is the custodian of heavily guarded information. Often, they give up key documents grudgingly, late, or—in one instance that I found out about after the fact—never. (See p. 51, "Open your eyes.") Knowing that, plaintiffs' lawyers should start compiling evidence from whatever public sources are available even before filing suit. The same goes for defense lawyers who know a suit is coming.

If you are out there interviewing witnesses and gathering up all manner of documentary evidence, you can shut off some claims or defenses—getting a huge leg up on the opposition. If you just get out of your office and investigate the case yourself, the outcome can be a foregone conclusion before you file or receive the original complaint.

I concede that criminal lawyers have their own built-in stimulus to investigate cases themselves: With few exceptions, there are no statutory discovery procedures of any consequence in criminal law on either the state or federal level. Criminal lawyers have no choice but to conduct extensive investigations. Nevertheless, you can do a great deal of good in civil cases by quickly shooting the scene of a client's accident, by searching the public record on the Internet, or by exploring deeds in a district clerk's office—to say nothing of the gold mine you can find if an opposing witness has been deposed in another case. Often, all it takes is a single document, photograph, or statement to turn a case around.

1. Visit the site.

Every case includes at least one site you should visit, whether it is the scene of an accident or the boardroom where merger documents were signed. A site visit forces you to walk in your client's shoes—or those of an opponent. You will see things through trial eyes—painting pictures in your mind that will make the case more vivid to a jury. During my career, I have found myself in the hold of a tiny refueling vessel in the middle of the Texas Gulf Coast, deep in the bowels of a dangerous prison unit in central Texas, and 6,000 miles from home visiting Samsung's offices in Seoul. I always learned something valuable to tell a jury. Having experienced it myself, I could convey the overwhelming smell of diesel fuel, the dangers of overcrowded cells, and the pride employees took in manufacturing electronic products that help run the world.

When I first started practicing, we called lawyers who knew the layout of a site cold "fact lawyers." Armed with a tape measure and Polaroid camera, they would spend hours accumulating details that enabled them to lacerate eyewitnesses with their superior knowledge of the scene. That was the training I received, and that was what led me to the cab of a Missouri Pacific engine one summer morning in 1991, investigating a wrongful death case for the family of the victim of a train-car collision.

a. The *Missouri Pacific* case.

For those who have not had the experience, railroads try lawsuits with a kind of nineteenth-century robber-baron mentality. If one is struck by a train, one is pronounced not only dead, but also unerringly stupid, by company executives. All train-car collisions, they reason, are the motorist's fault. That is true even if the railroad has (1) illegally parked a row of train cars half a mile long on the set of tracks nearest an intersection, (2) blocking an approaching driver's view of an oncoming locomotive on the inside set of tracks, and the train crew's view of her, (3) all in violation of state law and the railroad's own regulations. That is exactly what happened in the case of Sharon Elaine Lemon, who died one night at an unlit, four-track crossing in Sweeney, a tiny African-American community 100 miles south of Houston. The only warning sign at the intersection was a passive crossbuck, one of those white, X-shaped signs with "Train Crossing" in black letters. There was no automatic gate or flashing light. It was frightening to drive across those tracks during the day and even worse at night.

The family hired me to represent them against the railroad. One of the first things I did was get an order allowing me to inspect the cab of a typical engine—with a row of train cars parked on the next set of tracks. Standing in the cab, I could tell immediately that the crew's line of sight was cut off by those cars, that it would have been impossible for them to see Mrs. Lemon until it was too late—and doubly impossible to see how fast she approached the intersection. That was important because, on the night of the collision, the brakeman told the railroad investigator that he had been on the *lead* engine at the time of the accident, and that he first saw Mrs. Lemon 50 feet back from the crossbuck, "movin' fast." When I confronted him at his deposition about the parked train cars blocking his view, he suddenly remembered he wasn't on the lead engine, but on the *third* engine, and that he first saw Mrs. Lemon right at the crossbuck, not 50 feet down the road. But he still knew how fast she was driving: "She was really movin.' She was bumpin' over the tracks." Needless to say, I pointed out that it would have been even more difficult to see Mrs. Lemon from the third engine. I also pointed out his sudden change of memory.

Now, sometimes a witness who's been caught lying during his deposition will spend a great deal of time figuring out how to get even with the lawyer who made him look bad. Apparently the brakeman thought of little else. At trial, for reasons best known to the brakeman, his comeback seemed to start with his attire. He was wearing a black cape and black shirt unbuttoned to mid-chest, exposing a gold medallion on the end of a chain. He didn't just enter the courtroom; he swooped into it. Nor did he just sit in the witness chair; he draped himself over it.

As one would expect, the brakeman's change of position from the first to the third engine had the jurors looking at him skeptically. But at the moment I started in on the physical impossibility of his having seen Mrs. Lemon from the third engine, he rose from the witness chair, shushed me with upraised palms, turned to the wide-eyed panel, and announced: "I have reshuffled my thinking." Now he remembered that he was actually on the *second* engine pulling on some overalls at the time of the accident and that he first saw Mrs. Lemon when she was already on the tracks. Of course, she was "really flyin'." I pointed out that he had now ridden on all three engines and wondered aloud if there was any possibility he was actually riding lookout on the cowcatcher, watching for oncoming cars. As he slithered down from the stand, even casual observers noticed that the jury, once polite, had grown surly. When the brakeman left the room, they glowered at the defense lawyer.

Some cases are more satisfying than others. During mediation in this one, a railroad lawyer told me no black family "would get any money from an Angleton jury," the county seat where the case was tried. However, just before closing arguments, he more than quadrupled his earlier settlement offer. I advised the family to turn it down, which they did, readily.

After closing arguments were finished, the all-white jury deliberated into the evening before recessing. Just after lunch the next day they brought in a verdict of $12.5 million, including $10 million in punitive damages, disabusing the railroad lawyer, one assumes, of his misunderstanding about black families and white juries in Angleton, Texas.

2. Interview third-party witnesses.

I've already suggested that you get to know your client and her key witnesses. A face-to-face meeting with third-party witnesses is equally important. It can make a friend of someone critical to the outcome of your case, not under your control, who might not have been so friendly otherwise. Often, taking the time to meet with these "strangers" to your case can lead you to other important witnesses. You can also learn very quickly without the other side present whether your case has serious weaknesses that need to be addressed. Or better yet, that your opponent's case has a fatal flaw. Most important, you can find out what the witness is going to say long before it must be said under oath.

a.   Get a statement.

Of course, once you talk to the witness about your case, you have to make certain the version of events you just heard doesn't change when the witness testifies. By getting an affidavit, or, failing that, a signed statement, you nail down the witness's story and, should the story change, you are armed to impeach her.

Coaxing a witness into talking to you at all can be difficult, but getting her to swear to the truth of what she has told you is almost an art form. Witnesses are suspicious of the use you will make of a statement, fearing some unknown consequence. The key to getting a statement is to give the witness a reason to trust you before you ask for her to sign one. That means spending time over a cup of coffee talking about anything except the case, until the time is right. When that time comes, explain the process of pretrial discovery, the progress of the case, and the importance of the affidavit or statement you want the witness to sign. If the sworn statement may help resolve the case, thereby eliminating the need for her to testify, say so. That tradeoff—her signature for the possibility of avoiding a deposition or courtroom testimony—may be all it takes to get her cooperation.

Be paranoid about drafting the affidavit or statement. Everything you do or say may be subject to discovery. Imagine the witness being asked questions like: Who wrote that statement? Are those your words or the lawyer's? Whose thoughts are those? Did you feel pressure to sign? What did the lawyer tell you about why you should make this affidavit?

Talk to the witness about what she is going to say, and the questions you need answered. Let her write the statement out longhand, or have a court reporter take it down as you ask questions—even if you are in your office. If your assistant types up the statement, allow the witness every opportunity to make edits. Of course, you want the witness's first draft to be as close to final as possible, because a draft is discoverable. However, producing a slightly different draft is infinitely preferable to your writing out the statement yourself. If you do it, you are inviting brutal cross.

Remember, when you produce the affidavit, opposing counsel will have plenty of time to pore over every word, so don't create any extra fodder for her cross. Make certain the statement is concise, to the point, and absolutely accurate. Those witness statements, like those summary judgment affidavits so prevalent in the East Coast practice, can come back to haunt the witness and damage the case.

Make certain that the witness's statement contains language that it was given freely and without promise of benefit. Make certain those words are absolutely true, and that you have a witness to that fact. If questions are ever raised about your conduct, that court reporter or a notary can become a witness to what actually happened.

Notwithstanding all these precautions, do what you have to do to take the affidavit or statement on the spot, before the mood to cooperate changes. Don't let distances stop you. If a witness lives far away, get on a plane. If that's not possible, pick up the phone and ask the witness to give a statement in the presence of a court reporter or a colleague from the distant city. As uncomfortable as it may seem, calling is better than ignoring a witness, or worse, leaving her to the tender mercies of the other side. My partner and I have often talked about the cases we have won sitting at our desks, talking to a witness on the phone.

If the witness wants to take the statement to a lawyer or advisor for review, agree without hesitation. However, get the witness to dial you into that process, so that there will be no misunderstandings and no allegations of overreaching on your part. You may also be able to blunt a lawyer's knee-jerk inclination to "protect" his client by saying, "No statement."

In some states, procedural rules require statements to be produced to opposing counsel. If your case is in one of those states, then you're probably better off simply discussing the relevant information with the witness, or taking copious notes, instead of having her sign something. Bring a non-lawyer with you. If the witness changes her tune at trial, that person can be a witness to what was said. And if you get the sense during the interview that the witness isn't going to stick to her story, then revert to plan A: Get a signed statement and produce it to the other side.

The opportunity to personally interview witnesses varies greatly, depending on the area of law involved. Personal injury cases are obviously a fertile area. They often involve third-party eyewitnesses, all of whom should be interviewed as soon as you get into the case, no matter which side you are on. Police reports about the accident, including what witnesses supposedly said, are often wrong.

Finally, don't send an investigator to take statements, not unless he is a professional you know and trust. Investigators are often incapable of getting the kind of statement you need, and frequently—at least with the witnesses I've cross-examined—pressure them into signing an affidavit that misstates what was said. For the best result, interview the witness yourself. Or send a trusted associate. Otherwise, you run the risk of needlessly undermining your case with a flawed statement.

b.   Interview ex-employees.

In commercial cases, the most common nonparty witnesses are ex-employees. They may be disgruntled, as they are always described when they give harmful testimony, but if they have details and documents in admissible form, they can also be deadly. Having said that, there may be problems in talking to them informally. Corporations frequently offer to provide representation for ex-employees to regain some control over them. In those instances, you will have to settle for a deposition alone. Talking to a former employee informally in the presence of a lawyer hired by the company you've sued is not a formula for a productive conversation.

If a signed confidentiality agreement prohibits the employee from discussing job-related matters, you can't talk to him informally, either. While that stops you from interviewing him, it doesn't stop you from getting his testimony. Courts have consistently held that prohibiting testimony by confidentiality agreements violates public policy. Notice the witness's deposition and ask your judge to be on standby by phone to rule once the confidentiality agreement is invoked. I've never had a judge refuse to set one aside.

The former employer may also claim that the witness is covered by the attorney-client privilege related to his work and that it applies to your area of inquiry. Getting around a claim of privilege is a bit more dicey than getting around a confidentiality agreement. The court will weigh numerous factors to determine whether the privilege existed and, if so, whether it was waived. In commercial cases be alert to assertions of the attorney-client privilege, because what a lawyer said or did is often at the heart of the lawsuit.

3.   Compile documentary evidence.

The key to a solid cross-examination, especially for young lawyers, is to obtain any prior statements a witness has made that are contrary to their position in your case. The best source is a statement made under oath in a deposition or trial, followed by a document(s) that the witness authored. After that, for sheer fun, nothing equals a witness's contradictory statement in a speech, book, or article. Often, witnesses won't remember what they've said, and can be derisive about their own opinions. In addition to prior inconsistent statements, there are deeds and diagrams of scenes that contain undeniable facts.

With that kind of ammunition, witnesses can't run from the truth. If they do, facts and statements in hand, you can impeach them, and their credibility is shot.

I started practicing law when the only computer in America filled an entire room at IBM, so you can imagine how extraordinary it is to me to be able to do online research. There are any number of Internet data banks with information about expert witnesses, including copies of their depositions and trial testimony. The Internet is also a hotbed of public records potentially relevant to almost any witness.

But the Internet is just a starting point. After you hit the 'net, hit the road. Get out of your office and scorch the earth for any relevant evidence. There is nothing like poring through records in a clerk's dusky offices for hitting pay dirt. Just read on.

a.   The battle over the Howard Hughes estate.

The following example from my hardworking friend Wayne Fisher illustrates how personal investigation by a lawyer defeated a bogus $100-million claim. During a single deposition, Fisher destroyed a challenge to the billion-dollar Howard Hughes estate with evidence he'd compiled by relentlessly combing through records in county clerks' offices in California. Even a computer search today would be unlikely to turn up the evidence he found. If you really want to untangle a complicated or fraudulent transaction, you can't do it sitting at your desk—and rarely by waiting around for the production of a smoking gun.

When Howard Hughes died in 1976, Fisher was retained to represent his estate against a parade of obviously phony wills. But there was a troubling exception: a will witnessed by two seemingly credible Californians, one a businessman whom we shall call Harold Burton, and the other a physician we shall call Dr. Norman Frost. The will was written on stationery from the Beverly Hills Hotel, where Hughes had lived. It had an air of legitimacy, in that it left almost all of Hughes's money to charity, but reserved 10 percent as a bequest to Acme Mining, a company founded by a now-deceased lawyer who had actually done some work for Hughes. The will was filed for probate by the lawyer's former secretary, who, coincidentally, had inherited the Acme Mining stock from her boss.

Just the name, Acme Mining, was enough to raise a red flag. But neither witness to the will had any obvious motivation to lie, unless, of course, he was getting a kickback from the secretary-cum-heir to Hughes's $100 million. In prior pleadings, each swore he had never met the other, or Hughes, before the night that Hughes allegedly signed the will. They both claimed that a lawyer-friend called them at home, without warning, asking them to come to the Beverly Hills Hotel, on a matter of great personal importance. When they arrived at the hotel, they said they were escorted into Hughes's bedroom, where they witnessed him signing the will on Beverly Hills Hotel stationery. Shockingly, the stationery and ink proved to be of proper vintage, and a handwriting expert testified that Hughes's handwriting was genuine. If Fisher was unable to defeat the claim, Hughes's relatives in Houston, where he had been born, would lose the hundred million dollars and, under the terms of the "will," control of all the other bequests. With Harold Burton's deposition approaching, Fisher got to work.

The first step was to strip Burton of his credibility, so Fisher started searching those county clerks' offices in California. He found numerous notes, deeds, and mortgages signed by both men, relating to a complex real estate transaction they'd entered into as joint venturers. He also found pleadings from a lawsuit filed years before against the two men, alleging they had committed a stock swindle. In a deposition from that case, Burton swore that he'd *never* had any financial dealings with Dr. Frost. In short, Fisher found out that the two men knew each other quite well, and had a long track record of shady dealings.

Fisher organized his documents into several large binders. On the spine of each, he had printed the volume and Burton's initials. At the point those volumes stopped, a three-volume series marked with Dr. Frost's initials began. On the day of Burton's deposition, Fisher wheeled the binders into the conference room on a library cart, rolling it to an auspicious stop a foot away from the witness. The cameras caught Burton glancing nervously toward the cart.

Surrounded by a team of probate lawyers from around the country, some representing other beneficiaries under other suspicious wills, Fisher began by asking a series of precise personal questions: You are Harold Dennis Burton? Your house is located at 3576 Stony Brook Road here in Los Angeles? You were born at Wichita Memorial Hospital in 1931? I am not clear what year you graduated from Driscoll High School. Do you mind telling me? You are a 1953 graduate of UCLA with a major in business? Your social security number is 467-60-8391? It was issued in the State of Kansas in 1943?

You were married 36 years ago on November 5, 1953? You and your wife separated for 90 days beginning September 1964? She alleged in her petition . . . well, let's not get into that. You moved into your brother's house in the San Fernando Valley during that entire period? You have three children, ages 23, 27, and 34? Your youngest son works at HiTech Industries as a program manager? You own 22 percent of the outstanding shares of that company? Your two daughters are married, and neither works outside the house?

That went on for an hour. Occasionally, Fisher would ceremoniously pull down another volume (one of which was blank) and stare at it a few minutes before launching into some other area of the witness's life. Burton was already worried, and Fisher had done nothing but cover biographical information.

Fisher continued. "Mr. Burton, do you understand the nature of an oath?" The witness responded that indeed he did. "Do you understand that there are civil and criminal penalties for lying under oath?" Of course he did. "Harold," Fisher quickly responded, "I don't think you do."

There was a sudden gnashing of teeth among the assembled lawyers. Under the table, cordovan soles squeaked their concern. The lawyers had gotten a glimpse of Fisher's dark side, which emerges only when Schubert is performed badly or he intends to eviscerate a lying witness: "Mr. Burton," he said, "within 60 seconds you are going to lie under oath and then I am going to demonstrate to you what happens when you lie under oath. We really ought to start right now. Have you ever had financial dealings with Dr. Frost?"

The witness stammered a bit, then stalled. Finally he murmured, "Well, no, no." Fisher pounced.

"See, Harold—do you mind if I call you Harold?—that only took about, well, let me look at my watch, 45 seconds, give or take, and you already lied. Just like I predicted. Let me hand you these notes and deeds and mortgages and after you review them carefully, I want you to look into that camera and tell that judge and jury down in Houston, Texas, that you lied under oath."

A newly pensive Harold Burton busied himself for several minutes, rustling papers and reading small print. Finally, he looked up and stared expectantly into the camera, but said nothing. "Oh, go ahead, Harold.

You'll feel better," Fisher urged. "Oh, all right," the witness replied, "I lied under oath."

First, Fisher unsettled Burton with questions about his personal life, making him wonder just how much the lawyer knew—which would frankly worry me, once he got past my address. Pressed, Burton admitted committing a felony—perjury—as casually as if he had been asked to verify that the day was Tuesday. After the Los Angeles district attorney reviewed the evidence, all three of them—the businessman Burton, the doctor, and the secretary—were indicted. Burton and the secretary went to jail. The doctor was placed on probation.

Fisher didn't just impeach Burton; he ran over him. Then, noting slight movement in one finger, he backed the car up and parked on top of him. It was all made possible by Fisher getting off his duff and finding documents that put the lie to virtually everthing Burton could claim.

"We are not plumbers," Richard Haynes once said, "we are artists." That is an apt description of Fisher and his style. Perhaps few lawyers could have done what he did, but every lawyer ought to try.

IV. FORMAL DISCOVERY

A. Be a Bulldog about Documents

Compliance with document production is a troubling area of civil trial law. Technically, your opponent is required to produce all documents that are responsive to your request, provided your request is "not privileged," "relevant to the claim or defense" of your case, and "reasonably calculated to lead to admissible evidence." FED. R. CIV. P. 26 (b) (1). As a practical matter, it's self-defeating and often fatal to your chances if you fail to comply, unreasonably delaying production. Withheld documents tend to surface anyway, especially in multiparty cases or when third-party subpoenas are issued. It's very difficult to keep a bad document buried forever.

However, one of the dirty little secrets of our profession is that some parties, defendants especially, fail to produce critical documents or sit on them until after a key deposition has been taken. In my experience, they often wait until a trial has begun, on the assumption that the case will settle and no one will be the wiser. Sometimes, they never produce them at all. I would like to believe it is clients that withhold documents, not lawyers, but my experience tells me differently, at least in one astonishing case. (See p. 51, "Open your eyes.")

One reason parties and their lawyers think they can get away with that kind of unscrupulous conduct is that they often do. Too intimidated or lazy to follow up on discovery requests, the other side often does nothing more than send a couple letters requesting documents, and quit trying when they receive any kind of response. That is a huge mistake, and not just because of the possibility of getting sanctions. You can poison the well with the judge against the other side by arguing a motion to compel, especially when your opponent offers some lame excuse for failing to comply with a legitimate document request—including the old standby that he didn't think the request was relevant, as if that were the test. Wait until the judge rules on your adversary's summary judgment motion, motion in limine, or the jury charge. Judges have enormous power to even up the score, and most of them aren't afraid to use it, especially against a party who doesn't play by the rules.

Therefore, when it becomes clear that the other side is withholding documents you are entitled to, be a bulldog about getting them. When your opponent ignores production deadlines, asserts a phony claim of privilege, or fails to comply for whatever reason, don't let the matter slide. Send him *one* letter demand for compliance and set a drop-dead date for production. If that date passes without the documents being produced, file a motion to compel the next day. Set it for hearing, and, unless the hearing date itself scares your opponent into complying, which often happens, get the motion heard. Follow through consistently and I promise you, only good things will follow, like game-breaking documents. Besides, if you don't move to compel, you waive your right to the documents you wanted. The gaps in your story or your opponent's can never be filled.

B. Taking Depositions[1]

Depositions are the primary tool of meaningful discovery. To state the obvious, they provide an opportunity to obtain admissions, impeach wit-

---

1. Because the goals and techniques for deposing and cross-examining witnesses are nearly identical, this section should be read with chapter 6, "Killer Cross." To avoid repetition, only points unique to depositions are covered here. I cannot emphasize enough how important cross-examination skills are to depositions, and how valuable depositions are to learning them.

nesses, establish the facts of your story, and give meaning to all manner of evidence. If you are effective, you can break a case wide open by limiting the story your opponent can tell at trial. You can also defeat a dispositive motion before it is filed.

1.   Don't choose between "destructive" and "informational" depositions.

Depositions are now described as either "destructive" or "informational," a curious distinction that crept into the practice of law in the 1990s. The former has come to mean full-scale cross-examination designed to force a settlement, and the latter, that the lawyer didn't have time to prepare.

Actually, that's not altogether true. The main reason lawyers give for taking a strictly informational deposition is to set up a witness for cross at trial. The idea is to nail the witness down to positions that can easily be impeached, but wait until trial to surprise the witness with prior inconsistent testimony and/or documents.

In my experience, however, the depositions that do the most good for clients are the ones where you draw blood. Your aggression sends the right message. You will walk away from the deposition with the witness cowed and with powerful impeachment if you meet again in the courtroom. You are also more likely to get damaging admissions at a deposition than at trial, when witnesses are better prepared.

Asking nothing but anemic, open-ended questions, on the other hand, sends the wrong message: that you lack either talent or interest. Nor do you compromise your effectiveness at trial by showing the other side some of your strongest cross during a deposition. A witness who looks bad when deposed seldom improves at trial. Either he will fight you to no avail—given his deposition—or he will become compliant, to avoid going through *that* again. It really doesn't matter which course happens: Your case gets stronger either way.

Of course, you should always be prepared to ask some strictly informational questions during a deposition, but only to fill gaps in discovery. However, never pin yourself down to an "either-or" choice between the two forms of questioning. That eliminates flexibility, which trial lawyers need in depositions and at trial, especially when testimony takes an unexpected turn. So, before finishing a deposition, wreak a little havoc. Trust me. Your opponent may be stoic while you are shredding his client or expert witness, but inside he is praying for ways to end the massacre before trial begins.

2. Draft a jury charge first.

Drafting a jury charge before the first deposition helps you destroy your opponent's case. Not only will you ask questions in the words and phrases jurors will use to reach their verdict, you will force witnesses to do the same when they answer. That makes a huge difference when the jurors start deliberation. When you "talk the talk" from the first day of trial, they are conditioned to answer jury questions in your favor.

a. The E-Systems case.

In 1991, Carlos and Maria Fernanda Uribe, young Mexican nationals, traveled to El Paso, Texas, so that Maria could give birth to their child in the United States. Carlos was a successful businessman, and Maria, from all I later learned, a devoted mother. They planned to move to El Paso the following year, where Carlos owned a plant that manufactured clothing.

Recuperating in a hotel two days after her son's birth, Mrs. Uribe walked across the room to get a warm bottle. Her husband and two-year-old daughter played with the baby on a twin bed. It was, to paraphrase the poet W. H. Auden, their last moment as themselves. A shot rang out from the room next door, passed through the wall, and struck Mrs. Uribe, killing her almost instantly.

About 30 seconds later, a man burst into the room and tried to revive her. When it was clear she was dead, he identified himself as Truett Burney and said he was the one who had fired the gun. Later that night, he told the El Paso police he was "required" to carry the weapon and was "familiarizing himself" with it when it went off. The police thought he meant he was carrying the gun for work—and their report of the shooting said so. By the time Burney gave the police a handwritten statement at the jail that night, however, he had spoken to a criminal lawyer provided by his employer, E-Systems of Dallas. Burney repeated that he was "required" to carry the gun, but added, "for personal reasons."

A few weeks later, the El Paso lawyers the Uribes originally retained discovered they had a conflict of interest. As it turned out, in El Paso's small legal community, they also represented the insurance company that sold Truett Burney his homeowner's policy. For reasons I have never understood, when Burney made a claim against the insurance company based on the shooting, the insurer provided defense counsel for him. Because of the conflict, the Uribes' lawyers withdrew. The dead woman's father, a Houston businessman, contacted me about handling the case. I am still grateful that he did. Not only did I have the opportunity to help a wonderful family, but my trial team and I uncovered some of the most extraordinary evidence we have ever seen, before or since.

As a plaintiff, you have to find a defendant with liability *and* money. Burney had no real assets other than $100,000 in coverage under his home-owner's policy. The gun manufacturer, another defendant, proved to have no liability. Burney told the police that he had "dry-fired" the weapon, a Glock 45-caliber semiautomatic, in the direction of the wall, thinking it was unloaded. That wasn't a design defect in the gun; that was gross negligence on Burney's part. He had ignored gun-safety rules and flouted common sense.

That left his employer, E-Systems, as the "target" defendant. For the suit to have any financial value, we would have to prove the elements of *respondeat superior,* extending the liability of the servant to the master. Ultimately, we would have to persuade a jury to answer "yes" to this simple question, from our draft jury charge:

> On the occasion in question, that is, when he fired the weapon, was Truett Burney acting in the scope of his employment by E-Systems, Inc.? (Instruction: An employee is acting within the scope of his employment if he is acting in the furtherance of the business of his employer.)

Then, to get punitive or exemplary damages—the real leverage in many plaintiffs' cases—we would have to prove Burney was grossly negligent and impute that conduct to E-Systems. To do that, we would have to convince a jury that E-Systems "authorized" or "ratified or approved" Burney's gross negligence.[2]

Getting a jury to find that Burney was furthering the business of his employer was not going to be easy. He shot Mrs. Uribe hours after he left work, in a hotel room miles from his job. His statement to the police exonerated his employer. Nevertheless, it made no sense that he would be "required" to carry a 45-caliber semiautomatic weapon for personal reasons. My suspicions only deepened as I learned more about his mysterious employer.

---

2. Many jurisdictions follow some version of the Restatement (Second) of Torts, Section 909, which establishes four circumstances under which it is appropriate to impute an employee's gross negligence or malice to a corporate employer: (1) the corporation authorized the doing and manner of the act; or (2) the agent was unfit and the principal was reckless in employing him; or (3) the agent was employed in a managerial capacity and was acting in the scope of employment; or (4) the employer or a manager of the employer ratified or approved the act. We argued that the first and last conditions applied.

E-Systems's annual report boasted that 90 percent of its income was derived from the CIA. It manufactured surveillance equipment and was engaged in a murky public–private sector effort called Operation Alliance, involving high-tech interdiction of drug deals along the Texas-Mexico border. Operation Alliance was the job that brought Burney and his co-workers to El Paso. Maybe, from this intriguing information, evidence would emerge that Burney had the gun in his room for a job-related reason.

A few months into the representation, the Uribes' former lawyers sent us a copy of a signed statement Burney had given to an investigator for the insurance company they represented—the one that sold him his homeowner's policy. I am not certain to this day how or when they got it or why, however belatedly, they sent it to us. I knew they didn't get it through formal discovery because they got out of the case before discovery began. In any event, I'm glad they resolved whatever ethical issue the statement presented in favor of the Uribes, because it unraveled the mystery of Burney's gun and pushed E-Systems closer to liability.

In the statement, Burney admitted buying the gun because of his job, moving us a step closer to proving *respondeat superior.* Still, E-Systems had running room. Its executives would deny that they knew anything about the weapon, and Burney would back them up.

Ironically, Burney's deposition was scheduled for two days after we received the statement in the mail. What's more, our response to the defendants' production requests—and therefore our obligation to turn over the statement—wasn't due for two weeks. I wasn't about to volunteer that I had the statement until I questioned Burney—meaning, until I had given him a chance to lie about it. That seemed like poetic justice to me because I would never have seen that statement if my client's prior counsel hadn't sent it to me. As would soon become clear, Burney knew exactly how important it was.

At the beginning of his videotaped deposition, Burney played to E-Systems's director of security, who attended as the company's corporate representative. Burney was alternately cavalier and silly, which didn't bother us, because it surely would the jury, if they ever saw a video clip from the deposition. Even his appearance helped. He looked goofy, like Bozo the Clown, but with none of Bozo's fashion sense. The knot in his tie was the size of a small apple. If you were looking for a guy whose very existence suggested he would never do anything without an order from his boss, Burney was that man.

I asked Burney several times if he had given any statement other than the one that had been produced—the one he gave to the police exonerating his employers. Each time, he insisted that he had not. Then I started asking questions using the awkward language of the statement he gave his insurance carrier. "Isn't it true that you had this gun because of the 'type of equipment and areas you were employed in?'" Burney thought about the question for a while, then hesitantly responded, "No, I didn't." I asked if he bought the gun for "duty use," the next sentence of his statement. Before he could answer, the opposing lawyers were locked in a fugal chorus of complaints, demanding that I allow them to see the statement I obviously had. I handed it to them.

From the look on Burney's face on the tape, he might as well have blurted out, "How did you get this?" I continued questioning him:

Q: Yes or no, did you buy that Glock to use on the job in El Paso?
A: Yes, at the time if I thought I was in danger, I might carry it.
Q: That's why you were familiarizing yourself with the gun in the room, because of danger on your job?
A: Yes, sir.
Q: Thought you might have to use it once you were out on the job itself?
A: Yes, maybe.
Q: In the statement you mentioned before, the one you gave to the El Paso police, you said you bought that gun just for personal reasons. That's not correct, is it?
A: Well, I don't know. It was for personal use.
Q: Personal use by you on the job, true?
A: Well, that's right.
Q: You didn't have a girlfriend mad at you, or some jealous boyfriend, nothing like that?
A: No, sir. I bought it for duty use. But none of the higher-ups knew about it.

When you catch a witness lying, the smart move is to immediately get even more damaging testimony on the record, while he is too embarrassed or frightened to give you anything but honest answers. A few minutes' respite or a quick "break" with opposing counsel can chasten him into toeing the party line. I would have attempted to get more harmful testimony, but the next few minutes were like a scene out of a Salvador Dalí painting.

First, an alarm clock went off. Burney reached inside his briefcase and shut it off. Then he muttered, "I'll be danged," retrieved the "missing" statement, handed it to me, and said, "You know, it's been so long, I done forgot I gave it. You know how that goes." I responded honestly that I didn't know. Nor was I surprised he'd brought it with him, just that he gave it to me at all.

As rattled as Burney was, it nonetheless seemed odd for him to subsequently admit as readily as he did that his three co-workers on the El Paso job were all carrying guns. However, Burney knew something we didn't discover for several months. His criminal lawyer had sent affidavits executed by those co-workers to the El Paso grand jury investigating the shooting. Each admitted carrying weapons because of dangers on the job. Two of them said they had semiautomatics. Burney's criminal lawyer had also written a letter to the grand jury stating that the four men had participated in planting a listening device on a "known drug trafficker's home."

In one way, the grand jury strategy worked for Burney. The grand jurors no-billed him on a felony homicide and/or weapons violation, charging him instead with misdemeanor manslaughter. That also avoided publicity that could have pressured the CIA into suspending E-Systems's contracts.

What E-Systems executives had not banked on was that we would end up with those grand jury documents, which were provided to us by the insurance company lawyers representing Burney. That shifted the leverage dramatically in our direction. E-Systems could no longer credibly claim that Burney was some sort of *ultra vires* cowboy, out there doing his own thing. I was convinced jurors would believe the "higher-ups" at E-Systems had to know what was going on. We were clearly going to get a "yes" answer to the *respondeat* question, locking in compensatory damages.

To get punitive damages, however, was another matter, requiring us to prove Burney was grossly negligent, and then to impute that conduct to his employer, E-Systems. The company would fight punitives hard because, as is typical, its insurance coverage extended only to an employee's negligence—not gross negligence. Worse still for E-Systems, a finding of gross negligence would attract national media attention.

Proving gross negligence against Burney appeared easy. He fired a loaded weapon at a hotel room wall. The best opportunity to impute that conduct to E-Systems would be the deposition of a man we shall call Dan Rizzie, the vice president who negotiated the Operation Alliance contract with the CIA, and oversaw its execution. My wife, Kathryn, took his deposition, confronting Rizzie with the mounting evidence of E-Systems's complicity. She started with the criminal lawyer's letter to the grand jury:

Q: Is that what Burney and his co-workers went out to El Paso to do? To install a bugging device on a narcotic trafficker's home?

A: That was not what we contracted to do.

Q: That is not what I asked you. A government contract is not likely to put an illegal act in writing. What I asked was: Is the statement true or not?

A: I don't know if that statement is true or not. I know what we were contracted to do. I know what we sent them out there to do. If, in fact, they did what is stated here, that is beyond what we were contracted to do.

Q: That means the lawyer's letter could be true, right?

A: I don't know if it is true or not.

Rizzie defiantly added that he didn't believe the lawyer's letter. He did crack a little, however, admitting E-Systems knew there was an "element of danger" on the El Paso job but denying it would have required the employees to carry weapons. A jury could conclude from his "nondenial" denial of the wiretapping and his grudging acknowledgment of the "element of danger" that he could foresee that his employees would be carrying weapons on the job.

However, simply achieving the legal standards for obtaining punitives is never enough. You also have to make the jury mad enough to award them. Burney and his co-workers had given us a good start. During their depositions, each of them had denied the very words on the pages of their affidavits, claiming that they carried guns not because of dangers on the job, but because of the ordinary dangers of the highway, driving back and forth between company headquarters in Dallas and El Paso. That testimony would infuriate a jury, but we needed to make them mad at the "higher-ups," too. Rizzie wasn't disappointing us.

When shown the employees' affidavits, Rizzie testified that he believed them when they said they hadn't bought the weapons for work. Then he claimed that he'd never talked to any of them about the guns or even to Burney about the shooting. Given his high-level position, and his involvement in every aspect of Operation Alliance, that was too much distancing to be credible. Moreover, that none of the men was disciplined—not even

Burney, for the shooting—was additional proof of the company's ratification of Burney's gross negligence.

Kathryn had one more piece of evidence to show him. It led him into a ruinous admission, right out of the jury charge. Subsequent to Mrs. Uribe's death, E-Systems had issued a directive banning employees from carrying weapons "in the field," the term applied to jobs like the one in El Paso. While evidence of subsequent remedial action is usually inadmissible, there is an exception to show "control." Thus, the statement could be used to prove that E-Systems could have prevented the shooting by controlling its employees' conduct on and off the job, as it was doing with the directive.

At first, Rizzie denied the directive had anything to do with Mrs. Uribe's death, but he finally allowed that it "might have been spurred" by the incident. He did admit that the directive controlled the conduct of E-Systems employees before and after working hours once they were on assignment away from the home office. Kathryn asked if that meant E-Systems was removing the proximate cause (which she defined for him) of any future shooting, by prohibiting the weapons. His reply:

> The first purpose of the directive was to do everything we could reasonably do to ensure there was never a recurrence of the tragedy that happened; and secondly, *to even remove the proximate cause of such a recurrence*, and that is, having people exposed to danger who weren't trained to deal with that danger.

Rizzie had now gone from denying he knew anything about the weapons to admitting he could have stopped the shooting by acting sooner to prohibit the employees from carrying weapons. The jury charge would say the directive could be considered only on the issue of the company's ability to control its employees, but jurors wouldn't parse the words so thinly. Common sense would tell them that E-Systems had put its employees in harm's way, that it was foreseeable that they would arm themselves, and that the company had done nothing to prevent it until it was too late.

The case proceeded along until the Friday before trial, when we reached an extraordinary settlement with E-Systems. Filling in the draft jury charge played a big role. Rizzie's testimony and "60 Minutes" obtaining permission to put cameras in the courtroom didn't hurt, either.

I thought that would end the matter but, as you will see, it didn't. Three months later I received a startling call from E-Systems's former director of security, who had acted as the corporate representative and had been in charge of document production. He said he had quit the day before, and wanted to fly down—that he had something "disturbing" to show me. I had no idea what it would be. I told him to come as soon as he could. (See p. 51, "Open your eyes.")

C. Defending Depositions[3]

You should always prepare key witnesses for deposition testimony as if the case depended on it—because it does. Each one should be prepared as if he is about to take the stand at trial. Not only does that help prevent their making fatal admissions, it makes your life easier at trial. Having been prepared once before, and having given a deposition that may have lasted several days or even weeks, your witnesses will be much better prepared—and more confident—once they take the stand.

On the other hand, the price for inattention can be high, especially in commercial cases in which the facts and law are complex, and a wrong answer can admit you out of court. That happens all the time, and most often can be avoided.

1. Deposition testimony is trial testimony.

Make certain the witness understands the seriousness of deposition testimony. Tell him to look into the videographer's camera to underline important points, and to envision a judge and jury at the other end. Remind him repeatedly that he is not there to please the other party, her lawyer, or the court reporter. Ultimately, the only approval he is ever going to need is yours and the jury's.

2. Educate witnesses about their part of the case.

The extent to which you educate each witness is a judgment call, dictated by the nature of the testimony involved. The grieving widow whose husband was killed in a plant explosion doesn't need to know anything about the accident—but she does need to be ready to tell the jury how hard life has been ever since. That isn't meant to demean those types of witnesses. Their testimony is generally the most moving in all of law, especially when they describe the impact an accident has had on their lives.

On the other hand, key witnesses in a commercial case should know the entire transaction: everything from what they personally did to what they

---

3. Again, because the goals and techniques for defending a witness at a deposition and presenting a witness at trial are so similar, this section should be read with chapter 7, p. 217, "Preparing and Presenting Witnesses."

ordered done by others. That is especially true of the details of the deal documents, even if they signed them without reading a single word. You don't want your witness being impeached with obscure provisions, like a merger clause, that he didn't know existed.

You also need to make witnesses aware of the legal implications of their answers, especially in commercial cases, where the law is complex and the witnesses sometimes too smart by half. The last thing you want is some highly competitive executive testifying that he did his own due diligence on the business deal at issue and took the defendant's representations with a grain of salt—just to avoid letting anyone think that he could be out-smarted. Hello, big ego. Goodbye, detrimental reliance.

Witnesses need to know what other witnesses, on both sides of the case, have said prior to their own depositions, and, if possible, they need to be updated before they testify during trial. That provides your witnesses with a better understanding of what will be important in their own testimony and the likely topics of cross-examination. But don't encourage witnesses to conform their testimony to that of others just to avoid contradiction. Minor differences in the testimony of witnesses on the same side of a case are inevitable, honest, and only add to credibility. If they are major, how-ever, they are often fatal—a strong argument against having brought the case to begin with, or for the defense, for getting it settled.

Finally, witnesses must see all the documents or other evidence that applies to them in a material way. There is a terrible price to pay when lawyers leave witnesses—especially experts—vulnerable to the cross-examiner's ques-tions about "every piece of evidence you didn't get to see." The jury will con-clude that the witness doesn't know what he is talking about—and that his lawyer withheld the critical evidence for a sinister reason.

Pleadings bear special mention. A talented cross-examiner can turn a set of pleadings into the courtroom equivalent of the Holy Bible the minute a party or expert demonstrates ignorance about what is in them. I once briefly ducked in on a case Joe Jamail was trying in Galveston, just long enough to see him waving a petition in the air and barking at a defendant who obviously had contradicted something in it. "So you disagree with your own lawyer?" I heard him say as the jurors shook their heads at the defendant.

D. Let Them Eat Tape

Given that Americans receive most of their information from televi-sion, it follows that excerpts from videotaped depositions can be devastating at trial. Almost anything a witness says can be fixed when there is only a written transcript of his deposition, but nothing can repair an ill-timed grimace, snicker, or sneer, caught on tape—to say nothing of what you can do with a false statement. The camera never lies.

1. Creating persuasive videotaped excerpts.

There are two opportunities to use videotape excerpts during trial. You can always impeach with them, by far their most effective use. It is devastating when the man on the monitor makes a liar of the man in the witness chair—and they are the same man. Put the videotaped deposition on bar code, so that you can scroll right to the excerpt you need to impeach him, hit the button, and play it for the jury. Or anticipate the areas of the witness's testimony most likely to give rise to impeachment, prepare a few video clips ahead of trial, and pop them in the monitor at the appropriate time. No matter how good you are at impeaching a witness, you can never compete with the witness impeaching himself.

The second opportunity arises when the witness is unavailable, or, in one of those rare jurisdictions like New York or Texas that have no unavailability requirement,[4] you can play an excerpt during your case in chief. When you do, think like a director: videotapes, like network television shows, have to be interesting to the "audience." A dull live witness will appear even duller on tape. Unless you have questioned the witness to make a point, with inflection and conviction in your voice, don't bother playing an excerpt if it isn't absolutely necessary. Even if your deposition went great, keep the excerpt short—less than 30 or 40 minutes, tops. If not, you will lose the jurors. You also can use the tape as a well-poisoning introduction to a witness that you next call live. Even if the excerpt is no more than 10 or 15 minutes of terrible testimony and bad body language, it will prejudice the jurors against the witness before she takes the stand. No matter how good she is live, that excerpt can become a reminder of the way she really is—outside the courtroom.

In order for a tape to be effective, you must have long periods of uninterrupted impeachment. You just don't want your opponent to have any good tape at all. If the adverse witness has periods in which she has done well under cross, or if your opponent does create some self-serving direct,

---

4. Some states have created other exceptions for the use of depositions during the case-in-chief, primarily related to the deposition testimony of experts.

your good works can come to naught. If the judge orders the sides to combine their excerpts, your 30 minutes of great cross can be diluted or overcome by the witness's 10 good minutes of responses. Ironically, your strongest ally in creating a great excerpt is opposing counsel, who will most likely reserve questions until time of trial. Even when opposing counsel does create some self-serving direct, try to respond directly with even more stinging cross. Pound away from the beginning to the end of the deposition. Don't let the witness come up for air. Ask informational questions, which allow witnesses to ramble and make their case, only after you've created so much bad tape they can't recover. Quit when you've got what you need. In most cases, your opponent won't have any good counters.

Reverse your thinking when it's your own witness who's being deposed. Especially if he has done badly, assume that he will be hit by a bus between now and time of trial. Don't reserve your questions. Do a rehabilitative direct, if possible, that will create some good edits for you, and dilute your opponent's tape. If your direct just produces another round of withering cross, you haven't lost anything. He already looked bad.

Remember, it's not just witnesses who can come off sounding bad. During a trial several years ago, I sat disconsolate, watching a replay of my angry cross-examination of a particularly frustrating witness. The message wasn't lost on the jury: The incredibly charming lawyer who'd just smiled, tap-danced, and sung his way into their hearts was actually the Tony Soprano of the courtroom. Hearing my voice on only those few minutes of cross managed to make me sound mean, doubtless creating sympathy for an otherwise unsympathetic witness.

On the other hand, witnesses who get mad don't look any better. In the MoPac case, the camera caught the grade-crossing expert preparing to lunge at me across the table, beet-faced, pulling off his tie and shouting, "I, sir, am not over-coached," in response to my suggestion to the contrary. Then, suddenly becalmed, he looked directly into the camera and added, "As yet, sir. I have not been over-coached, as yet."

2. Edit only from the tape.

Always watch videotape as you edit it. If you use the transcript alone, you will miss the nonverbal communication that is often more persuasive than the spoken word. As I think about the videotaped depositions I have taken over the years, none is more vivid than one involving an arrogant economist (imagine that), who, having bragged about his four undergraduate and graduate degrees, responded to a simple math question by counting on his fingers. Or, the shooter in the E-Systems case grinning while he talked about buying the gun that killed Mrs. Uribe.

There is excellent software available that makes editing videotaped depositions easy. You can move back and forth quickly through the testimony, instantaneously splicing the segments together that you want to include. That is a huge improvement over the outmoded method of winding and rewinding the tape, making note of the excerpts you wanted from the timer on the screen, followed by a long delay while the videographer put it together for you, usually at great expense.

3. Excerpts must be accurate.

This is probably unnecessary advice because it is so obvious, but it is potentially so valuable that it bears stressing. If your opponent creates a video excerpt that takes a witness's statement out of context, you can win the case on the spot. When a trial lawyer does that with any document or deposition, even inadvertently, it can be deadly, but the impact is doubled with video, which is immediate, indisputable, and overwhelming. If that happens, all you have to do is show the jury what your opponent did—and his credibility will be destroyed.

In 1991, I represented Robert Sakowitz, Texas's onetime "merchant prince," and scion of a family retailing empire that collapsed with the oil and real estate markets in the 1980s. Ultimately, the retail stores, the primary asset of Robert's late father's estate, went bankrupt. Robert's nephew, Douglas Wyatt, sued Robert, alleging that he had breached his fiduciary duty by mismanaging the family business. The more destructive allegation was that Robert had diverted profits from secret side deals that should have gone to the family. Wyatt sought $8 million in actual damages and triple that amount in punitives.

Robert's sister, Lynn Wyatt, is a beautiful, internationally known socialite. She made the lawsuit possible by transferring her rights as a beneficiary under her father's estate to Douglas, her son. I told the jurors that she was like Daisy in *The Great Gatsby*, lighting a fuse and then retreating into her vast wealth so she wouldn't hear the explosion.[5]

---

5. I will refer to this case frequently in the book. Following is the family tree of the relevant players:

Bernard and Anne Sakowitz

Robert Sakowitz   Lynn Sakowitz (Mrs. Oscar) Wyatt

Douglas Wyatt

Lynn Wyatt was also the plaintiff's most important witness. She had served on the Sakowitz board of directors when her brother's personal business deals took place—the transactions that her son, Douglas, alleged were not disclosed. It was up to her to convince the jury that he hid those deals from her.

A woman of enormous charm and net worth to match (her husband, Oscar, was the founder of Coastal Corporation and one of America's richest men), Mrs. Wyatt did not like being challenged—and let it show. At one point during her deposition, I looked down after asking a question to glance at some notes. She snapped, "If you want me to answer that question, you look at me when I am talking." When I confronted her with minutes from board meetings showing that she was present when her brother disclosed many of his "secret deals" and absent when he disclosed others, her testimony rambled.

I always assumed Douglas's lawyer would call Mrs. Wyatt at trial and have her explain that she had a bad day when she gave her deposition. She was just smart and charming enough to pull it off. Instead, counsel announced in opening argument that she would appear through her videotaped deposition—as his first witness. She'd apparently had enough, and decided to let her son fend for himself.

After court that day, Douglas's lawyer faxed us his video edits. My associate and I discovered that even the slightest hint of testimony in Robert's favor had been edited out, and there had been plenty of it. In those days before editing software, we stayed up all night with a court reporter, gleefully creating a tape that completed the answers the other side intended to play. The next morning, the plaintiff's lawyer played his excerpts, which took about 25 minutes. I objected under Rule 106, the doctrine of optional completeness, arguing that the tape was misleading to the jury. The judge allowed me to play our tape immediately. As it started rolling, I whispered to my associate that the case would be over in 45 minutes. In retrospect, it really was.

Consider just this one "secret" transaction: Opposing counsel played an excerpt from Mrs. Wyatt's deposition in which she denied any knowledge of a deal involving RTS Leasing, a company owned by Robert that leased cars and trucks to Sakowitz, Inc., at below-market rates. In those days before tax reform, Robert got to take the depreciation on the vehicles personally. In addition to claiming ignorance of RTS Leasing, Mrs. Wyatt also stated that she would have voted against authorizing the deal had it been brought to the board.

That was all the jury saw about the RTS transaction in the plaintiff's tape. Our excerpt included theirs, but added everything the plaintiff had omitted. During the deposition, I had handed Mrs. Wyatt minutes from a board meeting in which the RTS Leasing deal was discussed at length. The minutes showed that Mrs. Wyatt was accompanied to the board meeting by her husband's personal lawyer, who explained how Robert's tax savings would work. Mrs. Wyatt had actually made the motion to approve the deal—a curious way of showing disapproval, as I pointed out at the deposition.

We completed Mrs. Wyatt's testimony on four or five more deals, each of which ended in unanimous board approval. Fifteen minutes into our tape, the jurors were already exchanging knowing glances.

We also inserted some moving, if irrelevant, testimony at the very end. In that segment, Lynn readily admitted that her brother had done "wonderful things for Sakowitz and for Houston." She also described with real emotion how grateful she was to Robert for what he'd done for her sons following her divorce from her first husband. She said that he became a surrogate father, took them everywhere, and even taught the litigious Douglas how to throw a football. The plaintiff never objected to the testimony.

I have a vivid memory of the reaction to the tapes. At the lunch break, the jury stormed out. At the same time, the press chased after Douglas's counsel, demanding to know if he was trying to mislead the jury. After only two hours of videotape, the plaintiff was out of the game and never got back in.

V. MAKING TRIAL EASIER

Finally, I have several practical suggestions. They have little in common except that each will enhance your performance at trial.

A. Get Evidence Preadmitted

It's the modern practice, anyway, but make certain to get your exhibits and deposition excerpts admitted prior to trial. If you wait until trial, you will interrupt the flow and rhythm of your examination every time you stop to admit evidence. Preadmitting evidence makes for a smoother trial and eliminates unnecessary evidentiary objections from your opening argument and examinations.

B. Collect Your Unhurried Thoughts

As soon as you get a case, open a working file for each aspect of the trial, such as opening and closing argument, the motion in limine, and so on. Throughout discovery, as you get ideas, dictate quick notes into the files. After trial each day, dictate a brief note into the closing file. Your passing thoughts are often likely to offer real insight about your case, and you don't want to let them slip through the cracks. This is not to dismiss the epiphanies achieved over scotch and water the night before your argument. It's just to underscore the importance of unhurried ideas; it is enormously beneficial to have them conveniently organized.

C. Diversity Sends Its Own Tailored Message

There will be all kinds of people on your juries, and simply put, people favor their own kind. If your trial team is diverse, and your witnesses, too, your chances of winning will improve. For instance, the jury needs to see the man who is lead counsel relying in earnest on the women on his team. Better yet, they need to see a woman as lead counsel, or taking important witnesses. The African-American juror needs to hear you praise your expert, the brilliant neurosurgeon. Later, she will be pleased to find out that he also is an African-American. I don't think it hurts that Jewish jurors figure out that I am, too, although that point is more for illustration than reality in my case, as I have had a total of maybe, two, jurors in Texas who were Jewish, during my career, while my friend, Jim Quinn, has had a total of two in New York, who weren't.

Jury Studies and Graphics

3

I. THE IMPORTANCE OF JURY SCIENCE

During the 1970s and 1980s, forensic experts refined their craft. Most important, they borrowed the concept of focus groups from marketing companies and applied it to jury trials, with great success. By presenting evidence accumulated during discovery to groups of people that reflected the demographics of a likely jury pool, and capitalizing on the feedback, they were able to identify the themes and issues most likely to affect the outcome of the trial. Jury science had come of age.

Soon, trial lawyers across the country were rehearsing their cases in focus groups and mock trials, and bringing forensic experts to court to assist them in jury selection. The advantages were apparent immediately. Armed with their skill, intuition, and jury research, these pioneering lawyers were far more likely to win than their less sophisticated opponents.

Additional tools of trial science have followed. Witness schools teach key witnesses how to improve their testimony and appear comfortable on the stand. Gallery ("shadow") juries provide daily feedback on how a trial is going and how the trial team can improve its performance. A panel of retired judges can be convened to test the issues for an upcoming evidentiary hearing or bench trial.

Yet this book is not about the *science* of trying cases. The trial of a lawsuit is at best an imprecise art, which makes the results of trial science so valuable. Rehearsing your case and feasting on the feedback helps you plot a winning strategy for trial, builds your confidence, and bolsters your skills. In fact, trial science has proven so effective that it is rare to find a trial lawyer who has not employed it in some form at least once. For many more, this lawyer included, it is standard practice in every case.

II. THE GOALS OF TRIAL SCIENCE

At its heart, trial science of all kinds has as its general goal diminished guesswork, reduced anxiety, and an improved outcome. But among all of its tools, none is more effective—or more amazing—than jury studies. By listening carefully to what panelists say during "deliberations" after a focus group or mock trial, you can identify winning themes and spot losing issues. You can also develop a profile of your ideal juror—and of jurors to be avoided. Finally, focus groups and mock trials can serve as a valuable wake-up call for the overconfident lawyer. It all adds up to a blueprint for winning at trial—or a list of reasons for settling.

III. EVERYTHING YOU NEED TO KNOW ABOUT JURY STUDIES

A. Understanding Focus Groups and Mock Trials

Although there are significant differences, focus groups and mock trials follow the same general structure. Forensic experts select "jurors" that reflect the likely demographics of the venire in the court where the case will be tried. The jurors sign confidentiality agreements to discourage leaks. Participants are not told whether the plaintiff or defendant is paying them, lest that knowledge influence their comments and votes.

To create an aura of authenticity, jury studies frequently are conducted in mock courtrooms. A robed "judge" reads an outline of both sides of the case and presides throughout the study. The panelists are told that they are helping to resolve the litigation as a service to the court where the case will actually be tried, thus impressing upon them the seriousness of their job.

The primary difference between focus groups and mock trials is the nature and length of presentation. The information they produce is the same, and in my view, equally reliable. During focus groups, lawyers argue their respective cases for about an hour each, presenting key evidence such as "hot docs" and videotaped deposition excerpts. The lawyer arguing for the plaintiff often makes a brief rebuttal, usually 15 minutes or less. Focus groups take only one day, including a few hours of deliberations. Mock trials, on the other hand, are minitrials, and generally require two or even three days to complete. Both sides argue, put on some number of their own witnesses, play videotaped deposition excerpts, and sometimes cross-examine actors or colleagues portraying adverse witnesses.[1] Graphics are tested in both focus groups and mock trials.

Following the presentation, panelists are divided into one or more "juries," depending on the number of participants. The lawyers eavesdrop on their deliberations through a two-way mirror or closed-circuit television. After they reach a "verdict," the panelists are debriefed by the forensic expert as the lawyers continue listening in secret. Then the lawyers visit with the panelists. In addition to hearing any criticism of their performance, the

---

1. I prefer focus groups to mock trials. They are shorter, less expensive, and by 6 P.M., you have the answers that you need. The upside of mock trials is that by the time you finish editing videos and preparing witnesses, you are virtually prepared for trial. The downside is you'll be too tired of the case to care.

lawyers can test the effect of additional evidence and arguments that were withheld from the presentation for strategic reasons or because of time constraints.

1.   Safeguards to ensure a valid result.

In scientific terms, the last thing you want from a jury study is a false positive, an unwarranted favorable result. To avoid that outcome, there are two things that you must do. First, choose a good trial lawyer to play opposing counsel. A mismatch will tell you nothing. Second, tilt the case in your opponent's favor. Present your side in the most unfavorable, but credible, way possible.

I realize that this advice is counterintuitive. As it is said in scientific circles, nobody likes to call their own baby ugly—especially with the client watching. But it is essential. If your case survives with the panelists despite a slanted presentation, you'll know you've got a strong hand. And remember, "surviving" doesn't necessarily mean winning. As long as you *could have* put on a case that would have convinced them, you're in good shape. It may go against the grain to withhold critical documents and arguments—but a fake loss can help avoid a real one.

In 1994, I tried a case involving a nuclear power plant with Jim Quinn, head of litigation at New York's Weil, Gotshal & Manges. We represented Westinghouse, which had sold the power plant to the South Texas Nuclear Project (STP). STP claimed the plant's nuclear steam generators were defective and threatened the life of the plant.

Quinn had successfully guided Westinghouse through a maze of similar litigation filed by other power plants for over a decade. I was in this suit because it was filed 100 miles south of Houston in Matagorda County, Texas, a region made famous back then by *The Wall Street Journal*, which labeled it a "plaintiff's paradise." As luck would have it, we weren't the plaintiff, and the actual one was asking for $800 million in actual damages and double that amount in punitives.

Dr. Robert Gordon, the forensic scientist I work with often, had 30 Matagorda County residents bused to his mock courtroom in Houston for a focus group. I argued for the plaintiff, STP. Quinn took Westinghouse. At Dr. Gordon's suggestion, I argued that leaks in the steam generators were so bad they created the possibility of a nuclear winter, and described the devastation an accident at the plant would cause. In reality, not even the plaintiff, STP, had suggested that possibility, but, given the accidents at Chernobyl and Three Mile Island, it was a credible argument—a great idea for getting feedback. On the defense side, Dr. Gordon told Quinn to pull his punches—to offer little resistance to the nuclear winter argument. If Westinghouse could survive without Quinn making a forceful rebuttal, our chances at trial would have to be good.

By the time I finished my presentation, talk of nuclear winter had left a distinct chill in the courtroom. I felt *really bad* that Quinn would have to argue under such pressure. I felt certain Westinghouse could never recover. However, as he rose to speak, he muttered something that sounded like a threat, and was off and running. I put on the best rebuttal I could but Quinn won, convincing many of the panelists that there was no need to replace the steam generators, a great result for our clients. Notwithstanding its huge hometown advantage—a problem we'd have to figure out how to face head-on—STP was not assured of a win.

The panelists couldn't have cared less about a nuclear winter; in fact, they were dismissive about it. They told us that the community had debated safety issues when STP announced its intention to build the nuclear plant there 20 years earlier. Because the region was dying, they chose economic growth over the risks of a nuclear accident. Apparently, they never looked back. Even now, with terrorist threats against nuclear power plants a reality, I doubt they would think any differently.

2.   Uncover compelling themes.

One of the primary goals of any jury study is to uncover the most compelling themes in your case. Themes are simple but powerful truths that emerge from the facts and motivate jurors to vote your way. By immediately introducing the themes that persuaded your focus group or mock trial jury, you will put your opponent on the defensive and set the agenda for the entire trial.

Some themes are self-evident. You don't need a focus group to tell you that a plant explosion that killed several workers is really about "doing things the right way and doing things the wrong way." It is far more difficult, but equally important, to uncover compelling themes in a document-intensive commercial case. Focus groups help you slice through the mountain of evidence characteristic of most commercial cases, to find the deeper truths buried within.

Consider a typical patent infringement case. Without the benefit of a focus group or mock trial, many plaintiffs lawyers would be tempted to argue the literal truth, that the defendant's product "reads on" certain claims in the plaintiff's patent. However, those claims are often incomprehensible to laypeople, and certainly to jurors hearing them for the first time. After listening to mock panelists analyze the case, however, you would appreciate that a patent infringement case is really about deceit and theft—of the plaintiff's idea.

On the other side, lawyers often argue that the defendant could not be guilty of infringing because its employees "reverse-engineered" the plaintiff's product, taking it apart, and then building its own similar product that was carefully designed to avoid the plaintiff's patent. Although perfectly legal, reverse-engineering just sounds sneaky. Taking another company's product apart, seeing how it's made, and claiming your company then built a product that does the same thing without copying, admits the defendant's abiding interest in whatever the plaintiff invented and moves it perilously close to infringement. Besides, if that "reverse-engineering" story were bullet-proof, the plaintiff's case would have been tossed out on summary judgment. Instead, a focus group jury would reveal that the case is really about false accusations of theft, character assassination of the defendants' team of distinguished engineers and scientists, and their justifiable anger. Then, with the jury psychologically prepared, as jury studies show, the defense lawyer can tell them about reverse engineering.

Ironically, the most powerful themes often come not from the forensics experts who put together jury studies, but from the panelists themselves. "If it ain't broke, don't fix it" leaps to mind—a remark made by a focus group juror in the science-laden Westinghouse power plant case. It made no difference to her that a team of nuclear scientists and engineers from STP would testify that the generators were corroding and would need to be replaced to avoid shutting down the plant. Once she learned that the plant was a world leader in producing electricity, she saw no point in the plaintiff's case. Her homespun observation told us what our case was really all about, and became a central theme of our successful defense.

3. Open your eyes.

Jury studies play an important psychological role: They open your eyes to the possibility that you could lose. Trial lawyers, who seldom suffer from a lack of confidence, need that kind of warning. It is far too easy to get caught up in the strengths of your case and lose sight that the other side has compelling arguments, too. Panelists, on the other hand, frequently spot weaknesses the entire trial team has missed. That can bring you back to reality while there's still time to correct the problem.

In the MoPac wrongful death case, focus group jurors held my client 35-percent responsible for the train-car collision that took her life. Until that moment—it was my first personal injury case—it never occurred to me that she was even partially at fault. Based on what the panelists said, I argued at trial more emphatically than I otherwise would have that she couldn't see the oncoming train because parked train cars blocked her view. I also emphasized the testimony of several nearby residents who testified that trains routinely passed through the intersection without sounding a whistle, and that they did not hear one the night of the accident. That did it. The jury assigned no liability to my deceased client. But for the focus group opening my eyes, the outcome on contributory negligence could have been different.

While a jury study "verdict" is not necessarily predictive of the real one, the issues that panelists struggle with are invariably at the heart of a typical juror's concerns—their doubts foreshadowing any great danger that lies ahead. Once you understand those concerns, you will be better equipped to allay them at trial—the earlier the better.

A friend of mine, and a student of Gerry Spence's psychodrama school of trial law, Stanley Schneider, represented a defendant in a child abuse case. "When you look at my client," Stanley said to a woman on the first row, "doesn't he look guilty? Like the kind of man who could commit this crime? I know that's what I thought when I first met him." The panelist, the wife of a Houston police officer, admitted that she thought the man was guilty the minute she laid eyes on him. His candor created a strong bond with the panelist, and an apparent predisposition among jurors to bend over backward to be fair. The panelist became the foreperson of the jury, which returned a verdict of not guilty.

Often, a trial lawyer is the last person to know what will give jurors pause. Schneider is the first to tell you: Without feedback from a prior jury study, it is unlikely that he would have known that his client's physical appearance would be the worst obstacle he would face—much less come up with such a bold plan to deal with it. (See, for an example of immediately confronting juror concerns in a commercial trial, p. 96, "Linkage and your worst weaknesses.")

On the other hand, some significant weaknesses can't be cured—the unmistakable signal that you ought to settle. To my amazement, that was the exact message our focus group sent in the Uribe case, the wrongful death action against E-Systems. In that case, an employee of E-Systems, who accidentally shot and killed our client (firing through his hotel room wall), admitted buying the weapon for use on the job. In addition, we had accumulated a mountain of incriminating evidence against his employer, the "deep-pocket" defendant, E-Systems.

As I expected, by the time I finished explaining the tragic circumstances of Mrs. Uribe's death, the focus group panelists were somber—and shaken. By the time my wife, Kathryn, finished arguing for E-Systems, the mood in the courtroom had changed. Worst sign of all, several panelists were shaking their heads in agreement with her. Kathryn began by magnifying E-Systems's government ties, and capitalizing on the border operation:

> E-Systems could make a lot more money manufacturing video games, but the company devotes its resources to fighting the war on drugs—in partnership with agencies of the U.S. government like Customs and the Drug Enforcement Agency. It manufactures electronic surveillance equipment designed to pick up light planes running drugs like cocaine across the Texas-Mexico border. Mr. Berg can call those E-Systems employees who installed that equipment out in El Paso a bunch of cowboys, but others might call them heroes. Anyone with a child who has had a drug problem knows the value of what they do.

Then she distanced E-Systems from Truett Burney, the shooter:

> Everyone in this company was sickened by Mrs. Uribe's tragic death. But E-Systems's employees aren't E-Systems's slaves. Mr. Burney was on his own. And he alone must answer for his incredible stupidity that night. He has to meet his Maker on this one.

Finally, she launched her attack on liability:

> Ladies and gentlemen, if every one of those employees out in El Paso was carrying a weapon, every one of them violated company policy. In the first place, E-Systems's managers would never put its own employees in harm's way. And consider this: E-Systems earns 90 percent of its income from the government. If a single executive or manager condoned those weapons, the company could be suspended or debarred—banned forever from contracting with the government. Perhaps Mr. Berg will explain to us why they would do that.

Divided into two "juries," the panelists found against Burney (who couldn't pay a judgment), but not E-Systems (which could). Several people mentioned drug problems with their children, and spoke of the E-Systems employees with great respect—almost as the heroes Kathryn had suggested they were. When a lawyer strikes a chord that resonates that deeply, it creates a psychological bond with jurors that is very difficult to break. Our "mountain of evidence" didn't faze them.

When I asked the panelists if anything would have changed their minds, several indicated that they would have needed stronger evidence that E-Systems's "higher-ups" knew that its employees would be in such great danger on the El Paso job that they would carry weapons. Many also said it made no sense that the company would jeopardize its relationship with the government by encouraging its employees to carry guns to the El Paso job.

When E-Systems made a substantial offer before trial, we took it. I was not going to be able to cure the weaknesses the panelists mentioned. Then, three months later, I received a call from E-Systems's ex-director of security, who had also been in charge of document production during our lawsuit. He had quit the day before. He told me he had something "disturbing" he wanted to show me, which turned out to include an E-Systems warning about the dangers on the El Paso job, referred to by its unclassified name of "Stallion":

E-Systems Warning Memo

HANDLE AS SECRET
LIMITED DISTRIBUTION

PROGRAM NAME: STALLION
UNCLASSIFIED NAME: STALLION

DESCRIPTION: "STALLION" is an activity at the E-Systems, Inc., Greenville Division to support a government agency. It's purpose is to provide a counternarcotics covert Van.

Operation Alliance – El Paso, TX

SECURITY: The name of company participants associated with this particular effort, and discussions with the other program cleared company personnel and the customer concerning matters are protected by this RAP.

This is an extremely dangerous program and may bring grave danger to the company employees and their families. This program will be discussed with only the program manager,   and those personnel annotated on the access roster. A master access list will be maintained in Vault F. This program is based on a limited distribution only.

HANDLE AS SECRET
LIMITED DISTRIBUTION

Of course, this was the very document our focus group had wanted to see. Had we been able to introduce it at trial, along with the judge's order to produce any E-Systems document related to danger on the El Paso job, the real jury would have turned into a lynch mob.

Ordinarily, I would have filed contempt charges with the judge who handled the suit, but frankly, he was once photographed by the *Houston Chronicle* sound asleep during a trial, and that was just about as excited as he ever got. Instead (given that I would be a witness), I asked Joe Jamail to institute a separate case, which would go to a different court, and he accepted. However, just after he filed against E-Systems and its outside counsel, alleging fraud in inducing the settlement, the law in Texas changed. To maintain suit, we would have to return the money the defendants paid. Given that Mrs. Uribe's survivors were financially fixed for life by the settlement, agreeing to do that would have been malpractice. So we dismissed the case, a frustrating result that rankles to this day. (Don't even ask what happened to the grievance Mr. Uribe filed against the outside counsel.)

4. Develop a juror profile.

Let me be clear about this: Nothing in this book remotely suggests avoiding the *Batson* Rule or its progeny, which precludes systematically eliminating panelists from a jury for reasons of race or gender alone. However, no trial lawyer who wants to win can do so while slavishly worrying about political correctness. At its heart, jury selection is an exercise in other people's bigotry—or lack of it—about a number of social and economic issues. That is yet another value of feedback from jury studies. You can find out how various people will react to your clients, and to your particular cause of action, based on factors such as gender, race, education, and employment.

Listen to the panelists "deliberate." What do the women say? The men? Minorities? Are the Anglos and Hispanics agreeing or at odds? How do African-Americans fit into the mix? How are the small businesspeople reacting? The executives? In the Bible Belt, religion is bound to be brought up. Who's quoting scripture? What does it mean for your side of the case? Short of going back to school to get a degree in psychology, there is nothing comparable for predicting human behavior.

Jury studies always seem to provide at least one or two surprises about people, which, if you didn't learn about them in advance, could cost you the case. As just one example, our focus groups consistently show that professional women, such as lawyers, financial consultants, and executives, are terrible plaintiffs' jurors in commercial litigation. Having had to work harder to get where they are, many "upwardly mobile" women tend to out-macho the men, to respond to whatever the plaintiff's facts might be with a dismissive "That's just business." That would not have been my assumption about successful women. The unpredictability teaches you caution—and alerts you to dig deeper about the panelists' attitudes during voir dire.

By observing who says what about your case, you and the jury special-ist can identify the kind of jurors you do and don't want. However, be aware: No matter how accurate a jury profile may seem, until you see and talk to the real panelists, nothing should be etched in stone. Once you get them talking, these "profiles" become human beings, sometimes a lot differ-ent from the ones you expected. (See p. 110, "Test the juror profile against the real panelists.") As Joe Jamail, the "King of Torts," is fond of saying, he'd put a banker with a heart on his jury—certainly not part of a plain-tiff's stereotypical juror profile. The problem, as he is quick to add, is that he has never met a banker with a heart.

B. When You Can't Pay the Freight

Full-scale jury studies and other forms of forensic help are too expen-sive for many clients. As a result, lawyers and forensics experts have created any number of cheaper alternatives.

1. Modified jury studies.

When money or time is at a premium, forensic experts can conduct modified versions of focus groups and mock trials, testing the most critical issues in your case in no more than 2 or 3 hours. The lawyers lay out the troubling issues in no time flat, and then listen to the panelists' reactions. The responses are as illuminating as a full-scale presentation, at least about the limited subject matter they've considered.

As far as I know, Dr. Gordon's firm was the first to do online jury studies, recruiting panelists in faraway jurisdictions, each of them at their computers at a secure web site that includes a chatroom. The procedure is the same as any focus group, but in writing. First, "jurors" read introduc-tory remarks, an outline of the case, and, finally, each side's presentation. Then the "jurors" respond to questions by the forensic experts and begin a dialogue among themselves in the chatroom. Usually, Dr. Gordon plants a provocateur among the panelists to stir their reactions.

Thus far, online focus groups are extremely successful in simple cases, and better than nothing, but not perfect, in complex ones. However, virtual studies are in their infancy, as traditional focus groups and mock trials once were. As the cost falls of such technology as video conferencing, online jury studies may prove to be the most cost-effective way to conduct a jury study, especially for trial lawyers with national practices.

2. Focus groups without the panelists.

To scale back even further, eliminate the panelists entirely and rely on the forensic expert alone. The night before I tried the Sakowitz case, Dr. Gordon came up with a great theme while we talked long-distance. This was the case in which his wealthy nephew sued Robert Sakowitz over the management of their family estate, a retail empire that had gone bankrupt.[2] Dr. Gordon's suggested theme—"Did he file this suit for sport or for spite?"—were among the first words, and the last, that I spoke at trial. That rhetorical question struck a chord with the jury and foreshadowed the evidence.

3. Focus groups without the experts.

Alternatively, you can keep the panelists and skip the experts. A trial lawyer friend of mine, with a string of extraordinary verdicts, does just that. He puts an ad in the paper soliciting individuals to participate in a discussion about whatever case he's working on. He invites a dozen of the respondents to sit around a table, listen to him outline the case, and give him their views. With the fees paid to the panelists, the total cost is about $1,000—including the donuts my parsimonious friend springs for. Without expensive pretrial bells and whistles, he goes to court as well prepared as any lawyer in this country.

4. Enlist academics.

You also can enlist academics to gather trial science, often with as much success as you would have with a forensic expert. On several occasions I have retained a highly respected political scientist from the University of Houston. He knows how to conduct focus groups because he does them for politicians. He knows voting patterns precinct-by-precinct, and sometimes block-by-block. His profession also requires him to study human behavior. Who better to help you vet a case or select a jury than a man with insight into the reasons people vote for one candidate or another? Better still, the professor's fees have always been less than half of what a

---

2. For a reminder of the Sakowitz family tree, see note 5, p. 41.

forensic specialist would charge—a strong reason for not sending him a copy of this book. In every part of the country, especially in college towns, there are plenty of academics who would jump at the chance to do this kind of work.

C. Nontraditional Uses of Forensic (and Other) Help

There are many other ways you can use outside help to your advantage, beyond just formal jury studies. Just about anyone you know who is sensitive and bright can offer valuable insight into your trial strategy, especially someone with a life different from your own.

1.   Focus-group a friend.

My secret weapon is Alex, who has little in common with forensic experts and trial lawyers, but everything in common with the typical juror. When I run my cases by him, I invariably get great insight. Our discussions force me to communicate complex issues in plain language, and to talk about the case in a way that people like Alex will trust.

Like many Southerners, Alex has traveled a long way in life. Born into a family of Klansmen, he left home in the late 1960s to fight in Vietnam. Since then, he has become a master craftsman. He can make anything out of wood, and make it beautiful. His political and racial views have softened, if not changed altogether. He also lives life to the fullest, racing souped-up cars on weekends. I met Alex when he began to remodel our house five years ago. I have come to think of him as a son, because I write a check to him every month and he won't go away.

The best help Alex ever gave me was in anticipation of a summary jury trial, a focus-group presentation before a pretend jury chosen from a real jury pool, and presided over by the real judge (who ordered it in hopes of settling the years-old litigation). In brief, Marriott Corporation sold hundreds of hotels in the 1980s to thousands of limited partners, in units that cost $100,000 each. I represented the investors years later, bringing suit against Marriott for fraudulently inducing them to make the investment.

Representing wealthy people is usually difficult—jurors automatically resent them. In this case, each limited partner signed a subscription agreement certifying that he had a net worth of $1 million or more, and, as a sophisticated investor, understood the risks he was taking. It would be easy for Marriott to characterize them as a bunch of spoiled rich people crying over losing money. That's why I was puzzled when two focus groups responded so favorably to my case. I needed a third opinion. I needed to talk to Alex. I thought that if anyone would resent rich people, he would.

Over our customary six-pack, I laid out Marriott's case as favorably as possible. I branded the limited partners as "a bunch of rich people whining about losing money," and pointed out that many people who invested in real estate in the 1980s lost money. I also told him that the management fees Marriott charged were within industry standards—the opposite of our actual contention. I added that the hotel business was improving and the investors would do fine if they would just show some patience.

Then I outlined my clients' side of the case, but without much conviction, telling Alex that the investors claimed they were misled, that Marriott's initial projections about the potential value of the deal were false, and that the company knew the projections were false when they made them. That was the extent of my argument on behalf of the limited partners. In particular, I never mentioned the pile of bad documents we had accumulated.

Alex stared at the ceiling for a long while. Then he asked, "How much money did Marriott make off this deal?" I told him the company had made substantial profits on the management fees the limited partners paid it, purposely avoiding the specific dollar amount. Alex asked me if he heard right, "that the investors hadn't even gotten their money back yet?" I confirmed that they had gotten back only a portion of their original investment over the 13 years of the partnership. "Well," he said, "Marriott isn't being straight with them. How can Marriott clean up like that and them not even get their money back? *They may be partners, but Marriott isn't acting like one.*"

That was the most compelling description of a breach of fiduciary duty I had ever heard. I used that exact language in the summary jury trial. The summary jury's "verdict" is confidential, but the $425-million settlement that followed a few months later is not.

2. Mock everything.

Forensic scientists have adapted jury studies to include mock everything. They can conduct a mock voir dire, mock arbitration, mock mediation, mock Markman hearings, and even the mock presentation of graphics—anything that you want to test before the real thing.

In 1998, a federal judge ordered an evidentiary hearing to determine whether the plaintiff, who alleged that my client, Samsung, had infringed his patent, had, in fact, obtained his patent by "inequitable conduct"—

defrauding the U.S. Patent Office into issuing it. If the judge found in Samsung's favor, he would declare the patent invalid and dismiss the case. Dr. Gordon convened a panel of three retired federal judges to test the issues in the potentially outcome-determinative hearing. As it turned out, the judges were dead-on about the questions and evidence that would matter most to the district judge, and in fact, about the favorable ruling that the judge ultimately issued.

Simulating various aspects of litigation helps formulate strategy, and builds your confidence. That is especially true when traveling in new territory—I had never tried a patent case before. Knowing how things played out during the rehearsal gave me a sense of what would really matter in the hearing.

Of course, jury studies are not the real thing. In an age of diminishing trial opportunities, however, they are an excellent training ground for young lawyers. I know this is true because both of my sons are learning the trial lawyer's craft, not only from depositions and jury trials, but also from presentations to focus groups.

3.   Vetting questions about representation and venue.

Some plaintiffs' lawyers consult with forensic experts before accepting representation, sometimes conducting a quick focus group study of any troubling issues in the case. If there's a problem that seems insurmountable, one that document production and depositions apparently can't change, then, for those lawyers, there's little reason to take the case.

Forensic specialists also can help with venue decisions, conducting online focus groups to test the attitudes of potential jurors in the remote jurisdictions where a case could be filed. They can tap colleagues in those locales who will have knowledge about how your type of case fares in those courts.

When filing a plaintiff's case, it borders on malpractice not to search for the most favorable jurisdiction. There's no point in filing a personal injury suit in an extreme tort-reform jurisdiction, where a bad outcome is all but preordained, if you can sue elsewhere. Even commercial cases justify a venue search. In *Marriott,* Dr. Gordon conducted a venue search, and, of three potential jurisdictions where the case could be filed, recommended San Antonio, based on recent verdicts in commercial cases. Four years later, following the "verdict" in our summary jury trial, and the settlement that followed, his advice was vindicated.

Of course, the defendant is stuck once the suit is filed, unless it has the option of contesting venue or jurisdiction. That may justify a venue study, and, if you contemplate removal, a comparison of your chances with the state versus federal court. The decision to move the case or not could be outcome-determinative.

D. A Word of Caution

There are plenty of lawyers who refuse to use forensic experts, focus groups, and mock trials, either because they think they don't need help to win, or they just don't believe in forensic science. I know of a San Antonio lawyer who vetoed a focus group before going to trial against Wal-Mart on the grounds that the client didn't hire him to try the case to a "phony" jury. I take a different view. With the exception of shadow juries, I am a strong advocate of jury science. Even so, I set real boundaries about who is in charge at trial. At the end of the day, it isn't a forensic expert that persuades the jury. It is you. Let them guide you, but don't give them the reins. You need help in formulating a winning strategy, but you don't need a Rasputin dictating what you do.

By the way, that San Antonio lawyer who refused forensic help won a $625-million verdict against Wal-Mart. Not bad—but think how well he might have done if he used a focus group.

IV. JURY EXPERTS AND OTHERS AT TRIAL

A. Striking the Jury

Armed with a juror profile from a focus group or mock trial, you should have a pretty good idea of the type of juror you're looking for—and the type to avoid. During voir dire, you can concentrate on making sure that prospective jurors who appear to match your profile really do—or whether they deviate from it for some reason unique to them.

1. You must be comfortable with the jurors.

Striking the jury is one of those times when a jury expert can prove invaluable. Nevertheless, if you have a difference of opinion about which panelists to strike, especially when it comes down to those final, difficult choices,[3] you must follow your own instincts.

---

3. See p. 109, "Exercising peremptory strikes."

Experienced forensic experts recognize the danger of pushing their choices too hard. In the MoPac case, I remember disagreeing with Dr. Gordon about a pleasant-looking man with a neatly trimmed mustache and beard, wearing a tweed coat. He looked like a plaintiff's juror, but something about him bothered me. Dr. Gordon wanted to keep him and I wanted to strike him. Finally, he asked, "You don't think you can work with him, do you?" I thought a moment and then struck him. Although I could never fully articulate my objection to the man, it didn't matter. If he had made it to the jury, he would have been a distraction to me during the trial. I would have worried from the moment that he was seated that I'd made a mistake.

Notwithstanding that example, remember that you ignore forensic experts without good reason at your own peril. Just ask Marcia Clark, the Los Angeles prosecutor in the O. J. Simpson trial. The papers reported that Don Vinson, a seminal figure in jury science, advised her following a jury study to avoid putting African-American women on the jury. Clark, who had won many prosecutions, ignored him. Without detracting from her considerable skills, I imagine that decision is one of Clark's greatest regrets.

2. Make the most of local talent.

In some parts of the country, especially in small cities and rural areas, you will want a former mayor or sheriff to help you select the jury. Not only do you get the benefit of someone who knows everyone in town, and who can predict how any given panelist will vote ("Old Tom hates your client"), but your case will have an implicit stamp of approval from an important local figure. That knowledge is as good as a focus group.

There's an added benefit to using well-known local figures. Even in a city as large as Houston, jurors immediately recognize the political scientist I mentioned because he frequently appears on local television as a political analyst. It never fails to create a favorable stir among panelists and add credibility to my case.

B. One Lawyer's Negative Opinion of Shadow Juries

Of all its tools, one of forensic science's least reliable, it seems to me, is shadow juries. Designed to be reflective of the demographics and responses of the real jury, shadow jurors watch the trial from the gallery by day and report their reactions each night to a person whose employer in the case is never disclosed. That person, in turn, relays what he learned to the trial lawyer, who, theoretically, adjusts her presentation accordingly.

I've used a shadow jury only once, got a nightly outpouring of compliments, was told we were "killing them," and damn near lost the case. But what if they were constantly criticizing instead? In a large commercial litigation, my opponent's shadow jury disappeared about a month into trial. "I fired 'em," he told me later. "I got tired of hearing what a jerk I was."

I can't give you a solid reason, but I just don't trust shadow juries. Maybe I was prejudiced by my bad experience. But at best, it seems that with everything else going on in a trial, they tip the information scale into overload.

V. SOME THOUGHTS ON GRAPHICS

A. *The Courtroom as Classroom*

If courtrooms are classrooms, then you must teach your "students" in a way that they won't forget. Studies show that jurors remember as much as 75 percent of what they hear and see, as opposed to 20 percent of what they just hear. Acting on the premise that those studies were not all done by graphics companies, I often use graphic designers to create a wide variety of demonstratives, especially time lines, computer animation, and models. In addition, like so many trial lawyers, I am a strong advocate of enlarging documents, or projecting them onto a screen with an Elmo, a projector that doesn't require transparencies, to emphasize the important parts. I have also done just fine with nothing but a black marker and butcher paper to write on.

1. The easiest cases to illustrate.

Personal injury cases easily lend themselves to demonstrative evidence. Defendants frequently have the advantage in getting still shots or videos of an accident scene because they know about it immediately. However, plaintiffs' lawyers, who come to the case late, can compensate. In addition to shooting the site or doing a reconstruction, they should photograph or video their clients' injuries as soon as they are retained. The tiny scars that remain by time of trial often understate what plaintiffs have been through, but contemporaneous photos and videotapes don't. Of course, for badly injured plaintiffs unable to come to court, there is nothing as moving as a "day-in-the life" video, showing the struggle life has become. If possible, the video should reflect the plaintiff trying to make a comeback. Jurors in some parts of the country have been hardened to claims of pain and suffering and may resent a video that depicts the plaintiff as a victim rather than a survivor.

Computer-animated reconstruction of an accident or operation is vivid, persuasive, inexpensive—and available to both sides. For about $1,000, you can create a computer animation that will give the jurors the sense that they were there.

2. Making commercial cases accessible.

Graphics are essential to winning commercial cases. Even the most complex technology can be presented in a way that brings it down to earth. If the object involved is too large to bring into the courtroom, you can build a model. In patent infringement or misappropriation of trade secrets cases, the technology may be so complicated that you have to do something dramatic to demonstrate the truth or falsity of the claim. Sometimes, all it takes is superimposing the relevant portions of an accused product's blueprints over the patented product's—to demonstrate their similarity or dissimilarity. When the products involve moving parts, their movements can be vividly replicated by computer animation, also to show similarity or dissimilarity.

Time lines are useful in *every* kind of case—especially complex ones. But keep them simple. You must cull the important dates and documents from your warehouse of evidence, and put only them on your time line. If there are too many data points, the time line will be distracting. To keep the jurors focused and to prevent them from reading ahead, my graphics expert places a magnetic cover over each entry, which I remove as I reach that event in the story.

As innocuous as they seem, time lines can also send a powerful message. In a case alleging deception, you can put critical events and excerpts from documents above and below a time line. The entries "above the line" show what the defendant was saying publicly, while the entries "below the line" reveal the dirty dealing that was really going on. Of course, knowing this is coming, the defendant can create its own own accusatory chart, showing the plaintiff's bad acts "above" and "below" the line.

3. Don't overspend.

As you've probably gathered, you're not dealing with a big spender. There's nothing I like more than to try a case without fancy graphics, especially in contrast to the opponent who brings in laser discs, PowerPoint, and a marching band.

It's more than sufficient during opening or voir dire to have someone with neat handwriting outline the elements of your case and the definition of the burden of proof on butcher paper. Moreover, there is nothing clearer, or easier to read, than a transparency, and if you think even those are too expensive, then you are as frugal as my grandfather, who turned the radio down so low you almost couldn't hear it, on the theory that he would save money on the electricity bill.

Even in commercial cases involving huge dollars, you don't have to spend a fortune. For a trip to Kinko's and $25, a blow-up of a "bad" document can become your opponent's worst nightmare. In the Westinghouse case, while the plaintiffs built a $75,000 model of their power plant, a balsa model of the real thing would have worked fine. Moreover, we used the model as much as the plaintiffs did, which had to leave jurors wondering to which side it belonged.

4. Graphics must be 100-percent accurate.

Be very careful to review the final draft or rough cut of any form of graphics you use. If inaccurate, your demonstrative will make deadly fodder for cross-examination. There is no more vivid example than the Microsoft antitrust trial, when David Boies, lead trial lawyer for the government, dismembered a defense video by proving that it was grossly misleading—just riddled with flaws. In an ordinary case, that's awful—but for Microsoft, the world's leading creator of software, it was an unmitigated disaster.

In the Sakowitz case, the plaintiff spent $2,500 on a chart that purported to trace $1 million from the Sakowitz family business to my client, Robert Sakowitz's, pocket. The one fact left off the shiny graphic was that Robert had previously made an offsetting loan of $1 million to the corporation. While cross-examining the plaintiff's damages expert, who admitted the mistake, I borrowed a black marker from plaintiff's counsel and drew a nasty looking X across the chart. Then I asked, politely, if that made it more accurate.

5. Test-drive your graphics.

Make certain you get feedback on your graphics before you go to court. As trivial as it may seem, always ask jury study panelists if they can read each line or see each detail from where they are sitting. At trial, ask the same thing, or have the court inquire. I learned that lesson the hard way. Following a trial in which I represented one of the world's leading manufacturers of electronics, jurors told me that our graphics, projected on a screen, were out of focus and sometimes unreadable. For good measure, they added that it took too long to get them in focus. That underscores why you have to test-drive your graphics. Those kinds of problems drive a wedge between you and the jurors, needlessly distracting them from the substance of the document, or whatever it is that you are attempting to display.

6. Adjustments on the fly.

The advances in software in the last ten years have created greater flexibility in modifying graphics and creating new ones. If there is a surprise in testimony that affects the accuracy of a chart you have created (which seems to happen in every trial), you should be able to immediately fix your graphic using a laptop computer and portable printer. If you can't, you are dangerously behind the times and need to get up to speed.

B. Overkill

If you are going to do a demonstration, don't get carried away. Court-room demonstrations can be the undoing, not just the making, of a good verdict. A lawyer for the cologne Brut won a case in a Texas district court, having decided to lay to rest once and for all the canard that the cologne was flammable. The plaintiff alleged that while wearing Brut, he leaned close to a stove and suffered significant burns when his face caught on fire. During closing argument, the defense lawyer doused his arms with a bottle of Brut, and, accompanied by this monologue, put a lighter to it:

> God, if I am wrong, burn me. My friends, ladies and gentlemen of the jury, I urge you to believe the evidence of your eyes. If you have any doubt about it, try it for yourselves. Upon normal application, the product is not flam-mable. That's issue number one: Is the product flammable upon application to the skin? My goodness, you just saw me do it. I tried it at home before I tried it here to make sure. I tried it a hundred times. If it had burned one time, I wouldn't have done it here. You don't try this sort of thing in the courtroom without knowing in advance what is going to happen.

Because there is no justice in the world, his arm did not catch fire. Despite the plaintiff's failure to object, the court of appeals reversed, call-ing it plain error, a decision aided in no small way by the fact that the Brut he poured on his arm wasn't even admitted into the evidence. He bought it on the way to court that morning. I have no idea what happened to the case after that, but I think I'll make a few calls to find out.

There are limits to the usefulness of graphics, too. You don't need a chart for every concept that you are trying to prove. In the *Marriott* case, one of my fellow lawyers, an otherwise capable hand, had prepared a chart showing J. W. Marriott in a bed with an appraiser, holding a sack of money. In case a juror might miss the point, the sack had green dollar signs all over it. I told him I'd pass on using the chart, which was a tad condescending. The moral of the story: If you are down to drawing an apple with a rotten core to prove your point, bag it.

Voir Diring for Dollars 4

I. THE IMPORTANCE OF VOIR DIRE

Settlement talks failed. The judge just rejected defense counsel's sixth motion for continuance because America does not celebrate St. Swithin's Day. After years of preparation and delay, the case is finally ready for trial. The panel shuffles into the courtroom. You don't know any of them, and they don't want to be there. As you rise to address them, it feels like a mass blind date.

"Who is he to Hecuba or Hecuba to him?" asks Hamlet, in wonder, about an actor's ability to connect with a fictional character. In voir dire, a trial lawyer's job is even more difficult. You have to connect with a group of strangers immediately, and without the benefit of a dress rehearsal. While jurors are impressed most by what they see and hear first *and* last—the psychological principle of primary and recency—primacy is the first among those two equals. If you are not persuasive from the start, it won't matter if you conclude your case with a powerful witness or the revelation of the Eleventh Commandment. It will be too late. Jurors make up their minds quickly.

Mastering lawyer voir dire is difficult. It takes commitment, experience, an understanding of human behavior, and that mass of intangibles, people skills. But it is worth the effort. Somewhere among that panel is your jury. During voir dire you get to talk about the essential issues in your case with the very people who will decide them—and to subtly sell the themes that can determine their verdict. By the time that conversation is over, you can be light years ahead of your opponent. Or not. It all turns on your ability to conduct effective voir dire.

II. THE GOALS OF LAWYER VOIR DIRE

A. Successful Challenges for Cause

The most important goal of voir dire is to successfully *challenge for cause* as many unacceptable panelists as possible. Once you demonstrate that a given panelist has already made up her mind about some significant aspect of your case, and won't change it, the judge should disqualify her from serving on the jury. Each time you are successful, it enhances your chance of winning exponentially.

To understand why this is so, consider the relationship between challenges for cause and *peremptory strikes*—the other method available to lawyers for eliminating panelists. Because you can exercise "peremptories" against a panelist for any reason (save race and gender), they are invaluable. However, you get so few peremptories (rarely more than six, often as few as three), there is little margin for error in the exercise of each one. One mistake, one bully-boy juror you should have struck but didn't, and you can ruin your chances of winning.

That is why successful challenges for cause are such a godsend. Each time the judge grants your challenge, it creates a "two-strike swing" in your favor. Not only do you save the peremptory strike that you would have used on the panelist that the judge disqualified, you also get to use it on someone else you don't want. That is when your strikes really start to count.

Moreover, the benefit is cumulative. With the departure of each panelist for cause, the venire becomes more favorable to your side of the case. Exercising strikes on a pool like that is like shooting big game in a zoo: It may not be sportsmanlike, but it's infinitely more effective.

B. Committing Panelists to Your Client's Case and Cause

To be "light years ahead" at the end of voir dire, you must not only convince the judge to disqualify undesirable panelists; you must also commit some number of those who remain to your client and his cause. Committing them is easier than it may appear. A profoundly psychological exercise, all you have to do is get the panel talking about experiences in their own lives that reflect the events that brought your client to court. As you will see, these shared experiences create an almost unbreakable bond between some panelists and your client, an emotional commitment that can last through deliberations. (See p. 92, "Link panelists' lives to your client's and his cause.")

III. THE MANY FACES OF VOIR DIRE

A. Lawyer Voir Dire

Lawyer voir dire is allowed in some form in most states, and is even allowed in a few federal courts.[1] In some jurisdictions, voir dire is so wide

---

1. Only six states make no statutory provision for lawyer voir dire: DE, IL, ME, MA, NH, and NJ. Nevertheless, it is allowed in IL, and NH is conducting a pilot program. The other 46 jurisdictions (including federal courts and D.C.) either: (1) mandate lawyer voir dire as the only form of voir dire, (2) allow lawyer voir dire in addition to voir dire by the judge, or (3) allow lawyer voir dire in the court's discretion. Those in category (1) are: CT, FL, GA, HI, IA, KS, MO, MT, NE, NY, ND, PA, TX, VT, WA, and WY (16 jurisdictions); category (2): AZ, CA, CO, ID, LA, NV, NC, OK, OR, VA, and WI (11 jurisdictions); category (3): AL, AK, AR, DC, IN, KY, MD, MI, MN, MS, NM, OH, RI, SC, SD, TN, UT, WV, and the federal courts (19 jurisdictions).

open that it fairly invites the filing of cases there. As a colleague of mine from deep East Texas drawled after selecting a jury in state court in New York City, "David, you won't believe what all they let you do up here." He was referring to the fact that judges aren't required to be present during voir dire in civil trials in New York state—the prevalent, if waning, practice in Manhattan.

In other jurisdictions, the judge presides over jury selection, usually beginning with some words of welcome and an explanation of voir dire. Then the judge questions panelists to determine if any of them should be disqualified for statutory reasons, such as a felony conviction, or because they will suffer undue hardship if selected, like a single parent with no one to pick up the children.

With those preliminary matters out of the way, each side is given an opportunity to ask questions of the panelists, starting with the plaintiff's counsel. When both sides finish, those panelists whose answers raised questions about their ability to serve impartially are brought up to the bench, where both sides can question them further about their views. At the conclusion of the questioning, the lawyers can move to challenge a panelist for cause, and the judge rules on the spot. If there are enough panelists remaining to fill the jury,[2] each side exercises its peremptory strikes. If there are not enough panelists left to fill the jury, the judge either brings in additional candidates from the jury assembly room or declares a mistrial and voir dire starts over at a later date.

B. Judge Voir Dire

I have never seen a meaningful voir dire when the judge does the questioning. They rarely elicit any valuable information about panelists, and certainly not enough to inform strikes or create challenges for cause. Granted, judges aren't supposed to be advocates, but that is little consolation when it comes time to strike the jury.

---

2. To calculate the number of panelists needed to fill the jury, simply add the total jurors required to the total strikes per side. For example, in a case requiring 13 jurors (including an alternate), and where each side has four strikes (including one for the alternate), the calculation is as follows:

Total number of jurors required for the case =	13 (12 + 1 alternate)
+ Total peremptory strikes	8 (3 per side + 1 each for alternate)
Total panelists needed to fill the jury =	21

Nevertheless, there is a way to be successful selecting juries when the judge conducts voir dire. Once you understand the goals and tactics of lawyer voir dire, as practiced in courts that allow it, you can apply a great deal of what you know in the courts where the judge asks the questions. While your opponent is flipping coins, your experience, understanding, and instinct will help you select a better jury. (See p. 119, "Emergency Room Voir Dire: When the Judge Asks the Questions.")

IV. LAYING THE GROUNDWORK

A. Before Trial Begins

Law schools don't teach voir dire, so new lawyers enter litigation sections unaware of the fundamentals and importance of the process. Even if they have studied the techniques of voir dire, the minute-to-minute reality of the courtroom can overwhelm beginners. The following suggestions are designed to give new lawyers a way to fill in that experience gap—long before the first question.

1. Watch a good lawyer conduct voir dire.

Young lawyers, especially, need to go to a courthouse and watch a good lawyer conduct voir dire. Not only will they begin to understand the principles of voir dire, they will also learn the answers to some basic but important questions, such as: Where do the panelists sit during voir dire? (In the gallery, facing the lawyers.) Where do I stand? (In the well of the court, facing the panelists.) How much time do I get from the judge? (Depends on the judge and jurisdiction.) When do I get the jury questionnaires back? (Probably just before the panel is seated.) How long do I have to review the questionnaires before starting voir dire? (As much time as the judge decides.)

2. Always request individual voir dire, even in federal court.

Individual voir dire is not allowed in most federal courts, but there are exceptions. For example, trial lawyers in the Southern District of Texas argued for individual voir dire so consistently for such a long period of time that at least half of the judges now allow it in some meaningful form. Given that success, trial lawyers everywhere ought to be encouraged to file a motion requesting some level of individual voir dire. Point to the Southern District of Texas for support, along with any other federal jurisdictions you happen to know about.

3. Always request a jury questionnaire.

The use of jury questionnaires is so commonplace that you and opposing counsel should be able to draft a single questionnaire that is acceptable to both sides. There is no good reason for a judge to deny a request for a questionnaire, whether it's a joint request or not, and they rarely do.[3] If the court provides a questionnaire that is superficial, ask to augment it or to provide one that is acceptable to both sides. (See p. 123, Appendix A, Sample Juror Questionnaire.) If the case justifies it, bring a forensic psychologist to court to explain the value of a detailed questionnaire. Let the judge know by your insistence how important the questionnaire is, and how it aids both sides.

4. Visit the locale.

With the increase in national practices, many lawyers try cases in jurisdictions where they've never appeared. Before you tee it up in a remote jurisdiction, it is imperative to spend some time there, learning about the judge, the residents, and local points of pride. If you don't know, or don't care, that the Kaiser Cats beat Ramona over the weekend, you ought to stay home. That is especially true in smaller towns and rural areas, where everyone talks to each other, and where trials are still a form of entertainment. Besides, you never know what you might learn. Ask Joe Jamail. He once stopped at a gas station as he entered a small Texas town where he was going to try a case against a local refinery. When the attendant learned why Jamail was in town, he said, "Well, don't worry none, son. We goin' to break it off in 'em."

Taking meals at the local diner is a good idea, although it is probably unwise to leave a $400 tip for the waitress who tells you that she's been called to jury duty for your trial. Folks who live in small-town America want to know that you are "good people." It follows that you should be friendly to everyone you encounter, even if it is for you, as it is for me, entirely out of character. You want to be sure the server invites you back to

---

3. In fact, Pennsylvania's voir dire statute encourages the use of juror questionnaires, so it might help to bring that statute to the court's attention. See Pa. R. Civ. P. 220.1(b)–(c).

the diner with some variation of the Southern farewell, "Now don't be a stranger." Translation: you passed the "good-people" test.

I could go on, but the following story makes the point better than anything I could ever write or say. A friend of mine, Mark Lanier, tried a case in a poor farming area about an hour south of Houston. The jury pool of 100 included only two college graduates and perhaps 50 others who had finished high school. Lanier's case alleged that Met Life was liable to some workers who had mesothelioma and other asbestos-related diseases, on the theory that the company knew about the dangers of asbestos as early as the 1940s, when it insured certain asbestos manufacturers, but did nothing about the danger. For a lot of reasons, not the least of which is what we sticklers would call a total absence of evidence, the insurance company had never paid anything but nuisance money, literally cents on the dollar, to settle one of these cases.

Within minutes of starting his voir dire, defense counsel lost the case. He began by introducing himself—the last thing, I am told, that went well. Then he asked, "How many of you have had an article peer-reviewed?" Undeterred by the blank looks and complete silence, he continued. "Well, let me ask this. Do you remember walking into your first biochem lab in college?" With that question, 200 eyes narrowed. Finally, he decided to try a sports question, asking how many of the panelists played golf. Again, utter silence. "Come on, fellows," MONY's lawyer said, "you're just embarrassed to admit you love the game. So, let me ask you this. When you get in your cart, have you ever noticed the little warning sticker above the panel on the left? There are seven warnings in all." According to *The Wall Street Journal*, the defendant paid $20 million to stop the trial.

B. Once the Panel Is Seated

In large measure, effective voir dire depends on your ability to stay on point and organized. Your chances of making cogent strikes, creating challenges for cause—or achieving any goal of voir dire—is about as good as the data about panelists that you and your colleagues collect on a jury chart.

1. Draw a jury chart.

Assume you have a panel of 24 people. Facing them, panelist 1 is usually the person seated farthest to your left on the first row. Obviously, if the panelists are seated eight across, there will be three rows. You and each member of your team must create a jury chart like the one in Figure 4.1, filling in each panelist's name and seat number. In addition, based on your jury profile and the answers to the questionnaires, tentatively rank as many of the panelists as your information allows, on a scale from 1 to 5, 1 being the worst potential juror, and 5 the best. For reasons that will become clear, also rank the panelists from your opponent's point of view. (See p. 112, "Identify your opponent's likely strikes.") In their squares on the chart, make note of any information you need to pursue with a particular panelist.

As voir dire progresses, summarize the panelists' relevant responses and nonverbal clues in their squares. Rank the panelists you couldn't categorize before questioning began. Keep updating your chart and fine-tuning the rankings. You'll make use of all this information when you strike the jury. Make a copy of this chart. You'll need it for the next section.

2. Identify panelists you must question.

Before you begin questioning, you must identify the last panelist who is eligible for jury duty, and, most important, where he is seated. That prevents you from questioning panelists who can't make it to the jury and skipping over those who can. For this calculation, first determine the total number of panelists required to fill your jury. Using the same formula as in

Figure 4.1
Sample Jury Chart

17	18	19	20	21	22	23	24
9	10	11	12	13	14	15	16
1 Name/ Bullet points/ Info from questionnaire/ ranking/	2	3	4	5	6	7	8

footnote 2, p. 74, assume your case requires 17 panelists (9 jurors including an alternate + 8 total strikes). Next, figure out where those 17 eligible panelists are seated. They won't necessarily be in the first 17 seats, because, by now, the judge has probably excused some people for statutory and hardship reasons. Grab your jury chart—and start making adjustments.

a. "X" out panelists excused before lawyer questioning began.

Assume that the judge has excused two panelists, 4 and 12. Mark an X through their squares on the chart, as in Figure 4.2 below, so that there won't be any question that they are off the panel. That means you must question the next two panelists beyond 17—those who will replace the two who've been excused. That takes you to panelist 19.

b. Mark a "?" for panelists who *might* be disqualified for cause.

Assume that two other panelists, 8 and 16, gave the plaintiff's lawyer answers that *could* result in their being disqualified for cause. Place question marks in their boxes on the chart, as in Figure 4.2 below. In order to question every panelist who could conceivably become a juror, you must assume that those two will be disqualified, which adds two more people to the eligible list, taking you to panelist 21. Remember, you won't know if those two panelists (8 and 16) will be disqualified until *after* you and your opponent complete voir dire, and they are brought to the bench for further questioning. Don't assume that they won't make it and skip over them. If you are wrong, you will have missed an opportunity to create a rapport with them, and perhaps created an enemy (or two) because of your unexplained slight in not questioning them.

There is one other, rolling adjustment that you must make—panelists whose answers to *your* questions leaves them susceptible to challenges for cause. Assume that panelists 5 and 15 give you such answers. That makes panelist 23 the last potential juror—two more people down the line. Panelists 5 and 15 should both receive question marks on your chart.

At this point, your jury chart will look something like the one in Figure 4.2. For purposes of clarity, I have included sample notes only for the panelists mentioned above—with rankings from the perspective of defense counsel. In a real trial, the chart would be covered with similar information.

Figure 4.2
Sample Working Jury Chart

17	18	19	20	21	22	23 Stop!	24
9	10	11	12 Port ✕	13	14	15 Tate? • Union Organizer 1	16 Hart? • Hates the plaintiff's lawyer 4+
1	2	3	4 Holt ✕	5 Polk ? • Won't give punitives 5	6	7	8 Kahn? • feels "bad" for plaintiff 2

3.   Never take notes during your own voir dire.

This is one of the few ironclad rules of this book. If you want to learn everything that you can about the panelists, don't take notes while you're on your feet. You must listen closely to the panelists' answers, and look them in the eyes while you do. Be on guard for body language that belies the words being spoken. If you are furiously scribbling notes, you will miss those clues. You will also make the panel nervous, when you should be calmly earning their trust.

It is impossible for one lawyer to pick up every significant answer or nonverbal response, anyway. Always have someone in court to help you, not only taking notes during your voir dire, but throughout the trial. If you don't have professionals to assist you, bring a family member or friend. Anyone who is smart and sensitive can be trusted to read the panelists' reactions, and make notes of significant verbal and nonverbal responses.

In addition, your colleagues can help keep the panelists straight, identifying who it was that said this or that, where that person was sitting, what they were wearing, and the color of their hair. Every good trial lawyer, including this one, has misidentified a panelist, allowing someone who should have been struck to sit on his jury. A second set of eyes can make a real difference.

V. GETTING A GREAT JURY

A. Take Real Command of the Courtroom

Power belongs to those who exercise it—a political lesson with unmistakable application to trials. The power vacuum in the courtroom is simply too large for the judge alone to fill. Talented trial lawyers step immediately into that breach, taking command of the courtroom, even when they are unaware that is what they are doing.

Taking real command, however, requires more than striding confidently to the lectern. That sort of nonverbal communication is critical, but it is also superficial. Anyone can look good for a while. I've watched many trial lawyers fade after a strong opening because they have little understanding of the underlying purpose of voir dire, no real interest in what the panelists have to say, and, consequently, little capacity to get them talking.

If you want panelists to respond, your effort must go deeper than just the appearance of empathy and interest. You must tap into the wiser part of yourself—the part that listens, tries to understand what is going on inside of people, and searches for the meaning hidden in a sudden smile or hesitant answer.

For defense lawyers, who are often analytical and detached, tapping into the wiser part of yourself means displaying compassion for a badly injured plaintiff, who may or may not be the victim of your client's conduct. You're not admitting liability by being kind. You're being smart by being human. Of course, when the suit is frivolous, your attitude can reflect it—even to the point of being disdainful. But be careful that you differentiate correctly between frivolous and nonfrivolous suits. If you are wrong, you will anger the jurors.

B. Six Steps to Successful Voir Dire

There are six stages of voir dire—at least on paper: (1) Putting the panelists at ease; (2) Humanizing your clients; (3) Asking open-ended questions of the panel as a whole, following up on their answers with questions directed to individuals; (4) Asking questions of individuals about their personal and work lives; (5) Creating challenges for cause; and (6) Striking the jury.

The reason I say "at least on paper" is because it is possible to get rolling on one question in the initial stages of voir dire, and keep a productive discussion going among the panelists for the entire time—right up to the point that you strike the jury. Nevertheless, it's not always that easy, so it is important to master each stage.

1. Put the panelists at ease.

Think about what you are asking of the panelists and the setting in which you are doing it. You want them to express real feelings about subjects they probably haven't discussed at home, much less in a room filled with strangers, or, in the case of small towns, with people they know.

To win them over, put them at ease. Don't jump into your questioning. Instead, start by explaining briefly what the process is about. Let the panelists know what you are going to do (ask questions) and what you expect of them (candid answers). Let them know that you are aware many of them are afraid of being called on—something every former law student should understand, and mention. Don't waste time translating "voir dire" from the French. There is no accurate translation and the panelists don't care what it means anyway.

Here's an example of how a plaintiff's lawyer might start:

Good morning, ladies and gentlemen. As Her Honor told you a few moments ago, I represent John Alexander and Fiona Waterstreet, and I am going to ask you some questions in a few minutes. But I know from your jury questionnaires that very few of you have served on a jury, so before I start asking questions, I am going to take a few minutes to expand on what the judge has said, and to explain what this process is all about.

Both sides get to ask you questions. The purpose is to try to understand your feelings about certain issues related to the case. Each side will have an hour, and at the end of that time, we want to have as much information as possible to help us make better decisions about who should serve on the jury. That will not be my decision alone. This is John and Fiona's jury and, as you will see, they will help make those decisions, too.

So, at this stage, the most important thing I can do to fulfill my responsibility to John and Fiona is to encourage you folks to answer my questions as openly as possible. All of us—the judge, John and Fiona, the defendants over there, and their lawyers—need you to be as open and candid as you can be when you respond. What we need to do our job is to get your impressions and ideas about the issues we are going to discuss this morning. Your candor makes this process work, and makes it fair.

Let me be clear about one thing: There are no right or wrong answers to these questions. We just want to get your views on some things that matter to both sides of this lawsuit. In short, the way it works is this: I have a responsibility to ask questions and you have a responsibility to answer them as openly as you can.

One other thing before I start. If there is anything you want to discuss in private, just raise your hand and we will go to the bench to discuss whatever it is with the judge. We always do that if there is a personal matter involved—or anything at all that you don't want to say in front of the entire panel. And don't worry about being nervous. In fact, I'm a bit nervous myself. As you can imagine, I don't want to let John and Fiona down.

In what amounts to a two- or three-minute opening statement, every word counts. If you make yourself more human ("I'm a bit nervous"), you make it easier for the panelists to talk to you, and the process becomes less daunting for them. If they believe that the case and your clients really matter to you ("I don't want to let John and Fiona down"), they may let go of the anti–trial-lawyer feelings they may have. Referring to your responsibility elevates your reason for being there. You don't want to sound sanctimonious, but trial lawyers can't afford to be cynical either—not if they want to establish a rapport with panelists. Wedding their duty to yours ("I have a responsibility—you have a responsibility") creates a kind of high-minded teamwork that elevates their reason for being there, too. The panel should see their service as a rare chance to make a difference in the lives of their neighbors, which, in fact, is the case. I often tell panels that I have rarely met anyone who actually served on a jury who didn't treasure the experience.

To avoid sounding too intrusive, I offer to take individual panelists to the bench to discuss anything they don't want to talk about in front of the rest of the panel. Telling them that is "always" how things are done makes discussing personal issues the everyday fare of jury selection—just another day at the office. In addition, showing concern for their privacy allows me to sound protective, a subtle step in breaking down the barriers between the panelists and me. Most important, making "up at the bench" a safe place to be is smart. It is there, out of the earshot of the other panelists, that you will have the opportunity to question an unwanted venireman more aggressively, and to do some of the most productive work of voir dire.

Voir dire is nothing if not subtle, especially when it comes to the words that you choose. Ask panelists to be "open," not "honest," which implies that they might lie to you—which, of course, some of them do. Nevertheless, you must attempt to convince them of the virtue of candor—even if it means their disqualification. Because it's honest answers you are after, never tell panelists that you are going to try to find out their "biases" and "prejudices." I hear lawyers make statements like that all the time. You might as well ask for a showing of hands of all the bigots on the panel.

Once questioning begins, take pains to reassure panelists even as you press them for their opinions. Show concern for any discomfort they have with your questions, and explain your reasons for asking. I frequently follow up an answer that may have been difficult for a panelist to provide, with a question that I have found to be as reliable as an old friend: "Mr. Jones, do you understand why I had to ask you that question?" This is a great question for reasons I have never been able to express entirely. There is just something respectful about it—as if the panelist and I are doing this difficult thing together. So far, the response has always been something like, "I understand. You have to do your job." Even if I someday get a hostile response, it will tell me a lot about the panelist—and provide an opportunity to ask a follow-up that allows him to get whatever is bothering him off his chest.

Before general questioning begins, I always make one other "confessional" comment, designed to ease their minds about admitting their own inability to serve. I tell them there are some juries I could not sit on:

> Look, I am a lawyer. I should be able to put my personal opinions to one side. But if I were sitting on a criminal case where child molesting was the charge, I would have to tell the court that I could not serve—that my feelings would affect my ability to deliberate fairly on the defendant's guilt or innocence. The defendant would start out way behind with me. Do you understand why I would do that?

This type of question is unlikely to get anyone dismissed for cause at this early stage of voir dire. Instead, it conditions panelists to think that there are certain cases where they could not be fair, and that admitting it is the honorable thing to do. The tricky part is to flush out confessions of bias only from the panelists you don't want—which is a function of knowing which questions to ask, and when, and what to do after—in other words, the point of this chapter.

Finally, as you prepare to move to another phase of voir dire, remind the panel one last time why they are there, and how important their role is:

> As I mentioned earlier, this case is very important to John and Fiona. This is their day in court—their *only* day in court. So all of us need to make certain we do this right. If anything occurs to you that you feel is important, anything that affects your ability to sit as a juror in this case, please let us know. There is no other way for John and Fiona to get a fair jury and a fair trial. That's all I'm trying to accomplish by asking these questions. I'm trying to get a fair jury.

Well, not exactly. As an advocate, the last thing I want is a fair jury. I'm trying to seat twelve people so biased against the other side that the trial will be all but over by the time they are sworn in to serve.

2. Humanize your clients.

After making your opening remarks, introduce your clients, but in a way that shows your relationship with them really matters: "My name is

David Berg and I am proud to represent John Alexander and Fiona Water-street." That pride should be apparent in your words *and* body language. Stand next to your clients. Never point at them across the room. Whether your clients are individuals or corporations, never refer to them as "defendants" or "plaintiffs." Those are the impersonal, vaguely pejorative-sounding labels reserved for the opposition. From time to time, call your clients by their first names, including the senior-most corporate officer in your case.[4]

Not just during jury selection, but throughout the trial, do all that you can to convey the message that you like and respect your clients. If the jurors grow to like them—as you obviously do—it makes a decision against them harder. It's difficult for anyone to say "no" to people they like.

While humanizing the client is critical to your success in any kind of case, it is especially so when representing corporations. You have to give potential jurors—already suspicious of big business—reason to believe that the business that you represent is no Enron, and deserves to be judged on its own merits. To accomplish that, you must equate the company with the good people who work there: individuals with first names, personalities, pride in their company, and a real stake in the outcome of the case.

In my practice, humanizing a corporation was never more critical than when I represented Westinghouse in the case filed against it by the South Texas Project ("STP"). STP filed the suit in Matagorda County, Texas, where it is the largest employer, taxpayer, and an exemplary corporate citizen. STP's claim was that Westinghouse had sold it defective nuclear steam generators. Not only did STP have a huge home-court advantage, but some of its employees had waged an anti-Westinghouse campaign throughout the county during the four years prior to trial. An award in the billions against Westinghouse was a real possibility.

Prior to sending out jury notices, the sheriff assured us that he had removed anyone from the list who worked for the power plant—thereby leaving 250 of their closest friends and relatives to fill the cavernous courtroom.

---

4. In Texas, incidentally, our bovine friends get the same treatment. In the early 1980s, a Houston personal injury lawyer, John O'Quinn, won an $8.5-million verdict for the owner of a deceased stud bull, "Superman," who was felled midstream of an enviable career by cruel circumstance and an apparently lethal pesticide. When I asked O'Quinn how he had persuaded the jury to return such a large award for the beloved bovine, he draped his arm over my shoulder, kicked the dirt with his pointy-toe boots, and said, with understandable pride, "I just humanized the bull."

During voir dire, the judge allowed Daryl Bristow, lead lawyer for the plaintiffs (and later a member of President Bush's trial team in Florida following the 2000 election), to use videotaped deposition excerpts, documents, and graphics. My New York colleague, Jim Quinn, could not believe what he was witnessing. Bristow's voir dire, interrupted only for an occasional question of the panelists, was like a prosecutor's closing argument in a murder case.

I recognize that the extraordinary latitude we enjoyed during voir dire doesn't exist in many courtrooms—not even in Texas. Therefore, I have chosen examples from that voir dire that apply in all kinds of cases.

A few minutes into my voir dire, I began humanizing Westinghouse. I had a half-dozen of its nuclear scientists and engineers seated in the row just beyond the venire. Some were coatless, some sported pocket protectors, and several looked scared. Holding a hand mike, I walked through the swinging gates that separated me from the panelists, down the aisle to where they were seated. Each man took the mike, said "hello" or "good morning," and introduced himself. I then explained that each of these men was present at the birth of nuclear power in our country:

> Every one of them had something to do with putting Westinghouse nuclear engines on Navy submarines in the '60s. They are very proud of that history. And so are their families. In fact, Ernie here is a second-generation Westinghouse engineer himself, and guess where his daughter works?
>
> These are the men who designed and helped install much of the equipment in the power plant here. They are as proud of what they have accomplished as any job they've done, except maybe the one for the Navy, because that involved national security. This suit may be against Westinghouse, but *they* are the ones accused of committing fraud.

If my client was going to get slammed with a big verdict, I wanted the panelists to understand that the consequences went beyond the corporation to the people who worked there—that reputations, and perhaps jobs, were at stake—something that the men and women of a blue-collar county like Matagorda would identify with and understand. I also wanted to make the implicit point that the only real difference between Westinghouse and STP engineers and scientists was the company they worked for. Similar points should be made representing any company.

Lawyers have to make themselves human, too. My colleague in the Westinghouse case, Jim Quinn, practices in New York City. We worried how he would play in South Texas, a concern I tested during voir dire when a venireman asked me an esoteric question about radioactive materials at the plant. I didn't know what the answer was, so, without warning to Quinn, I said, "Jim, why don't you answer that one?" Then I introduced him to the panel. "This is my co-counsel, Jim Quinn, who, despite being from New York, is a relatively decent human being. He's going to try this case, too, so I want you to get to meet him." I sat down, curious to see if Quinn had Texas-sized anything.

Jim wriggled the hand mike free and walked around the lectern, leaning against the plaintiff's counsel table. After a long moment, he said, "Howdy, y'all. How ya' dune?" Well, buckaroos, they say you could hear the "yee-haws" all the way to Mount Pleasant. "Do I sound like a Texan?" he added, and they roared.

Now, Quinn claims *I* fake sincerity better than anyone he knows, but folks, that day he was really on. He even managed to tell the predominantly Catholic jury pool that he had gone to Notre Dame. When he got to a story about Sister Ignatius, his favorite high school teacher, I had to resume the voir dire myself. Even I felt shame for him, because the man obviously had none of his own. The jury loved him. In fact, fears of geographic bias against lawyers are exaggerated. Jurors respect lawyers who are good at what they do, regardless of where the lawyers hang their hats when the case is over.

One final word before moving on: This entire exercise, from putting panelists at ease to introducing and humanizing your clients, takes no more than six or seven minutes. It's a great investment of time.

3. Ask questions of the panel as a whole.

This is the guts of voir dire. During this stage, you can (1) commit panelists to your client and his cause, and (2) create challenges for cause. The key to achieving these goals is to encourage panelists to speak their minds by asking them provocative, open-ended questions. As *laissez-faire* as that may sound, it is anything but that. By their very nature, open-ended questions allow you to direct the panelists' "freewheeling" discussion to your ends (committing panelists and creating challenges)—while appearing to do no more than letting them roam free.

a. Ask open-ended questions.

In an effort to avoid "bad" answers that might poison the panel, many trial lawyers ask questions that stifle discussion, rather than encouraging it. Yet, by eliminating "bad" answers, these lawyers also eliminate honest ones, a huge mistake. It's *reliable information* you are after, not the panel's forced or mindless agreement. Besides, it's not going to destroy your case if someone says aloud that he would never award punitive damages, that trial lawyers are greedy, or that tobacco company executives are criminals. Quite the opposite. Without knowing what panelists really think, you risk putting one or more spoilers on your jury.

How can you encourage panelists to speak freely and to give honest answers? Assure them that there are no right or wrong answers—and really mean it. Whenever possible, especially when you begin your voir dire, ask open-ended questions—never forcing a favorable answer. Let the panelists talk—not just to you, but to each other as well.

Trial lawyers didn't ask open-ended questions during voir dire when I started practicing.[5] I learned to treat jury selection as an opportunity to

---

5. Back then, lawyers learned to ask four types of questions, which were designed to (1) educate, (2) condition, (3) commit, and (4) select (out) panelists. Because the goals served by those four categories of questions are valuable (although more easily attained by open-ended questioning), and because they are an excellent teaching tool for beginning lawyers, I have included a discussion of each one.

1. Questions that educate. These questions are asked in conjunction with explanatory comments about the law related to your case, such as the burden of proof or elements of your main cause of action or defense. Plaintiffs' lawyers often start by explaining the burden to the panelists, with the textbook definition written on a piece of butcher paper mounted on an easel. Then they explain it in plain language, using their hands to create the familiar imagery of the scales of justice:

   What proving the case by a preponderance of evidence means, very simply, is that when the evidence is in, we only have to tip the scales ever so slightly, by a tiny grain of sand, to win. Is there anyone who would require more proof than this [lowering one hand and raising the other slightly]?

   Without more, this form of questioning is useless. No panelist would disagree with that proposition without some motivation from you to do so. Using a more sophisticated approach, you can get panelists to admit that they can't follow the law, by saying that they would require the plaintiff to introduce more proof than that tiny grain of sand to win, or, that they would require the defendant to produce any proof at all. (See p. 98, "Flush out unacceptable panelists, all at once.")

2. Questions that condition. Traditionally, questions that condition panelists are anything but open-ended. They are designed to force panelists to think your way about key issues in your case. For example, in a case alleging fraud in the inducement to sign a contract, you would introduce the idea that what is said prior to signing the contract is more important than the written document itself—and then gauge the reaction: "Of course, there are all kinds of provisions written into a contract, but we believe that what people promised to each other during negotiations—before it was signed—is more important than the written words. We believe a man's word is his bond. Do you agree, Ms. Johnson?" However tempting such an approach might be, the lopsided emotional content precludes informative answers. It would take a very strong panelist to say that she didn't believe

make an opening argument and hammer panelists into voting my way. Asking questions in a way that sold the case, I would try to commit panelists to a verdict: "If I prove by a preponderance of the evidence that Mr. Johnson's broken neck was a result of the defendant's negligence, would you follow the law that permits you to award money damages for his pain and suffering?"

---

that a man's word is his bond. To make the response more predictive, balance the emotion: "Or do you believe that a contract must be in writing—in other words, if it's not in the contract, it doesn't matter what else is said?" That combination of questions is far more likely to expose what the panelists really believe—especially those critical few on every panel who think everything must be in writing. By minimizing the coercive element in your questions, you can still get panelists thinking your way about the case—and uncover panelists you won't want.

3. Questions that commit. Commitment questions are barely distinguishable from conditioning questions, except that they are generally asked in order to nail down the verdict. For example:

   You heard what the plaintiff's lawyer said about the burden of proof, Mr. Johnson. He said that he had to tip the scales in his favor. Now, if he fails to do that, can you look the plaintiff in the eyes and tell him, "I feel badly for you. I know you are terribly injured. But I cannot award damages to you"?

   Here—much like the salesperson who asks before making his sales pitch, "If the price is right, and the terms are acceptable, will you buy the carpet?"—the lawyer attempts to "prequalify," or commit, the panelists. That question is not terrible. However, because of its coercive nature, the answer could prove unreliable. Ask instead, "How would you feel about voting against the plaintiff if he fails to prove his case?" That gives the panelist, not you, the opportunity to bring up whether it would be difficult or not to tell a badly injured plaintiff, "no." Note also that the question is predicated on what the plaintiff's lawyer said about the burden of proof—it's never too early to take on your opponent.

4. Questions that select (litmus-test questions). The answers to these questions tell you whether a panelist should stay or go. Racehorse Haynes used to say that all he needed to know to make that decision was how a panelist voted in the 1964 presidential election (Lyndon Johnson versus Barry Goldwater), and he wouldn't have to ask anything else. However, since many panelists now were not born before that election, must less voted in it, a more mainstream example is in order. For instance, plaintiffs' lawyers must ask how panelists feel about punitive and noneconomic damages, given widespread public hostility toward awarding either. Litmus-test questions and, in fact, all generalizations about people have become far less reliable since the 1960s, and the sea change of social conditions in this country. In most jurisdictions, the old stereotypes about people from different races or religions voting a particular way no longer hold true. Those lines were blurred long ago.

"Would you actually do that—return a verdict awarding substantial money damages?" What answer can a venireman give but "yes"? Committing panelists to your cause is a primary goal of voir dire, but that's not the way to do it. Questions like that all but state that panelists would be breaking the law if they don't agree to an award. Besides, with everyone listening, a panelist doesn't want to sound callous.

According to Ronny Krist, past-president of the International Academy of Trial Lawyers, this sort of browbeating question produces a "transitory" juror, one willing to give the answer suggested by the question, but one who could easily change his mind during trial. It costs a panelist nothing, emotionally or in the eyes of other panel members, to agree to an obvious answer. There is no commitment to the answer. If the plaintiff's lawyer took him at his word, she would never strike him. Yet, he may lead the charge against her client—something that she couldn't know until the jury returns.

A far more effective strategy is to ask that same panelist how he *feels* about awarding money for pain and suffering. The difference is not merely semantic. This question is open-ended. Rather than suggesting the answer, it encourages the panelist to say what is on his mind.

Of course, there are many people (often referred to as "men") who are frightened by the prospect of talking about their feelings, especially in a courtroom filled with strangers or in a small town, where everyone knows everyone. For such a panelist, you may have to take the concept of "feelings" down an emotional notch or two. Try asking them about their "beliefs" or "ideas" instead.

I concede there are risks when you allow panelists to speak their minds. Occasionally, answers to open-ended questions will reveal that someone is completely committed to your position, so much so that you lose him to an opponent's challenge for cause or peremptory strike. Nor am I dismissive of those lawyers who fear that a bad answer will poison the panel. I heard about an old gentleman on a panel in Dallas who asked the plaintiff's lawyer seeking punitive damages, "Son, why do you need all that money?" A comment like that, rare as it may be, is difficult to overcome. Yet, you're seldom at a total loss for a remedy. There are antidotes for even that toxic a poison, including offering evidence at trial that decisively answers his question—and striking him so that he never gets a chance to hear and ignore such evidence.

Not even the staunchest advocate of open-ended questioning believes that every question can be open-ended. There are times when a more traditional, somewhat coercive series of questions will serve your purpose—but only at the right time. (See, e.g., p. 106, "Elevate what was said to a matter of principle.") If you let the panelists talk freely first, getting their concerns out in the open, they will be far more receptive to questions that none-too-subtly sell some part of your case. When you do move away from open-ended questions, however, make certain that you have a good reason, and cushion the blow. Never pressure panelists into agreeing with you. Reassure them often that there are no right or wrong answers, and that their candor is what makes the process work.

Since you have asked the panelists to be open and assured them that there are no right or wrong answers, you should rarely disagree with anything they say. However, there is a limit to what you have to indulge. If someone constantly interrupts you or other panelists, you have to cut them off. Ronnie Krist once told a hostile, nonstop talker on his panel, "Sir, each lawyer in this case has six strikes. I can use mine to get rid of any panelist I don't want for any reason at all. So sit down and quit talking because you ain't going to be on my jury." There may be subtler ways of shutting up a panelist, but none, I would guess, is more effective.

i.   *Loop answers into alliances.*

By asking open-ended questions, you encourage answers that lend themselves to what forensic scientists call "looping." The rest of us would call it "conversation." The lawyer simply bats an answer from the panelist who gave it to another who disputes it or agrees with it. Having started the conversation, the lawyer then withdraws from the fray. For example: "Mr. Johnson, what did you think of Ms. Jones's answer that she would never award punitive damages?"

Whether there is a widespread discussion or just two panelists agreeing or disagreeing with each other, it is not idle conversation. Panelists who agree will form an alliance—one that almost certainly will last throughout trial, assuming they both make it to the jury. If they disagree, they provide valuable information about themselves. For example, a discussion about punitive damages is certain to inflame ideologues on both sides of the issue—and reveal disqualifying opinions on the subject as well.

If the argument gets heated, that's great. If it becomes chaotic, with everyone talking at once, step in to restore order. Remind the panel that your time is limited, repeat someone's position on the hot topic ("Who disagrees with what Ms. Jones said about tobacco companies?"), and get them back to responding one person at a time.

Looping also allows panelists to develop the themes of your case for themselves, building on each other's comments. When that happens, the trial strategy you have worked on for years becomes their idea. The evidence that they later hear will confirm what they began to suspect during voir dire.

Some forensic experts suggest that you must end these round-robin discussions on a favorable note, hearing last from a panelist who expressed views aligned with your case, but I don't think that is critical. The object is to get the issue out there, whatever it might be, and to find out where *each* panelist stands, if it's humanly possible. If you are running out of time, and there are still some panelists who haven't let their feelings be known, you can always put an issue to a vote, row by row: "Raise your hand if you agree with Mr. Jones, about never awarding punitive damages." Make certain no one is lying behind the log: "Now raise your hand if you disagree." That should elicit a response from everyone.

Watch the panelists who make it to the jury buddy up once the trial begins. Those who agreed during voir dire will become fast friends, sitting next to one another in the box and taking breaks together. Their impact on the panel's deliberations will be greater because they will act together, supporting and rescuing one another when necessary. They almost certainly will vote alike. If there are more than two who bonded during voir dire, even better. They will probably cast their votes in a bloc.

ii.   Test the reliability of answers.

When a panelist expresses an opinion about a significant matter, ask how strongly she feels about what she has said, on a scale of one to ten. You will learn from her answer whether she can be moved by the evidence to a different view, or if she is so deeply committed to her position that she is unlikely to budge. Knowing the depth of their feelings about a given issue is invaluable when you rank the panelists. The more accurate the rankings are, the more accurate your strikes.

Consider the venireman in a capital murder case Racehorse Haynes tried in New Braunfels, a heavily German settlement in Central Texas. When Haynes asked the panelist if he could "personally give the death penalty," the man glanced at his watch and responded in a thick accent, "Vell, Mr. Haynes, not today. But I can be back Thursday, after verk." There, you had your basic ten.

b.   Link panelists' lives to your client's and his cause.

By committing panelists, I mean persuading some or all of them, during voir dire, that your client should win the case. To do that, you must encourage them to open up about personal experiences that mirror the events that brought your client to court. It is that common ground—having lived through similar experiences—that allows panelists to identify with your client and to feel that there is a bond between them.

i. *Linkage and the law.*

To create that bond, you must trigger appropriate answers from the panelists, a strategy I stumbled onto during voir dire in a murder trial in 1979.

The basic facts of that case were undisputed. My client shot and killed her husband, dismembered his body, then drove from Texas to California to bury him on her father's ranch. What had not been reported in the highly publicized case was that my client had been brutalized by her husband. In fact—a rarity in those days—he had actually had been convicted of (misdemeanor) assault after beating her so badly he put her in the hospital. My client's testimony would be that, prior to the shooting, her husband had kept her awake for 72 hours, poking her breasts with an ice pick and frequently holding a gun to her head. After three days of tormenting her, he handed her the gun and challenged her to kill him before he killed her and their kids. She took the gun and pulled the trigger. Immediately thereafter, she used a chainsaw to dismember his body, and when the first blade broke, she drove to the hardware store and bought another one.

Early in my voir dire, I discussed the elements of self-defense, intending, I am sure, to "sell" the panel on the right of a wife to use deadly force against an abusive husband. That concept was far from a given in Texas in the 1970s. Nevertheless, just mentioning that my client would assert self-defense cast the case in a different light, hinting that the lurid "dismemberment" headlines didn't tell the whole story. The panelists became increasingly responsive to my questions. When I asked if anyone had known the deceased, I made certain to describe him, telling the panelists: "He was a man about 6'2" and 225 pounds"—a stark contrast to my diminutive client. I could see the heads shaking sympathetically. Without "selling" the case, the panelists were shifting my way. Then—and this is the part I can see as if it happened yesterday—a hand shot up in the rear of the courtroom. A man on the aisle pointed down the row to a woman who sat crying quietly. She was so far in the back of the panel there was no chance she'd make it to the jury. I almost suggested that she be excused. Instead, I handed her a glass of water and asked if she was okay—a combination of instinct, manners, and dumb luck. The woman took a moment to compose herself, and then said, "I wish my daughter had the courage to do what she did," gesturing toward my client, "because my daughter would still be alive today."

Following voir dire, the judge, a former prosecutor, predicted that the jurors, who decide punishment in Texas, would give my client probation. They never even got that far, acquitting her in 45 minutes. The woman who lost her daughter to spousal abuse had told my client's story for her, far more eloquently than I ever could. She wasn't even on the jury, yet she all but decided the case.

Talk about conditioning and committing panelists! I am philosophically opposed to exclamation points, but that's how significant the lesson was that I learned that day. The panelist identified so completely with my client's experience that she could not conceivably have found her guilty. Had she been seated closer in, so that she was eligible for the jury, the judge would have excused her for cause. But it wouldn't have mattered. She galvanized the panel, creating empathy for my client and the opposite for the deceased husband. The similarity between the grieving mother's life and that of my client, and the lesson her comment taught about a woman and self-defense, convinced some of the panelists to acquit before testimony began.

Over the years, I have thought a great deal about how to get panelists to open up about their personal experiences. What triggers the needed response varies from case to case. Most often, it is open-ended questions about the (1) the *law* (as in the murder case), (2) the *themes,* or (3) the *worst weaknesses* in your case that is the trigger. An example of (2) and (3) follows.

What makes this strategy so valuable is that you can use it in all kinds of trials—including the most complex commercial cases. What makes it so successful is that, while you aren't allowed to argue your facts during voir dire, the panelists' responses tell your client's story for him. Moreover, your open-ended question about self-defense, or whatever topic you choose to trigger the response, implies what your facts will be. Why would you ask the question if you don't intend to argue self-defense? By the end of voir dire, panelists may not know your facts, but they know your story. That is how, so early on, panelists can identify so deeply with your client.

ii.   *Linkage and your themes.*

In 2002, my son Gabe and I represented Eric Fleisher and his company, Assist Sports Management (ASM), against ASM's former president, who, after resigning in 1999, took with him some of the agency's best-known players, including Minnesota Timberwolves superstar Kevin Garnett. The suit, tried in New York Supreme Court in Manhattan, alleged that the former president breached his fiduciary duty to ASM and Fleisher by improperly soliciting those players to join him at a new agency.

While the phrase "breach of fiduciary duty" means a great deal to lawyers, to laypeople it's little more than confusing legal jargon. At the heart of every breach of fiduciary duty, however, is a betrayal—and that's a theme anyone can understand. That's why I used it during voir dire:

> At some point, all of us have been betrayed—including me. Someone we trusted has stabbed us in the back. Now, I don't want you to tell me the facts, but will someone tell me how you felt when that happened to you? Again, I'm not asking for specifics.

Note that the question assumes everyone in the courtroom has been betrayed. If, instead, you first ask something like, "What is a betrayal?" or "Haven't we all been betrayed?" the panel will waste 30 minutes answering the wrong question before they get to the one you really wanted answered.

Note also that the occasional admission, such as your having been betrayed, makes you more human—someone panelists can talk to even if they don't have an advanced degree and an expensive suit. Equally important, you send a message about the level of candor that you expect. If you can open up in front of a group of strangers, so can they.

Most important, the concept of betrayal is so universal and provocative that it is likely to jolt several panelists into talking. It is a rare human being who has never been betrayed, and rarer still, one who has forgotten how it felt when it happened. Invariably, someone on the panel will tell you how devastating the experience was, and with a little urging, discuss the details. That is what happened in the Fleisher case. A big firm defense lawyer on the panel—not exactly the type you would expect to bare his soul in front of strangers—told us about a close friend who brought an investment to him. The lawyer put together a group of his clients, and along with them, invested the money his friend needed to close the deal:

> Q: I take it from your bringing this up now that the investment turned out badly?
>
> A: Yes, but that was not the problem. Sometimes, investments go bad. But my friend misled us about the investment. He gave us phony financial information.
>
> Q: You trusted your friend?
>
> A: Yes, that's the main reason I did the deal.
>
> Q: He misrepresented the transaction?
>
> A: Yes.

Q: How did that make you feel?

A: I was sick about it. It cost me the clients and a great deal of money. It also cost me a friend, because I can't talk to him anymore. I can't stand to be in the same room with him.

Q: Did you sue?

A: No, but we should have.

At the core, stories of betrayal are all the same: A "friend" stabs a friend in the back. That's what the panelists's friend had done to him, and that's what the former president of ASM had done to Eric Fleisher. In recounting his own bitter experience, the defense lawyer was telling my client's story, and, without realizing it, stirring other panelists' own difficult memories. When they realized that Eric had been stabbed in the back by a trusted "friend," as they once were, they identified deeply with him. The multimillion-dollar verdict they returned in his favor three weeks later was set in motion on that first day of trial.[6]

iii. Linkage and your worst weaknesses.

Being a defense lawyer can be a thankless task. If you win, you were supposed to win. Your client never owed the plaintiff any money to begin with. If you lose, it is your fault, and the client often goes to another firm. That leaves many defense lawyers risk-averse, content to avoid losing, rather than trying to win. The result is often a lackluster representation, including the predictable litany of "yeah, buts" that sink so many defendants with juries.

Instead, defense counsel, no less than plaintiff's lawyers, should strike an emotional chord with panelists. While there are obstacles—jurors often think "a pox on both your houses" when corporate behemoths go at it—there are effective ways to overcome them. One of the best is to question panelists about the worst weakness in your case.

As Matagorda County's largest employer, taxpayer, and leading corporate citizen, STP (the power plant) dominated the business and social life of the community. Moreover, when the plant was built, it reversed years of economic decline in the area. As a result, the city felt an emotional commitment to the power plant and its employees. It was a serious problem in representing Westinghouse—and one that wasn't going to just go away.

---

6. As of the date of this writing, the trial court had not ruled on the pending motions for new trial, and therefore, the verdict is not yet final.

I dealt with the issue early on in voir dire, telling panelists that I was worried: "The power plant has sued Westinghouse for $800 million, plus two times that amount in punitive damages. As you know, the plant is the largest employer here. They pay a lot of taxes and support a lot of good things, like little league teams and the United Way."

I turned to a pleasant-looking man in the front row. From the questionnaires, I knew he was one of the few panelists who owned his own business. I asked if he ever worried about being sued. He answered, "Yes, everyone does." I continued:

> I want you to assume that you had a business dispute with Westinghouse and that the company sued you for millions of dollars—in Pittsburgh, where the company is headquartered. They have thousands of employees there. And when it came time to select a jury, many of the people on the panel had relatives and friends working for Westinghouse. How would you feel?

The entire panel was listening intently. "I'd be scared to death," the panelist answered. "I could lose my business." With his help, I was beginning to make a delicate point. Gesturing toward my clients, I asked, "How do you think these guys feel? I mean being here, in Bay City." Without hesitating, he said, "They have to be scared." Westinghouse's general counsel leaned forward. Suddenly, the elephant was no longer under the coffee table. "Why should they be scared?" I asked. The panelist replied: "Because they don't know if they can get a fair trial."

Bingo. The panelist gave us the exact answer we needed. I continued: "Then, let me ask you this, sir. Is Westinghouse's fear justified?" This time, the man hesitated, looked around the room at his friends and neighbors, and said, "I think it might be tough." Then I said: "I'm sure you know *The Wall Street Journal* called Matagorda County a 'plaintiff's paradise.' How did that make you feel?" He answered, "That was bad. Folks here aren't proud of that. These are real fair people." When I looked around, heads were nodding in agreement. I didn't have to ask him another question on the subject. We had the next-best thing to a change of venue—potential jurors who were committed to proving that Matagorda County could be fair to defendants, a quaint if little-honored tradition in that jurisdiction. With the help of the venireman, I had turned the plaintiff's greatest strength on its head. Kissing panelists is generally frowned on in Texas— bailiffs have been known to shoot lawyers for less—so I moved on.

That technique—turning weaknesses to assets—can be effective in all types of cases, although, for defendants, especially, it frequently needs to be toned down—for instance, when the plaintiff in a personal injury case has been seriously injured. I recall reading the transcript from a medical malpractice case, in which the defense counsel struck just the right tone. The young plaintiff had suffered brain damage during an operation. The lawyer began his voir dire by saying that his situation reminded him of when he played Little League as a boy and the score would be 9–0 before his team even got up to bat. His mother, he said, would have to assure him that the game wasn't lost and his team still had a chance to catch up. He told the panel that he hoped the same would be true in the trial. I don't remember which side ultimately won the case, but I do recall thinking how reasonable that sounded, and how inclined jurors would be to hear him out, despite the brain-damaged plaintiff.

c. Create challenges for cause.

To create challenges for cause, you must learn to ask questions that flush out unwanted panelists, eliciting answers that cast doubt on their ability to be fair and impartial. Following individual questioning, panelists whose responses raise such doubts are brought to the bench and, if they aren't automatically disqualified based on what they've already said, are questioned further by the lawyers, and sometimes, the judge. If their answers reveal bias, they may be disqualified. (See p. 104, "Disqualify panelists for cause.")

Knowing how to create challenges is important because in most cases, there will be panelists whose hidden agendas could doom your chances from the start. Jury studies and your common sense can highlight the potential issues, which most often involve a controversial client, a hometown bias, tort-reform activism, or the like. These are the panelists who will be laying for you and, if you don't know how to expose them, will skate, unchallenged, onto your jury.

i. *Flush out unacceptable panelists, all at once.*

I learned from trying criminal cases that if there is an explosive issue in your case, explode it, as soon as you face the panel. Asbestos cases are a prime example. Granted, they are easy for plaintiffs to win (there is only one known cause of asbestosis and mesothelioma: exposure to asbestos), but they still have a complicating factor. If the plaintiff smoked, some panelists will believe that he contributed to his own illness, asbestos-related or not. These anti-tobacco panelists, ordinarily good plaintiff's jurors, are unlikely to hold an asbestos company solely liable for the plaintiff's illness—because that would absolve big tobacco. In other words, these panelists are predisposed to finding contributory negligence by the smoker-plaintiff.

Mark Lanier, an asbestos lawyer, handles the problem by embracing the anti-tobacco predisposition instead of arguing about it:

> Ladies and gentlemen, my clients filed this lawsuit because they were exposed to asbestos on the job and now they have lung disease. Now, no one will dispute that asbestos causes lung disease. But, so does tobacco. Those lawyers over there are going to tell you that these men are responsible for their own disease to some degree, because they smoked. I will tell you now, it is a fact, that each of them has smoked for years.

Note that Lanier seems to be crediting his opponent's theory of the case. During trial, he will set the record straight about smoking and contributory negligence, but for now he has implied that smoking *did* contribute to his clients' lung disease.

Next, palms up, he demonstrates how little he must tip the scales for his clients to win. By implying that their anti-tobacco views won't keep him from winning, indeed, that they will hardly matter, Lanier rouses the panelists to defend their beliefs—unaware that by doing so, they are admitting that they can't follow the law, and, as a result, will probably be disqualified for cause. Lanier uses old-fashioned educational questions as a platform, and builds from there:

> I told you before, all I have to do to win was tilt the scales this way, as if there were one tiny grain of sand on my side of the scale. That is all I have to do to show that smoking did not contribute to my clients' illness. Now, knowing that my clients not only were exposed to asbestos, but also, that each of them smoked—how many of you are saying to yourself, "Lanier, if you're going to prove to me that it was asbestos and not cigarettes that caused their lung disease, you're going to have to do better than that. You're going to have to prove it by more than a grain of sand. No, sir, Lanier, you're not getting off that easy."

This demonstration invariably incites panelists who hate big tobacco. Inevitably, Lanier tells me, several panelists admit that they would require him to prove his case by more than that grain of sand—more proof than the law requires.

At a minimum, panelists who make that sort of admission will be brought to the bench, and if the judge doesn't disqualify them automatically, you can question them further, nail down their predisposition to ignore the law, and challenge them for cause. (See p. 104, "Disqualify panelists for cause.") Note that this entire series of questions, which may eliminate several panelists, takes only a few minutes.

ii.   *Flush out unacceptable panelists, one at a time.*

Not all issues can be handled globally as in the asbestos cases. Nevertheless, when feelings about parties, entities, legal concepts, or any matter, are stacked against you, ask questions that encourage panelists to speak freely about them—even if you have to go down the row, one person at a time.

Personal injury lawyers must ask panelists how they feel about punitive damages and about plaintiffs' lawyers. Defense lawyers must ask potential jurors how they feel about the unpopular defendant they represent, be it a tobacco company, a gun manufacturer, or whatever the case might be. In my experience, some number of the biased panelists will talk themselves up to the bench and off the panel. Even if you can't get rid of all of them for cause, you will still know by their answers whether particular people should stay or go.

Note that getting biased panelists up to the bench doesn't always entail exposing angry feelings, as in the asbestos case example. You can approach the problem in a completely opposite way. In *Westinghouse,* for example, I asked how panelists felt about the power plant. That question unleashed a flood of complimentary responses about STP—many of them sufficient to get the panelists up to the bench for further questioning, and disqualification.

However, for all my advocacy of allowing panelists to speak freely, there are limits, and this is one of them. If a panelist praises an opposing party to high heaven, elicit just enough of their response to justify taking them up to the bench, and politely shut them down ("Thank you for your answer, Mrs. Jones. I don't mean to cut you off, but we can discuss your answer further at the bench."). You don't need a crippling testimonial, such as the one Richard Haynes elicited in a different context from the church lady on the panel whose answers about her fellow parishioner, Haynes's client, won him an acquittal. (See p. 11, "You'll learn something useful for trial.")

d. Prod unresponsive panels.

As a word of encouragement, since I began asking open-ended questions, I've never had a panel clam up, although some, obviously, have been less talkative than others. Nevertheless, assume that no one responds—the worst-case scenario. How do you get them to open up? First, try modifying the questions that you've asked. Make them less personal. Ask if anyone *knows* someone who's been betrayed, and how that person felt when it happened. Or, as an even less threatening question, ask how they *think* it feels when someone is betrayed. The added virtue of this type of question is that it offers panelists the opportunity to shine by displaying their wisdom about human behavior. Their observations may or may not be profound, but they will be genuine—and instructive about your strikes.

If you are still unable to get them talking, you can always move on to the next phase of voir dire—individual questions about comfortable subjects. (See below, "Don't accept silence.") If, during that effort, a previously silent panelist loosens up, return to the open-ended questions that you asked of the panel as a whole, and try to elicit their more informative answers.

4. Ask questions of individual jurors.

Voir dire may assume many forms, but it always comes down to the same problem: so many panelists, so little time. After you finish asking the panel general questions and follow-ups, you need to be certain that you have heard from everyone who could be on the jury.

a. Don't accept silence.

Start with the panelists who haven't said anything—or anything informative. Ironically, the silent types frequently make it to the jury, simply because they haven't said anything bad. Yet, they can kill you—stampeding the jury in the wrong direction. For that reason alone, do all that you can to get these panelists talking—and watch them like a hawk for nonverbal clues.

To identify the strongest among them, scour the questionnaires for supervisors, professionals, and anyone else who is used to being in charge. Ask them work-related questions: Do they supervise others? If so, how many? Do they hire and fire? Do they make decisions? What sort? Whom do they answer to in the chain of command? What is their relationship like with their superiors? With the employees who work under them? The answers to these questions should give you a good idea if the panelist is going to overpower the others—and whether she will be able to identify with your client.

Prior jury duty can also be very revealing. How recently did the panelist serve? Was it a criminal or civil case? Was she the foreperson? Did the jury reach a verdict? Did it hang? If so, and you're allowed, find out if she was the panelist who did the hanging.

Similarly, attitudes toward lawyers and the legal system can be predictive. Does the panelist have a family lawyer? Has she ever brought suit? What was the reason? Has she ever been sued? Did the case go to court? Was there a jury trial? Was there a verdict? Did she think the verdict was fair? Was there anything that left her unhappy with her lawyer, the courts, or judges? Did the experience increase or decrease her faith in the jury system?

If, after all your efforts, there are still panelists who won't open up, point out their silence to them—and how much you need their answers. Pick someone and ask if she could help you out. Ask about the things that would get most people talking. Does she have children and grandchildren? Does she believe in corporal punishment? Of course, the answer to that latter question can tell you a lot. If the answer is yes, she is probably quick to hold people responsible and punish misbehavior. This could be the first person you'd want on your jury—or the first you'd choose to strike.

Failing all that, if you are still unable to get them talking, put the onus on the panel. Remind them without apology that you've got a responsibility to your client to get some meaningful answers or you can't help her select a fair jury. When doing so, avoid obsequious comments like, "Let me pick on you, first, Mrs. Johnson." You're not picking on anyone. You're doing all you can to get the panelists talking and if you're not successful, your client will suffer unfairly.

b.   Question panelists who raised concerns.

If a panelist's answers or body language left you concerned that he might be against you, pick up where he left off: "Mr. Smith, when you were discussing punitive damages, you mentioned at the same time that your wife is politically active. I got the sense those answers were related. Is that true?" "What did you mean when you said that about your wife?" "Is she involved with an organization that is concerned in any way with tort reform?"

Frequently, when you are fighting to get rid of a panelist, the panelist is looking for a way out, too. Sometimes, all they need is your invitation, especially if their prior response, verbal or nonverbal, indicated reservations about some aspect of your case: "Mrs. Jones, earlier I asked a question about bringing lawsuits to settle business disputes. You didn't say anything, but you seemed concerned. Frankly, I picked that up from your expression when I asked the question. Am I right about that?" If she opens up, you may be headed for a successful challenge for cause, and an unexpected two-strike swing in your favor.

c. Try head fakes.

If you kiss up to a favorable panelist, it's like yelling "Yahoo" every time you draw a good hand in poker. Don't give your opponent that kind of information. When a panelist gives you a good answer, disguise your feelings. Remain impassive or, if you can do so without offending the panelist, appear puzzled. That head fake may confuse your opponent into not striking a panelist you like.

Even more important, don't give away your feelings about people you don't want on your jury, especially those few panelists "at play," the ones you *and* your opponent might strike. Assume that you represent the defendant in a personal injury case and that panelist 14 underlined on her questionnaire that she was an accident victim, and had sued over her injuries. Assume further that during voir dire, she also said that she was concerned about excessive jury awards. As the quintessential panelist at play, 14 could spell trouble for either side, identifying with the plaintiff's pain and suffering, yet refusing to award much money at all. Moreover, after questioning her, you really don't want her on your jury, ranking her no higher than a 3. That doesn't necessarily mean that you will use a strike on her, especially if you have other panelists you'd rather eliminate—a decision made easier if you can convincingly head fake your opponent into striking her for you when the time comes. (See p. 112, "Identify your opponent's likely strikes.") For now, however, preserve your options. Don't give away how much you want her gone. Instead, linger approvingly over her answers; ask her a few extra questions. Create the impression that you'd like her on your jury—and that your opponent would be better off without her.

Don't waste time on head fakes no one will believe. If you represent a corporate defendant, your opponent isn't going to strike a union worker who has been scowling at you the whole time, no matter how good your acting skills.

d. Nominate the "presiding juror."

Ask a couple of panelists how they would feel if asked to serve as "foreperson" or "presiding juror"—a not-so-subtle way of nominating a favored panelist or two for the job. If it happens that one them is chosen, you may have a significant voice on the jury and a vote on your side. However, by asking the question, you might tip off an opponent to your favorites. Therefore, ask the same question of a couple of your adversary's best panelists—so long as you feel certain that they will either be disqualified for cause, or that you will strike them yourself. The last thing you want is to get one of your opponent's favorites elected to the job.

5. Disqualify panelists for cause.

When group voir dire is finished, the panelists whose answers raised doubt about their ability to be impartial are brought to the bench, one at a time. Each side is then given an opportunity to ask more questions, and, if desired, to challenge the panelist for cause. As discussed at the beginning of this chapter, disqualifying panelists for cause is the most important goal of voir dire. Each time the judge grants a challenge, the jury pool becomes more favorable, and the danger of running out of peremptory strikes becomes smaller.

a. The standard for disqualification for cause.

Challenges for cause require you to prove to the court that the panelist has a "fixed state of mind" that will prevent her from being fair about a significant aspect of your case, be it the law, the facts, your client, or you. To develop a successful challenge, you must entice panelists you don't want to expand on their comments, admit a disqualifying opinion, and then, pin them down so that they can't backpedal.

b. Eliminating panelists at the bench.

Challenging panelists at the bench is far different from conducting group voir dire. You are no longer facilitating the panelists' discussion at a polite distance. Now, you are face to face with someone who almost certainly should not serve on your jury. You must do all you can to get rid of this panelist, even if you have to make the person mad to do it.

The judge, on the other hand, is going to be concerned about filling the jury as quickly as possible, so that the trial can start. To avoid disqualifying so many panelists that you run out of the number needed to fill the jury, close calls will go against you. In fact, the judge will try to rehabilitate panelists who ought to be disqualified, getting them to agree that they can set aside their personal feelings, listen to the evidence, and then make up their minds.

What happens, therefore, is a struggle for control—polite and civil, to be sure, but a struggle nonetheless. Following are the steps for winning that battle. They are among the most important rules in all of trial law.

i.   *Praise the panelist's candor.*

Once at the bench, you would think that panelists would admit to anything to get out of jury duty—but, generally, they don't. In fact, unless they have expressed an opinion that, *ipso facto,* disqualifies them, panelists often resist admitting their true feelings for fear of being disqualified. That is a very human response. They don't think of themselves as unfair or biased, and they don't want to appear that way to others. Knowing that, you must assure them that any opinion they hold is acceptable to you, no matter how adverse it is to your case—especially (you don't tell them this) if they are disqualified because of it.

Assume that the panelist has said during voir dire that he has "some concerns" about punitive damages and "doesn't know" if he can award them. While it is clear he has failed the plaintiff's litmus test, he hasn't failed the court's: His comments will not get him disqualified. As a result, you must coax or cross-examine him into admitting an opinion that will. It is a subtle process that begins with praising his candor:

> This process wouldn't work without people like you. We all realize you have given your answers knowing that they were not going to make some of us happy. But that is the point, isn't it? Everyone involved in this case is grateful that you have been so honest. In fact, we hope your candor will rub off on some of the other panelists.

ii.   *Make disqualification commendable.*

Next, remind the panelist that confessing his bias (without using that word) is the right thing to do, and offer him a carrot—the chance to go home:

> Earlier, I mentioned that if I were called as a juror in a child-molesting case, I'd have to tell the judge I shouldn't serve—that I couldn't be fair to the defendant. I take it you would agree that whenever a person feels he can't be fair—for whatever reason—that person just should not serve on the jury. In fairness to one side or the other, those people should take themselves out of the running—and head on home. You would agree with that, I take it?

These comments help condition the panelist to think differently about how he can best be fair. He now understands, if he didn't before, that admitting what he really feels may be the *only* fair thing to do—even if it results in his disqualification.

iii. Get agreement on what the panelist said.

Repeat the statement that brought the panelist to the bench in the first place, as close to verbatim as you can. If you are using real-time court reporting, read the statement to him from the transcript, or from a verbatim note. That saves you time establishing what was said and makes any attempt at backpedaling less likely:

> Let me check this note my colleague just handed me, because I want to be absolutely accurate about what you said earlier about punitive damages. According to this note, you said, "I don't know if I could award punitive damages. I have some concerns about them." That is correct, isn't it?

When you appear to be reading their comments, most panelists are loathe to challenge their accuracy. But be aware: If you have trouble just getting him to admit what he said, you're going to have to hammer him into admitting what he feels.

iv. Elevate what was said to a matter of principle.

Remember: Every panelist brought to the bench has said something sufficiently troubling to raise doubt about his ability to be impartial. The panelist's own words are the starting point for disqualification. Seize on whatever was said, and elevate it to a matter of principle:

> Now, when you say that you "don't know" if you can award punitive damages, that you've got "some concerns" about awarding them, I take it you didn't just make up that view as you walked into the courtroom to get out of jury duty—that you have given some thought to the subject of punitive damages before you came here today?

It doesn't matter that the question is coercive. What you are after is the panelist's acknowledgment that his opinion is sincere—not something that he invented on the spot. No panelist in my experience has ever said he was making up an answer to get out of jury duty.

v. Elevate the principle to a disqualifying opinion.

Given his (inevitable) agreement that his views are sincere, or deeply held, or however you get him to describe them, you have the answer you need to demonstrate that he can't be fair. After all, if he has principled reservations about awarding punitive damages, how can he put them out of his mind when he gets into that jury room?

> Mr. Smith, my clients are going to ask this jury for a large money award to compensate their company for the losses they've suffered. They are also going to ask for an award of punitive damages to punish the defendant for its conduct. Given the kind of debate we've had in America about punitive damages, your concerns about awarding them are understandable. But, isn't it a fair statement that if you are selected for this jury, that you aren't just going to forget your views about punitive damages—simply erase them from your mind? That when you enter that jury room to deliberate, your views would have to affect your decision in this case, wouldn't they?

There is something very compelling to panelists when you force them to see themselves in that jury room, deliberating. Cornered by their own answers during voir dire, or motivated by honesty, most panelists will agree that their thoughts will affect their decisions. Placing the panelist there, in the midst of deliberations, head filled with bias, possibly influencing other panelists, also has an effect on the judge, vividly demonstrating why she should disqualify him. But you're not quite there yet.

The next step is to get the panelist to admit the obvious: that his reservations about awarding punitive damages put your client at "something of a disadvantage" or gives the opposing party "something of an advantage" with him. You don't have to get him to agree in the exact wording of the statute or case law of your jurisdiction that he is not qualified to serve (for example, that he has a fixed state of mind). All you need is his acknowledgment that the sides won't be on equal footing with him once deliberations begin; indeed, even as "you stand here now," before testimony has even begun.

Be ready for a common response: that the panelist didn't mean that he favored one side over the other, only that he would need to hear the evidence before making up his mind. Did you misjudge him? Not a chance. As the Freudians say, "I heard you the first time." He wants to get on the jury to kill your client. And he won't be happy until you're back to driving a Ford Escort.

If the panelist won't admit his disqualifying opinion, cross-examine him until he does—or until the judge stops you. And don't worry about offending the panelist. You'll have to strike him if you can't get him dismissed for cause, anyway. At the same time, don't be too aggressive. The judge will cut you off if you treat him like an adverse witness.

The best approach to a backtracking panelist is to question him about the basis of his views—the ones that he now tells you won't affect his decision in the case. Since he's already said that they didn't come to him out of the blue, find out what he's read about punitive damages, what discussions he has had about them, and with whom. "What did you say when your wife said she thought that punitive damages were excessive? Surely you must have agreed with her, given your concerns." Once you get him talking about what he's read and said, I would be surprised if he didn't admit to being disgusted by huge punitive awards and greedy plaintiffs lawyers.

No matter how you approach a panelist with troubling opinions for your side of the case, there is always the chance he won't budge, and you will have to strike him. But assuming that he agrees his views will keep him from being fair, or words to that effect, you still have one more critical step.

vi.   Preempt rehabilitation.

In some jurisdictions, once you get a panelist to admit a preexisting bias about a significant aspect of your case, neither the court nor opposing counsel can rehabilitate him—as in the Texas of old: "You mean to tell this court you hate the plaintiff just because he cheated you in a business deal? Come on, podner, you can follow the law as I give it, or face contempt charges, can't you? Well, I thought so. Now, go sit down." Or, the modern version: "Can you think of any reason you can't be fair or follow my instructions on the law?" In jurisdictions where this practice is outlawed (as it ought to be everywhere), once the panelist indicates a disqualifying opinion, the challenge should be granted. However, even when the case law of your jurisdiction permits rehabilitation, you can still preclude it. Commit the panelist unalterably to what he has said, so that no one can make him change his mind:

> Mr. Smith, it is clear from what you have said that you are a thoughtful person, that you haven't arrived at your opinion lightly. Whether I agree with you, or the judge does, or anyone else, those are your views. Having said that, is it a fair statement that your views are your own—that you won't abandon or back away from those views, just to serve on this jury?

There are many ways of asking this question, but the point is the same. Having agreed that he wouldn't manufacture an opinion to get out of jury duty, it seems certain he will agree that he wouldn't abandon his principled beliefs, just to get on one. That makes it all but impossible for him to credibly assure the judge or opposing counsel that he could set aside his opinions and follow the law on punitive damages. With those admissions, your challenge should be granted. If not, you may be able to use the adverse ruling to your advantage, later, when striking the jury. (See p. 115, "Request an extra strike.")

c. "Busting" the panel.

Obviously, judges don't like it when you force them to "bust" the panel—disqualifying so many panelists for cause that, after both sides exercise their peremptory strikes, there won't be enough panelists left to fill the jury. When that happens, the judge must call for more panelists or declare a mistrial. Nevertheless, you are obligated to risk busting the panel when, for whatever reason, you know you will have a significant number of enemies in the venire going in. The more hostile panelists you disqualify for cause, the greater your chances of winning.

In that regard, here is a tip for the final minutes of voir dire: As you come close to the end, the judge may become a bit more lenient about granting your challenges—if she has more than enough panelists to fill the jury. So, even if a panelist's answers are not quite sufficient for disqualification, make your motion anyway.

6. Exercising peremptory strikes.

There is some room for error in almost every phase of trial. A lawyer who performs poorly one day may do well the next. A witness who gets taken apart on cross occasionally may be rehabilitated on direct. That is not true about jury selection. One serious mistake about a panelist can cost you the verdict—a lesson that every lawyer who tries a lot of cases learns sooner or later.

a. Common methods of striking a jury.

There are two basic methods of striking juries. Under one practice, a typed list of all the panelists, numbered, and in the order they are seated, is provided to both sides at the conclusion of questioning. The sides then retire to separate areas to discuss the panelists, marking through the names of each undesirable one, until their strikes are exhausted. The sides turn in their lists to the clerk, who marks each side's strikes on a clean list of the panelists. Then, as the lawyers hold their breath, the clerk reads off the first 12 people (or six, or whatever number is required to fill the jury) who do not have a line drawn through their name. The next unmarked name(s) becomes the alternate(s).

The other basic method, striking panelists one by one, comes in many varieties. Generally, lawyers assemble around the bench, and, on a rotating basis starting with the plaintiff, either accept (pass) or reject each panelist as their names are called. When their strikes are exhausted or waived, the first 8 or 12 remaining panelists (or, again, however many are required) become the jury. In other jurisdictions, panelists are struck at random ("the struck method"), one by one, until both sides exhaust their strikes. If eight jurors are needed, the first eight remaining panelists in order of seating become the jury.

I personally witnessed one of the more intriguing variations on jury selection while trying a case in Manhattan. There, on a hallway bench, sat two lawyers, privately striking a jury. They passed a "breadboard"—a 2-foot-by-3-foot wooden panel covered with fabric and mounted with kangaroo-like pouches—back and forth. In each pouch was a file card with a panelist's name, arranged in seating order. One by one, the lawyers removed the cards of panelists they wanted to eliminate, until both sides exhausted their peremptories. Voila, they had a jury. Who knows what's next in the Big Apple? Maybe they'll try their cases over lunch and mail in their verdicts.

b.   Ten rules for striking juries.[7]

The brief time that you will have to exercise your peremptory strikes will have an outsized influence on the outcome of your case. Take your time and be deliberate about each one, especially when you are down to those last few, difficult strikes. At every step, listen to your instincts. No rule can capture them, and no rule can trump them.

i.   Test the juror profile against the real panelists.

What a juror profile does best is to isolate categories of people you don't want on your jury. That negative information is what you will recall when you get ready to exercise your strikes. However, like all generalizations, juror profiles can be wrong. The big firm lawyer who opened up to us during the Fleisher voir dire about a back-stabbing friend is a case

---

7. Unless otherwise indicated, these ten rules apply to both basic methods of jury selection.

in point. Had the other side not struck him, he'd have made an excellent juror for us, even though our juror profile would have advised striking him.

So, before you make a final decision about a panelist's ranking or whether to strike him, based on the juror profile, ask yourself a fundamental question: How did the real panelist stack up against the profile of ideal and undesirable jurors? How do you harmonize the profile's advice to strike middle-aged executives with the fact that there was a middle-aged executive on the panel whom you really liked? Why shouldn't you strike the hostile young taxi driver the profile says you want, when you didn't like him? "Trust," as President Reagan was fond of quoting the Russians, "but verify." Test the juror profile against the real-life panelists before you decide to keep or strike anyone.

ii.　*Categorize the panelists.*

Based on all the information at hand, finalize your rankings of each panelist on a scale of 1 to 5; 5 being the best. Then, separate them into three broad categories: (1) those you definitely *don't want* ("no"); (2) those you definitely *do want* ("yes"); and (3) those you are *not certain about* ("maybe"). Be as deliberate as possible. The more accurate those categories and rankings, the better your strikes, and the more likely you are to select a favorable jury.

iii.　*Compare panelists constantly.*

If there is one abiding principle of jury selection, it is this: Striking jurors is an exercise in constant comparisons. Your first few strikes (the unwanted "1's") may be obvious, but they are obvious only in comparison to other panelists—the ones who would be, in varying degrees, better suited for your jury.

Things get considerably more difficult when you get down to your last few strikes. Typically, you won't have enough left to get rid of all the panelists you don't want. When you get ready to exercise a strike, take a moment to compare the rankings of the remaining undesirable panelists one last time. You may not be entirely comfortable with your decision, but by constantly comparing your strikes to the bitter end, you will have done all that you can.

iv.　*Get rid of the "1's."*

Unless you are *certain* your opponent is going to strike a panelist you must strike, get rid of that panelist yourself, immediately.

There are no more-important targets among those unwanted "1's" than the strong-willed panelists whom you believe are against you. During deliberations, they can turn a favorable jury completely around, stampeding them in the wrong direction. They are the deal-breakers—and must be struck. If your opponent is any good at all, he will be doing the same thing, striking the strong panelists who were for you.

Because both sides tend to strike strong people, juries frequently include several nondescript "3's," usually people about whom little is known. But the point of this chapter is not to teach you how to select nondescript juries. By disqualifying even a few panelists for cause, you make your opponent's choices increasingly difficult. As a result, you are likely to end up with one or two of your "5's" on the jury. That's all it takes to tip the scales heavily in your favor.

v.   Identify your opponent's likely strikes.

Earlier, I suggested that you rank each panelist from your opponent's point of view. Not one lawyer in a hundred does that—which gives you an advantage no matter which method of striking jurors you are using.

It's not that difficult to figure out your opponent's likely strikes. For example, if you flip your "5's," your dream jurors, you will have located most, if not all, of her "1's"—unless counsel doesn't know what she is doing. But "1's" and "5's" are usually obvious. The real value comes when you figure out the panelists "at play," those few people that *both* of you might strike. Making an accurate, if educated, guess about even one of them, and letting your opponent strike an unwanted panelist for you, can change the composition of your jury, and thus the outcome of the trial.

Because this strategy is so valuable, let me build on an earlier, related example to underscore its importance. Recall panelist 14, the at-play panelist who sent mixed signals in a personal injury case, indicating that she was concerned about large damage awards, but had been an accident victim, and had brought suit over her injuries. (See p. 103, "Try head fakes.") After questioning her, you really don't want her on your jury, ranking her no higher than a 3. To encourage your opponent to strike her, you tried a head fake, indicating by your feigned approval of her answers that you want her on your jury. Now, you must answer the hard questions: Can you live with her on the jury or not? Did your opponent take the bait? What is the likelihood, realistically, that your opponent will strike her, either because of your head fake or some other reason? Or, must you use a strike of your own? Two scenarios tell you to use your own strike. If you have enough peremptory strikes to eliminate her and every other unwanted panelist, you have done a terrific job during voir dire, and the answer is easy. Or, even if you are 90 percent certain that your opponent will strike her, but she would be a disaster for you if he didn't, then you must strike her. However, the most realistic scenario is more ambiguous—that you are running out of strikes, and, despite not wanting her on your jury, you are uncertain whether to use a "peremptory" on her or some other panelist you don't want. When that time comes, open up your options. Don't confine yourself to traditional hand-wringing decisions about "the lesser of evils" on your list of unwanted panelists. Take a peek at your opponent's cards. Ask yourself the same questions about his choices that you would ask yourself about your own: Is panelist 14 a "1" or "2" from his standpoint? How does she stack up against the others your opponent might strike? Is she the worst of his potential strikes? How many strikes must he use on his "1's"? How many strikes will he have left? Answering these questions correctly reduces the risk of making a bad decision; not asking them leaves your choice more to chance. Given her conflicted feelings, and your ostensible eagerness to have her on the jury, the other side just might strike her for you. If you make the right decision, and your opponent strikes 14, you will have created a late-in-the-day, two-strike swing in your favor. If you are wrong, you are no worse off than before.

vi. *Limit strategic back-strikes.*

Of the two basic methods for striking juries, striking them one at a time is the more challenging, because you go head-to-head against your opponent and announce your decision about each panelist in each other's presence—often making that decision based on what you think that lawyer will or will not do. In jurisdictions that allow back-striking, lawyers who accept a panelist may go back later to eliminate him. That leads to strategic back-striking, passing on a panelist at play whom you don't want on your jury, to see if your opponent will strike that panelist for you. If you are wrong, and still have a peremptory left, you can go back and strike him.

There are limits to this strategy. You could always pass every panelist, waiting to see if your opponent is going to strike *any* panelists you don't want, and then go back to eliminate the ones that opposing counsel didn't. However, if your opponent is doing the same thing, waiting you out by passing every panelist, voir dire could last until one of you dies. There are ways, as one Florida judge put it, to put an end to the "game playing." The judge can rule that each time you pass, you forfeit a strike, or she can simply shut voir dire down altogether, leaving the sides with a handful of unused peremptories, and a handful of jurors each side would have struck. Given the judge's broad powers over voir dire, it is smarter to limit your strategic passes to those few at-play panelists. That eliminates the suspicion that you are playing games, and leaves strategic back-striking a viable option.

Take note, however: Some jurisdictions don't allow back-strikes, which means that your decision to pass is final. If you roll the dice on a panelist that you think is at play, you'd better be certain you can live with him. If you are wrong, and your opponent passes him, too, he's on the jury.

There is another variation on striking panelists one at a time that is worth noting. I have never done it, but Robert Hirschhorn, a jury consultant, has helped select juries in courts where, once both sides accept a single panelist ("consecutive pass"), it's all over. You may have 3 strikes left, but you can't use them. The first 12 eligible panelists, or whatever number is required, fill the jury. Still, that doesn't eliminate the possibility that your opponent will strike a panelist for you. Not only that, but there is the very real possibility that you can force her to strike her favorite panelist. Assume that your opponent loves panelist 7—your worst nightmare as a juror. It's your turn to go first, and if you both pass, jury selection ends and 7 is on the jury. However, so are 8, 9, and 10, all of whom your opponent *dis*likes. Therefore, you pass, and calmly wait for your opponent to strike 7, so that she can keep jury selection alive and eliminate the next three.

vii. Avoid double-strikes.

There is no more harmful error when striking from a list of all the panelists than double-strikes—eliminating the same person as your opponent. When that happens, one of you has made a serious error, wasting one of your precious few peremptories. The effect is the opposite of a two-strike swing, costing you a strike that you could have used on someone else. However, by attempting to predict the other side's strikes, you can at least minimize the possibility that you will strike the same person.

viii. Forfeit a strike.

This is another valuable tactic that is not employed widely—but is available no matter the method of jury selection. The goal is not so much to put panelists you want on the jury, but to deny your opponent a juror whom he would want very much. All you have to do is forfeit one (or more) of your strikes. That suggestion is probably completely counterintuitive, so let me sell you on its value. Here's how it works.

This is the simplest example. Assume that you are striking from a list of all the panelists. You know that 21 is the last eligible panelist, and believe that she is the worst person for your jury. This is a no-brainer. Forfeit a strike. That makes 20 the final panelist eligible for the jury—21 is gone.

Now, a little more complex situation. Assume that you are striking panelists one by one, in order of their seating, that your case requires seven jurors (the alternate won't be chosen until deliberations begin), and that you have five panelists in the box already. That leaves two more jurors to go. You and your opponent each have only one strike left, and it's your turn to go first—on panelist 12—someone you really don't want.

Your first instinct is to strike panelist 12. Most lawyers would. But first, get a good sense of the possibilities. Compare 12 to the other panelists who can make it to the jury. Since you and your opponent have a total of two strikes, two of the next four panelists will become jurors—if both of you exercise your remaining strike. The jury chart (Figure 4.3) depicts only those four panelists eligible for jury duty, and comments and rankings from your viewpoint about each of them.

Figure 4.3
Sample Jury Chart Segment Showing Four Eligible Panelists

12	13	14	15	16	17	18
bad	best	good	awful must strike			
2	5	4	1			

Grab your jury chart. For this exercise to make the most sense, make the strikes yourself.

If you strike panelist 12, panelist 15—a nightmare for you—will make it to the jury. That's because your opponent is certain to strike either 13 or 14, and the remaining panelist between those two becomes the sixth juror. Since you are out of strikes, panelist 15 is the seventh and final juror. If, however, you forfeit your final strike, 15 cannot conceivably make it to the panel—no matter what your opponent does. True, you are stuck with 12, but 15 was going to be far worse.

ix. *Request an extra strike.*

Losing a challenge for cause can be turned to your advantage. You can use that adverse decision as a platform to obtain an extra strike. (To keep this discussion realistic, it refers only to a request for one additional strike, because you will be fortunate to get even that.)

In my experience, judges are initially dismissive when you approach them for an extra strike, often because they have never had a lawyer make such a request. To be persuasive, you must make the case that (1) the judge's decision denying your challenge for cause was wrong, and has caused you harm, and that (2) down to your final strike, you are being forced to accept the panelist the judge should have disqualified, or someone else whom you want even less. No matter which choice you make, you must emphasize that the court's decision has cost you a strike that you desperately need.

It doesn't matter whether you are in a jurisdiction that requires that you demonstrate harm to show reversible error, or if you are in one where such a showing is unnecessary, because the mistaken denial of a challenge for cause is itself reversible error. The object is to pressure the court into giving you that extra strike—not to worry about niceties of the law on appeal.[8]

At every step, you must be deliberate. First, you must go on the record with your request for an additional strike *before* the jury is struck—or it will be too late. No judge will allow you to take a peek at the jury, decide that you don't like it, and then ask for an additional strike. Once it's struck, you're stuck.

Next, be specific about which panelists are involved. For example, assume that you have one strike and there are two panelists you unsuccessfully challenged for cause. Remind the judge who they are and the arguments you made about each of them. Tell him that by striking one, you are being forced to take the other. If the judge denies your request for an extra strike, the appellate court will know from the record that an unacceptable panelist made it to the jury.

Note: You aren't revealing your strikes when your opponent knows you tried to challenge both panelists for cause. Things get a little trickier when that final choice is between a panelist you were unsuccessful in disqualifying, and someone else that you don't want but had no grounds to challenge for cause. The reason for your extra strike is the same. Explain to the court that because he improperly denied your challenge for cause, you are being forced to make a choice between the two, which will leave one unwanted

---

8. In jurisdictions where you must demonstrate harm resulting from the judge's incorrect decision, the failure to request an additional strike waives the error.

panelist on the jury. However, to create a complete record, you must inform the appellate court who that "other" panelist is, without letting your opponent know. This time, when you go on the record, do so *in camera,* under seal, and tell the court the other panelist's name. Otherwise, in attempting to complete your record, you would tell your opponent how you are likely to use one of your strikes.

When you make a record that complete, the judge may relent, for fear of being reversed. By the simple expedient of granting you an extra strike, he can cure any potential error related to his decision. It is the ultimate in creating the two-strike swing—effectively disqualifying a panelist when you thought that window had closed.

x. Consult with clients in front of the venire.

Make it clear that you *and* your clients are selecting the jury, exactly as you said at the beginning of your voir dire. To reinforce that, confer with the clients in front of the panel. Take time to look over the venire one last time, clients in tow. That way, you can tell the jurors in opening and closing argument, "you are John and Fiona's jury. I am sure many of you saw how involved they were in selecting you." The jurors will be flattered. It is another way of saying to them, "You are our kind of people." By doing so, you hope they will conclude that your clients are their kind of people, too.

VI. VOIR DIRE IN HANDCUFFS

With an understanding of how to conduct lawyer voir dire, you should be capable of overcoming the challenges of time limits and judge-only voir dire. It all comes down to your adjusting to the handcuffs, and selecting a better jury than your opponent.

A. Zip Disk Voir Dire: Time Limits

With broad power over the conduct of voir dire, trial judges often impose strict time limits. However, as jury consultant Robert Hirschhorn states,[9] "[A] 30-minute *voir dire* does not have to be a deathblow to a case if each of those 30 minutes is treated as if they are an attorney's precious last

---

9. Robert Hirschhorn & Stacie M. Screiber, *How to Conduct Meaningful and Effective Voir Dire in Thirty Minutes*, 15 ADVOC. 102, 111 (1996).

dime. As one would plan a budget down to the last expenditure, so should an attorney budget *voir dire* time wisely to make sure that not one second is spent frivolously." So, as restrictive as your voir dire might be—I've been given as little as 15 minutes—it is still better than judge-only voir dire. You just have to learn to compress your voir dire into Zip disk format. Get your initial rankings done as soon as possible. Plan your questions and comments to avoid wasting any time. Do everything that you would ordinarily do during voir dire—but do it double-time.

Begin by making comments that put the panelists at ease and by introducing your clients warmly—but in no more than two or three minutes. Then, out of the two or three topics that you could ask the panelists about, choose the one most likely to strike it rich with the first persons you question, the one designed to provoke responses that create empathy and identification immediately. (See p. 92, "Link panelists' lives to your client's and his cause.") If you are running out of time, put a quick end to the round-robin discussion, ask for a show of hands row by row of those who agree and disagree with what has been said, or, if the judge is pounding the gavel, ask for a show of hands all at once.

In cases with particularly difficult issues, use the method of the asbestos case voir dire, flushing out the largest number of unacceptable panelists in the shortest period of time. (See p. 98, "Flush out unacceptable panelists, all at once.") That technique is likely to get panelists up to the bench, a huge asset in any case, but especially when your time is so limited. You get to ask them more questions—and the time doesn't count against yours. Once at the bench, you have a right to test for bias in a meaningful way, so seize the opportunity to expand your questions beyond the panelist's troubling answer.

As Hirschhorn emphasizes, be careful not to repeat questions that the judge or your opponent has asked, or the judge may cut you off. When your time is up, if you still have relevant questions, request additional time to ask them. Argue that you are being deprived of an opportunity to conduct a meaningful voir dire, and be ready to back up what you say. If the judge refuses your request, dictate those additional questions into the record. Be sure to proffer your additional questions *prior* to striking the jury, or it will be too late for the judge to take any remedial action, and you will have waived any error. If you are timely, and the questions reasonable, the judge may relent.

B. Emergency Room Voir Dire: When the Judge Asks the Questions

In most federal courts and in several state courts,[10] only the judge questions the panelists, or, as the practice is more widely known, no voir dire at all. In these restrictive courts, some of the lessons learned from doing lawyer voir dire will help you select a favorable jury. To put you in the right frame of mind, imagine that you are the only doctor in a hospital emergency room. A patient walks in complaining of severe indigestion and then loses consciousness. There's no time to consult or run tests. Based on your intuition, skill, and training, you treat the patient for a heart attack and save her life. That's the way you have to operate when the judge conducts voir dire. You have to trust that your instincts and ability will lead you to make the right decisions. But how? As the forensic expert Dr. Gordon says, "Welcome to Emergency Room voir dire."

If you can afford it, conduct a mock, "hurry-up" jury study. Make it as realistic as possible. Put a retired judge or seasoned colleague on the "bench." Beg, borrow, or recreate the typical questions your real judge asks of the venire. Have the stand-in conduct a 15-minute voir dire. At the end of his questioning, give yourself ten minutes to strike the panel. This type of practice will hone your ability to make split-second decisions when you strike the real panel. Selecting an actual jury is not the time for on-the-job training.

In many federal jurisdictions, the same panelists serve for several weeks, sitting on several panels, and often on more than one jury. Since they are already in the courthouse, request that panelists who will be assigned to your case on Monday be allowed to fill out the questionnaires the preceding Friday. In the best of all worlds, the judge will return the questionnaires to you to study over the weekend. Almost certainly, however, the panelists will fill them out while sitting in the courtroom on the morning of the trial.

As soon as you get a list of the panelists, have someone on your team conduct an online search for any and all *public* information they can find. Anything about a venireman's personal and professional history (from such sites as http://www.google.com) or recorded instruments, such as deeds or liens, is fair game and potential pay dirt. In those federal jurisdictions that

---

10. See note 1, p. 73, for the type of voir dire available in all courts.

"recycle" panelists, the lawyers who have tried cases in that courthouse recently are an excellent source of information. Before trial begins, find out who they are, and ask them to be ready to accept your call so that they can share any information or thoughts they have on the panelists you've drawn.

While the judge is questioning the panelists, observe everything the panelists say or do. The judge's questions may be useless, but the panelists' occasional answers never are. Be hyperalert for reaction time, tone of voice, and whatever other meaning you discern from their responses. There is no clue too subtle to go unnoticed—not when you have so few firsthand observations to rely on, and not when your first impressions can change the composition of your jury.

After she is finished, the judge may allow you to ask some follow-up questions about things the panelists said—so don't fail to request permission to do so. Even federal judges must allow you to question panelists individually who have heard about your case before coming to court—if what they've heard has influenced their thinking about the case. However, before you get to question the panelist, most judges will ask if the panelist can put that information out of his mind and follow the law as instructed—which usually results in intimidating the panelist into saying that he can. Nevertheless, it never hurts to request permission to ask a couple questions of the panelist at the bench. The worst the judge can do is say no. Once there, you know what to do.

As you would with any other venire, categorize and rank the panelists. Especially when you don't get to question them yourself, those rankings will be critical when you exercise your strikes.

VII. WHEN THEY ARE SEATED IN THE BOX

Much of what you have worked for during the months and years of pretrial prep will have been determined by what you have accomplished during voir dire. You should have selected a jury that likes you, and have a great chance of winning. Once they are sworn, you will move on, turning your attention to opening and the first witness. But the jurors will have formed impressions in these first few hours that almost certainly won't change. The emotions you stirred and the promises implicit in all that you said will resonate within them throughout trial. Deliver on what you promised—don't let them down.

VIII. VOIR DIRE CHECKLIST

The following checklist is divided chronologically, with the rules within them listed roughly in order of importance. However, familiarity with those rules tells you that those differences are generally insignificant.

A. **Prior to Trial**
   1. Always request individual voir dire, even in federal court.
   2. Always request a jury questionnaire.
   3. Visit the locale.
B. **Once the Panel Is Seated**
   1. Draw a jury chart.
   2. Identify panelists you must question.
      a. "X" out panelists excused before lawyer questioning began.
      b. Mark a "?" for panelists who *might* be disqualified for cause.
   3. Never take notes during your own voir dire.
C. **The Six Stages of Voir Dire**
   1. Put the panelists at ease.
   2. Humanize your clients.
   3. Ask questions of the panel as a whole.
      a. Ask open-ended questions.
         i. Loop their answers into alliances.
         ii. Test the reliability of answers.
      b. Link panelists' lives to your client's and her cause.
         i. Linkage and the law.
         ii. Linkage and your themes.
         iii. Linkage and your worst weaknesses.
      c. Develop challenges for cause.
         i. Flush out unacceptable panelists, all at once.
         ii. Flush out unacceptable panelists, one at a time.
      d. Prod unresponsive panels.
   4. Ask questions of individual jurors.
      a. Don't accept silence.
      b. Question panelists whose answers raised concern.
      c. Try head fakes.
      d. Nominate the "presiding juror."
   5. Disqualify panelists for cause.
      a. Establish a fixed state of mind.

    b. Eliminate panelists at the bench.
        i.   Praise the panelist's candor.
        ii. Make disqualification commendable.
        iii. Get agreement on what the panelist said.
        iv. Elevate what was said to a matter of principle.
        v.   Elevate the principle to a disqualifying opinion.
        vi. Preempt rehabilitation.

6. Ten rules for striking juries.
    a. Test the juror profile against the real panelists.
    b. Categorize the panelists.
    c. Consult with clients in front of the venire.
    d. Compare panelists constantly.
    e. Get rid of the "1's."
    f. Identify your opponent's likely strikes.
    g. Limit strategic back-strikes.
    h. Avoid double-strikes.
    i. Forfeit a strike.
    j. Request an extra strike.

APPENDIX A
Sample Juror Questionnaire

Juror #

1. Full name _____ Age _____

2. Where do you live?_____

3. Where do you work and what is your job (if unemployed or retired, where did you last work)? _____

4. Length of employment: _____ Title or position: _____

5. What are/were your main job responsibilities?_____

6. What jobs have you held in the past? _____

7. Have you ever held a job that required you to hire, fire, or supervise employees? ___ YES ___ NO

8. How far did you go in school (if college, name school(s) and any degree(s) received)? _____

9. Marital Status:_____

10. If you are married, for how many years? _____ How many times have you been married? _____

11. Regarding your spouse, ex-spouse, or the person with whom you are living, where do these people work and what are their jobs (if unemployed or retired, where have they worked in the past)?_____

12. Please list the sex, age, and occupation for each of your:

CHILDREN			STEPCHILDREN		
Sex	Age	Occupation	Sex	Age	Occupation

13. Have you attended any lecture(s), seminar(s), or course(s) in any of the following areas: accounting, aviation mechanics, business law, engineering, finance, flight safety, insurance, law, medicine, or psychology?
    ___ YES ___ NO If yes, what lecture(s), seminar(s), or course(s)?

14. Have you or any of your family members or friends ever worked for an insurance company or in the field of insurance or claims?
    ___ YES ___ NO If YES, who, for what company(ies), and in what job?

15. Have you or any of your family members or friends ever worked for XYZ Engineering or any other engineering or manufacturing company?
___ YES ___ NO If YES, who, and what was this person's job?

_____

16. Have you or any family member ever owned a business?
___ YES ___ NO If YES, who, when, and what type of business?

_____

17. If the business is no longer open, why was it sold or closed?

_____

18. Have you or anyone you know ever applied for work with or worked for any lawyer(s) or law firm(s)?
___ YES ___ NO If YES, who and for which lawyer(s) or law firm(s)?

_____

19. Do you know any lawyer(s)? ___ YES ___ NO
If YES, whom do you know and how do you know this person?

_____

20. Have you or any family members ever been a Plaintiff (the person suing) or a Defendant (the person being sued) in a lawsuit?
___ YES ___ NO If YES, please explain:

_____

21. How many times have you served as a juror in a:
Criminal case ___ times   Civil case ___ times
Grand Jury ___ times   ___ Never served
a. What type(s) of civil case(s)?
b. What was the verdict(s)?
c. Were you the foreperson? ___ YES ___ NO

22. Have you ever used or purchased a product that you felt was defective?
___ YES ___ NO If YES, please explain:

_____

23. Have you or any of your family members or close friends ever been involved in an accident (automobile, airplane, boat, etc.)?
___ YES ___ NO If YES:
a. Who had the accident?
b. Whose fault was the accident?
c. Was anyone injured or killed as a result of this accident?
___ YES ___ NO
d. Was there a lawsuit filed? ___ YES ___ NO
e. What was the outcome of the lawsuit?
f. How did you feel about the outcome of the lawsuit?

24. Please tell us how safe you believe the following modes of transportation are:

	Very Safe	Safe	Somewhat Safe	Unsafe	Very Unsafe
a. Automobile	___	___	___	___	___
b. Airplane	___	___	___	___	___
c. Train	___	___	___	___	___
d. Bus	___	___	___	___	___

25. Do you know anyone who has been injured or killed in any type of accident? ___ YES ___ NO If YES, please explain:

_____

26. Have you or any of your family members or close friends ever built an ultra-light aircraft from a kit? ___ YES ___ NO If YES, please explain:

_____

27. Have you or any of your family members or close friends ever flown in an aircraft built from a kit? ___ YES ___ NO If YES, please explain:

_____

28. What do you believe causes most crashes of aircraft built from kits?
___ Poor design by the manufacturer ___ Improperly built by Owner
___ Other
PLEASE EXPLAIN YOUR ANSWER:_____

29. In general, what are your feelings or opinions about people who bring wrongful-death lawsuits? _____

_____

30. Generally speaking, do you feel that jury verdicts or settlements are:
___ Too High ___ About Right ___ Too Low
PLEASE EXPLAIN YOUR ANSWER:_____

31. At the end of this case, the Court may instruct the jury to consider certain damages. If supported by the evidence, could you award damages for:
Physical Pain ___ YES ___ NO
Mental Anguish ___ YES ___ NO
Medical Expenses ___ YES ___ NO
Lost Income ___ YES ___ NO
Physical Impairment ___ YES ___ NO
Loss of Companionship ___ YES ___ NO
IF YOU ANSWERED "NO" FOR ANY OF THE ABOVE, PLEASE EXPLAIN YOUR ANSWER:

_____

32. What are your feelings or opinions about awarding money for the pain and suffering a person experiences prior to dying in an accident? _____

_____

33. In a case where a husband is killed when his ultra-light aircraft crashes, how do you feel about awarding money to his spouse for mental anguish and loss of companionship?_____

_____

34. What would be important to you in deciding how much money, if any, a spouse should receive for:
a. Emotional pain and mental anguish:_____
b. Loss of companionship, love, and comfort:_____

35. Which of the words below would you use to describe yourself? (please check (_) all that apply):

___ Analytical	___ Outspoken
___ Careful	___ Practical
___ Compassionate	___ Private
___ Compulsive	___ Quiet
___ Creative	___ Selfish
___ Emotional	___ Sensitive
___ Generous	___ Skeptical
___ Impulsive	___ Smart
___ Judgmental	___ Strict
___ Logical	___ Successful
___ Naive	___ Technical
___ Old-fashioned	___ Thoughtful
___ Open-minded	___ Trusting
___ Opinionated	___ Other

36. Please list any unions or civic, social, professional, or religious organizations to which you now belong or have belonged: _____

_____

37. Are you or any of your family members or friends a member of any other group(s) or organization(s) favoring tort reform?
    ___ YES ___ NO   If YES, who and what group(s) or organization(s)?

38. Please list the newspapers, magazines, professional journals, or periodicals to which you subscribe or read on a regular basis: _____

_____

39. How many hours per week do you spend watching television?
40. Please list your three favorite television shows:
    (1) _____ (2) _____ (3) _____
41. Please list the three people you admire most:
    (1) _____ (2) _____ (3) _____
42. Please list the three people you admire least:
    (1) _____ (2) _____ (3) _____
43. What do you enjoy doing in your spare time? _____
44. Is there anything else that you feel is important for the parties to know about you? _____

JUROR OATH

I hereby swear or affirm that all the answers given in this juror questionnaire are true, correct, and complete to the best of my knowledge.

Opening Argument 5

I. THE IMPORTANCE OF OPENING ARGUMENT

Opening is trial law's most underrated weapon. Until closing, it is the only chance you will have to tell your client's story uninterrupted, save the occasional objection. If your opening is persuasive, it can have more impact than summation, especially in long trials where many jurors will have already made up their minds. Obviously, even if you are ahead following opening, you can still lose—no different from a successful voir dire. If your client comes off badly on direct, or gets killed on cross, it can alter the course of a trial. But, also like voir dire, if you don't get off to a good start with the jury, your odds of winning are diminished. A bad early impression is likely to last throughout the trial.

Besides, it is not just jurors who are moved by a compelling opening argument. It is surprisingly cathartic for your client to hear someone, finally, tell his side of the story—someone who is speaking without notes, who believes so passionately what she is saying that it comes from her heart and not a legal pad. That strengthens the bond between you—a bond not likely to be lost on the jury.

II. THE GOALS OF OPENING ARGUMENT

A. Trial Lawyers Must Be Good Storytellers

The degree to which jurors are persuaded is in direct proportion to your performance: You must be a good storyteller. In Marshall McLuhan's famous phrase about television, "the medium is the message." In a jury trial, the medium is you.

B. Cicero Is Not Just a City Near Chicago

At first blush, you might think that Cicero, the Roman statesman, and Mollie Martin, my high school debate coach, have little to do with opening argument, but you would be wrong. There is no better training for a trial lawyer than on a high school debate team, and no better teacher than my debate coach's idol, Cicero.

"Miz Mollie" was right. Cicero took the time to understand jurors and what it takes to sway their minds. His observations about delivery and structure of argument have endured since the first century B.C., when he was the most acclaimed public speaker and trial lawyer in Rome. Even today, the best trial lawyers do what Cicero did back then, except that he did it in Latin, while wearing only a toga.

III. DELIVERY

There is no more important aspect of argument than the way it's delivered. Yet, for all its significance, there is no easier skill to master or improve. Follow Cicero's advice about persuasion and your opening can set the agenda for the entire trial.

A. Tone

Cicero believed that argument must be delivered "agreeably" and "feelingly," that the manner in which a case is presented is "often to be worth more than the merits of the case."[1] The more cases I try, the more brilliant I believe that advice to be. *How* things are said is often more important than *what* is said. This advice applies not only to opening but throughout a trial, and not just to lawyers, but also to parties and witnesses. Sooner or later, every good trial lawyer I know "discovers" this principle, and after the epiphany thinks that he made it up.

1. Jurors give verdicts to people they like.

In the television industry, they speak of the "Q" factor, that intangible quality that makes viewers tune in to a performer because they like her. Trial lawyers, contentious by nature, ought to remember that: Jurors give verdicts to people they like.

Anger and arrogance are not your allies in a courtroom. In a forum where things can—and inevitably do—go wrong, a certain degree of humility is required. Too many jurors are bullied at work or at home to be a fan of a bully in the courtroom. Don't get me wrong. You're not running for cheerleader. There is nothing in Cicero's suggestion to present your case "agreeably" and "feelingly" that implies being a pushover. Being tough and aggressive (as was Cicero) is essential to winning the case. But being tough and aggressive is one thing; being constantly angry and arrogant, quite another.

---

1. MARTHA K. LEVINE, CICERO ON APPEALS, available at http://courses.smsu.edu/mk1808f/eng625s00/Cicero%20onAppeals.eng625s00/Cicero%20on20Appeals.htm (on file with author).

I could write a treatise about attitude in the courtroom, but Cicero said it best in a single paragraph: Anger, the great Roman suggests, has its time and place, but opening is not one of them:

> The [juror's] feelings are not likely to be kindled by what I call the ardent and impassioned onset. For vigorous language is not always wanted, but often such as is calm, gentle, mild: this the kind that commends the parties. *Id.*

I was not an early follower of this advice. At the beginning of my career, the "ardent and impassioned onset" was my favored style. Some of the cases I handled early in my career—the often brutal arrests of young people for war protests and marijuana possession—would have angered a saint. But the jury didn't know what I knew when I made my opening argument. I learned quickly not to get ahead of them emotionally—advice that applies throughout each stage of trial. Make sure they are up to speed before you turn up the heat. Be patient and let their emotions build as the facts unfold. If instead, you alienate jurors with your attitude, it will be difficult to regain their respect.

Let the facts of the case dictate the emotion you display. I don't mean being phony—I mean being realistic about your case. If the other side has mistreated your client, a little emotion as you explain the transgression is fine. Getting hysterical over an easement issue is not.

Remember, the facts alone—without your help—can sometimes stir overwhelming emotion. If you represent the paralyzed victim of a drunk driver, you need only to recite the facts objectively to be persuasive. On the other hand, if you are representing the drunk driver, it is not likely you could be righteously indignant and effective at the same time. You just have to adjust accordingly.

There are exceptions. Joe Jamail once represented a driver paralyzed in an accident with an 18-wheeler. His client, however, blew a .20 on the Breathalyzer, twice the legal limit. Unlike the typical case, it was the drunk driver who brought suit. Rising in indignation to make his opening statement, Jamail argued without blinking, "I don't care how much he had to drink, the accident was not his fault." Leaning forward, voice filled with emotion, he added, "Hell, it ain't open season on drunks." On that jury, drunks apparently had a large following. The verdict was $14 million—enough to keep anyone in single malt scotch for years to come.

2. Speak with conviction.

Obviously, your voice is your most powerful weapon. The proper inflection or tone can draw jurors in and hold them. Yet the fundamental power is the not the pitch of your voice, but the conviction in it. Listen closely to the best trial lawyers. Their voices convey a sense of moral urgency and absolute belief in the justness of their cause.

Morris Dees, the founder of the Southern Poverty Law Center, could talk about weed removal and you'd be in tears sooner or later. Standing stock still throughout opening, he speaks so quietly that jurors are forced to lean forward to hear him. His delivery builds in intensity as the facts of his case unfold. Yet, it isn't skillful oratory alone that makes him so effective. It is conviction—his faith in the righteousness of his cause. It is almost religious. True, his cases are against neo-Nazi groups and the Klan, and jurors will be with him from the start. But I have heard him speak inside and outside the courtroom, and that soft voice coupled with an unadorned belief in what he is saying makes it is impossible not to be moved.

The converse is also true: Speak without conviction and you will lose the jury. If you don't believe in your client's cause, or are merely pretending to be a true believer, the panel will know it. Whether your voice is soft or fills the courtroom will be irrelevant. Your greatest weapon will be turned against you—a dead giveaway of your insincerity.

You're not playing make-believe, but do what actors do: Stay in focus. Remember while you speak why you are there. Concentrate on things that matter. Stay in focus, and your voice will never betray you.

B. Nonverbal Communication

Communication occurs on several levels at once, like fishing with several hooks on your line. Nonverbal communication is one of those hooks—unspoken signals that influence jurors separate and apart from your words. Nonverbal communication can be as persuasive as the spoken word, and, in a jury trial, creates a secret advantage: No matter how strictly a judge applies the rules against argument, he can't stop you from using this arsenal of silent weapons.

1. Make eye contact.

Jurors need to hear conviction in your voice, but they also need to see it in your eyes. Even if only for a moment, make eye contact with each of them while you speak. It will serve as a signal that what you are saying really matters—and that each of them matters, too. If your eyes wander or you look down, you send the wrong message: that you are disinterested or discouraged.

While you should establish eye contact with each juror, resist the temptation to look too long at your favorites—the ones who are obviously receptive to you and to your case. You risk making them feel uncomfortable, and the others, neglected and resentful. Besides, those skeptical-looking panelists merit your attention, too—perhaps more than the others. It's human nature: If you don't establish eye contact with them, the slight fortifies their resistance.

Parenthetically, nonverbal communication is a two-way street. Opening is an especially good time to get a read on the jurors. You will watch them for their reactions throughout the trial, but you cannot be obvious about it, or you risk offending them. During opening, you are *supposed* to be looking at them. So glance at their faces and watch their body language for those early clues. Try to figure out which ones appear to be with you, and which ones don't.

2. Stand still.

Get out from behind the lectern. It's just one more barrier between you and the jurors, and it's easily overcome. Find a comfortable spot to stand—one that doesn't "invade their space." Once you find that spot, stand still for as much of your argument as possible. If you move, do so for a specific purpose, such as getting closer to the jurors at the far end of the box, or pointing out something on a timeline. When you move, never appear rushed. And never pace nervously up and down in front of the jury box. That's a terrible image. Not only will you appear unsure of yourself, you will also look like one of those moving ducks in a shooting gallery. If there is one thing you don't want to be during a trial, it's the target.

3. Be quiet.

It's not just the sound of your voice that can mesmerize jurors. Silence can be powerful, too. Pausing to let a point sink in, or to announce the importance of what's coming, is the nonverbal equivalent of an exclamation point.

4. Gesture.

The right gesture, no matter how slight, can make a point memorable. Put your hand on your client's shoulder as you introduce him or her to the jury. That presents a clear image about the closeness of your relationship.

Pointing to your client across the room, on the other hand, creates a distance the jury should not even *think* exists. When you argue the facts, don't just tell the jury that the defense will attempt to mislead them. Instead, show them, pointing skyward toward "what they want you to see," and with the other hand, downward, toward "what they don't want you to see."

5. Power ties and other urban legends.

Trial lawyers should dress conservatively. Dark clothing is a sign of respect for the jury and the legal system. Blue shirts and blouses are warmer than white ones, and therefore more likely to draw the jury toward you rather than keep them away. Flashy jewelry should be left at home.

While many lawyers consult image consultants to develop their wardrobe, and I don't profess to be an expert in color coordination, there is a limit to the value of clothing as weapons of nonverbal communication. I'm referring now to such concepts as "power ties." Jury consultants will tell you that these ties announce to the panel that you are in charge, or that something important like a big cross-examination is about to happen. But what if you blow the cross? Assuming the consultants are right, your power tie underscores the importance of your defeat. (Almost as bad, what if the jury thinks that you have terrible taste?)

Let me explain why I react this viscerally to the idea that power clothing can make a big difference at trial. I used to know this guy, Dwayne, who practiced down the hall from me. He spent most of his working day trying to figure out a shortcut to a large practice—some gimmick that would put him on the map. One day, he called me all excited. "I've got it, buddy," he said. "My new phone number is 222-2222."

"Well, of course, Dwayne," I thought to myself, "why wouldn't *that* start a stampede of clients to your door? I'll bet IBM is dialing your number at this very moment." If Dwayne could have somehow combined the slightest bit of legal talent and hard work with his penchant for catchy phone numbers, he might not have left the law to become an optician about a year after he changed his phone number.

My point here is that I am suspicious of any strategy that feels like a gimmick. Power ties strike me as an attempt to compensate for a lack of courtroom skills, or to avoid the hard work it takes to create a real relationship with a jury. In my experience, there are no such shortcuts. It's far more effective to be prepared and be yourself in the courtroom than it is to rely on your juror-friendly aftershave to win the case.

At the same time, if you feel more confident when wearing a power tie, by all means, wear one. But remember: You still have to defeat your opponent. Try as I might, I can't recall a single tie ever taking apart a witness on cross-examination.

C. Watch Your Words

This is where I part company with Cicero. He favored flowery words and ornate sentences. Modern juries are turned off by unnecessary flourishes. When it comes to word choice, I prefer to follow the advice of a former president of the United States, himself, ironically, one of the worst speakers in the history of the Republic.

1. Keep it simple.

President Carter may have been a terrible public speaker, but he had the right idea. He used to say he gave speeches so the guy who pumped gas at the corner station could understand them. He knew that communication is most effective when it is kept simple.[2] All that information about your client's case, which you know so well, is new to the jury. Help them follow it. Don't telegraph your thoughts. Explain fully what you mean with words everyone understands.

Keeping it simple doesn't mean sacrificing eloquence; quite the opposite. Was there anyone in this country who did not understand what Martin Luther King meant when he said, "I have a dream"? Did anyone doubt Winston Churchill's resolve to defeat the Nazis when he vowed to "fight them on the beaches"? Many of the great speeches of history stand out not for their polysyllabic flourishes, but for their simplicity and clarity.

2. Choose forceful words.

Jurors are not offended if you speak bluntly—so long as what you tell them proves true. The last thing they want to hear is a weak-kneed lawyer tiptoeing around the truth. Choose words that are forceful, descriptive, and down-to-earth—words that sell your case and undermine your opponent's. For that reason, your opponent never "says" anything about a significant issue. She "claims" or "wants you to believe." She never "agrees";

---

2. The best work on simplifying language is Strunk & White, *Elements of Style*, which, at only 87 pages, takes its own advice.

she "admits." Defense counsel never "offers a defense." She "comes up with a bunch of excuses" and "won't accept responsibility." The defendant didn't "commit fraud." He "betrayed" your client and "stabbed him in the back." The plaintiff isn't "seeking damages." She "only wants what she has coming to her." When appropriate, the plaintiff isn't seeking compensation, but "a pot of gold."

Highly charged and shed of legalisms, these are the kinds of words you should use as you put together any argument. In the words of the *New York Times Manual of Style and Usage*, "Verbs work hardest, and adjectives little."[3] Add punch to your opening by selecting a verb that creates a lasting impression. For ideas, try *Words That Make a Difference*.[4] The author lists hundreds of nouns, verbs, adjectives, and adverbs that send an unmistakable message.

That said, be careful. A word or phrase that might be perfect in one context can be a disaster in another. In the early 1990s—long before scientific studies undermined their validity—the nation's first breast implant case was tried in Houston. I watched a snippet of the defense lawyer's opening on local television and knew immediately that he was going to get killed. Pointing toward one of the two plaintiffs, a kind-looking woman around 50, he snarled, "She *claims* she's got *some kind of disease* from the implants. Let her tell you about that." I've never forgotten how coarse he sounded. Whether illness associated with implants later turned out to be junk science or not, that was awful lawyering. The jury awarded the woman $25 million, which came as no surprise to anyone who watched the lawyer's opening.

3. Analogize.

Analogies are powerful tools. With the right reference, you can capture your case in a way that will stick with the jurors when they leave the courthouse. In even the most complex litigation, use comparisons that involve everyday things, like food, or home, or sports. (See p. 238, "Experts must communicate.") Jurors will think about your point as they drive up their driveways, open the refrigerator, or attend a Little League game.

3. ALLAN M. SIEGAL & WILLIAM G. CONNOLLY, THE NEW YORK TIMES MANUAL OF STYLE AND USAGE: THE OFFICIAL STYLE GUIDE USED BY THE WRITERS AND EDITORS OF THE WORLD'S MOST AUTHORITATIVE NEWSPAPER (1999).

4. ROBERT GREENMAN, WORDS THAT MAKE A DIFFERENCE (2002).

In 1998, I was involved in a case so complicated that it cried out for a good analogy. I represented Samsung against Texas Instruments in a suit alleging TI had violated a most-favored-nations clause in a royalty-related agreement. In the clause, Texas Instruments promised to charge Samsung no more for microchips than it charged Samsung's Japanese competitors. During opening, I compared TI to a dishonest butcher who sells your neighbor hamburger meat at a secret, cheaper price than he sells it to you—something jurors would be reminded of whenever they walked into their grocery store or drove through a McDonald's.

D. Teaching Tools

Graphics and documents help you simplify and organize your opening, particularly in complex commercial cases. Having something to look at can also give jurors a needed break in the middle of listening. But use these teaching tools wisely.

1. Streamline timelines.

By their nature, timelines teach. Pared down to the most critical dates and events, a timeline can help jurors grasp the essence of even the most complex cases. If, however, a timeline is too detailed, the important facts that really matter will get swamped. (See p. 64, "Making commercial cases accessible.") Timelines also perform double duty, serving as an outline for your opening argument. Relying on a timeline instead of a legal pad removes one of the barriers between you and the jury. It also forces you to talk to the jurors, instead of reading to them.

2. Circulate very few documents.

In the past, whenever I had killer documents in a case, I circulated all of them to the panel during opening. Jurors had told me over the years that they appreciated being able to read key documents to themselves, to verify their contents and importance. They said it helped them understand the case. Handing documents to jurors when I was allowed to do so myself also gave me the chance to establish a physical bond with them—something I learned from Richard Haynes.

Nevertheless, there are too many potential problems—and I have experienced them all—to circulate all the "hot docs" in your case. In the first place, you can't speak while the jurors are reading. You have to wait while the document makes the rounds from the first juror to the last. Silence may be a powerful weapon, but not when it complicates your presentation and destroys your momentum.

So as a rule, circulate only one or two of the briefest, most important documents. To minimize time-consuming delays, circulate one copy per person instead of a single copy for the entire panel. Put the remaining documents on overhead projectors—if they are truly important. At trial, less is always more—especially when it comes to documents. (See p. 166, "Cross *about* documents, not *out of* them.")

IV. STRUCTURE

Cicero structured argument around three fundamental principles of persuasion: appeals to ethos, logos, and pathos. That technique is as valid today as it was in ancient Rome:

> Under my whole oratorical system lie three principles: First, the winning of men's favor [ethos], second, their enlightenment [logos] and third, their excitement [pathos]. . . . Of these three, the first calls for gentleness of style, the second for acuteness, the third for energy. For, of necessity, the [juror] who is to decide in our favor must either lean to our side by natural inclination, or be won over by the arguments for the defense, or constrained by stirring his feelings.[5]

Note that Cicero wrote from the perspective of a defense lawyer, yet he placed a premium on emotions. That's a valuable lesson from one of their own for the less passionate half of the modern bar.

In short, Cicero recommends beginning and ending with an appeal to the jurors' emotions (ethos and pathos). In between, squeeze in evidence that will give the jury an intellectual basis for their decision (logos). Although it probably never occurred to him, Cicero structured his arguments like an Oreo cookie. Following is an examination of the ingredients of each layer.

A. Ethos

Opening isn't closing. Neither the rules nor common sense allow you to argue as passionately. But if you want a decisive verdict, you must engage jurors emotionally from the start.

---

5. Levine, *supra* note 1.

1. Don't bury your lead.

Cicero recommends restraint at the beginning, but that doesn't mean burying your lead. The most effective opening arguments begin with a stirring "headline"—a *shorthand* statement that captures the essence of your case. You will never find a shorter or more persuasive opening comment than defense counsel's in *Chiron v. Genentech,* a patent-infringement case tried to a verdict in 2002.

In that case, Chiron, a pharmaceutical company, alleged that its rival, Genentech, manufactured two drugs that infringed its patent on a "humanized" mouse antibody that "binds to HER-2, a protein that protrudes from the surface of many breast cancer cells."[6] However germane, that's just not the level of detail any juror needs at the beginning of a trial, unless sleep has been a problem. Instead, Genentech's lead defense counsel, Leora Ben-Ami, walked to the jury box, held up two medicine bottles, and said, "This case is about two medical miracles." I love that beginning. By holding the two bottles in her hands, Ms. Ben-Ami established physical control over the drugs—a powerful image for a jury whose decision would decide their ownership. By calling them "medical miracles" she communicated how important the case was. The net effect was to make precisely the appeal to ethos Cicero envisioned: It is in everyone's interest to develop wonder drugs, especially Genentech's pursuit of a cure for breast cancer and non-Hodgkins lymphoma. Ms. Ben-Ami staked out that (common) ground for her client and won her case, proving that Chiron's patent was invalid.

I learned the value of crystallizing the most powerful aspect of the case years ago, from a source that remained a mystery for ten years. In 1973, I represented Houston's fire chief, who had been indicted for allegedly rigging bids for fire engines. Highly publicized, the case was tried on a change of venue in Ft. Worth, which, parenthetically, is an odd city filled with strange people.

I reserved opening until after the state presented its case. Moments before I started, I found a note taped to the defense table with my name written on the front. I assumed it came from my co-counsel. It read, "The only conspiracy proven so far is the one against the fire chief. His mortal enemies in the labor union and city hall have teamed up to destroy him. They have been very successful. He is a broken man on the verge of losing the only job he ever

---

6. *Chiron Loses Patent Lawsuit Against Genentech Cancer Drug,* N.Y. TIMES, September 22, 2002, Section C, at 2.

wanted. They should be on trial, not him." Those words were the first ones I spoke during my opening. After that, I put the fire chief on, rested, and won a quick acquittal. Several jurors later commented that my opening really put the case in perspective.

A decade later, I returned to the Ft. Worth courthouse for an unrelated hearing. When it concluded, I went to the office of the judge who tried the fire chief's case. I told him that I had thought of him many times, that I had learned a great deal in his court, and that the win had been a big one for me. He listened for a while and then asked if I had found his note.

2.   Inoculate your argument against objections.

Much trial literature is devoted to the "debate" over whether you should argue during opening. To most trial lawyers, there is no debate. The best opening statement is a good closing argument in disguise. That does not mean, however, that you have to break the rule against argument in opening—a rule that is rarely enforced anyway. You just have to inoculate your opening against the objection that you are arguing. It is simple to do. Early in your argument, repeat what the judge has probably already said: that what the lawyers say is not evidence. That single disclaimer creates great latitude with most courts. By repeating the instruction, you demonstrate your willingness to play by the rules while pushing back their boundaries. If opposing counsel objects to something in your opening, it will probably be to no avail. In my experience, the judge will say something like, "Counsel has already said this isn't evidence," or, "The jury will hear the evidence." Get past a couple of those objections, and the lawyer will give up, leaving you free to make an uninterrupted argument. Just don't be too enthusiastic when you tell the jury that what you say isn't evidence. They might believe you.

There's one more thing you can do to minimize objections during opening. Getting all the exhibits and deposition transcripts admitted prior to trial eliminates the objection during opening that the document you are arguing, or the video excerpt that you are playing, hasn't been admitted into the evidence, because it already has.

3.   Humanize your client.

Build on what you began in voir dire. Refer to your client warmly, by first name. If it's comfortable, introduce him again, and not at a distance. Then let the jurors know something commendable about him. They will view the crusty CEO locked in a bitter dispute with a customer more favorably when they learn that he is also involved in his community, volunteering as a Big Brother and serving as a deacon in his church.

How much you have to do to humanize a client depends on a number of factors, primarily how closely he matches up with the demographics of the jury and how well his type of person plays in that part of the country. As one example, humanizing my acerbic, Harvard-educated client in Orlando, where his case was tried, was far more difficult than it would have been in New York City.

One thing is certain: the more difficult it is to humanize your client, the greater the threat to your chances of winning—and the more critical it is to get it done. I faced such a situation in 1989, when a law school classmate asked me to help him try a case in federal court. He was an experienced trial lawyer, but he had never tried a federal case. I had tried many white-collar cases in federal court, but never a civil suit for money damages. Separately, we each had our strengths; together, we made an entire trial lawyer.

If that wasn't enough to worry our clients, we were also latecomers to the case. My friend was called in the Thursday before trial, and he called me the following night. The case was very complicated. Our clients alleged that a law firm had failed to provide them with adequate securities advice in a complicated real estate syndication.

Most difficult of all, our clients were Iranian-born. Americans still harbor bitter memories of 52 of their countrymen being held hostage in Iran by the Ayatollah Khomeini, from 1979 to 1980, so you can imagine how potential jurors felt about all things Iranian in 1989. If tough cases are the ones that really teach you something, I should have gotten a Ph.D.

The morning of trial, I met Dr. Bob Gordon, a forensic psychologist, for the first time. Under Bob's tutelage, my classmate had gone from shy and inarticulate to a polished trial lawyer with powerful jury skills and a winning track record.

Ever diplomatic, Dr. Gordon asked if I would "mind" talking to him about my opening argument. I'd been a trial lawyer for more than 20 years, and had never used forensic help. I jumped at the chance. It was a pleasant December day, so we each grabbed a Coke and walked several times around the courthouse block. That walk changed my practice. I can't remember everything Dr. Gordon said, but the gist of it is embedded in my memory. We talked about how imperative it was to humanize our Iranian clients. The jurors needed to be able to see the two of them as real people—not Middle Eastern stereotypes. I remember distinctly Bob's elegant phrase: "They must become part of the American family." That job was made easier because they already had, long since. I tried to follow Bob's advice starting in the opening minutes of the case:

In the dead of night in January 1980, these two men, Ali Ebrahimi and Yousef Panahpour, loaded their wives and children into their cars, and, with their headlights turned off, drove silently into the Iranian night. They left loved ones and virtually every penny they had behind. To save their lives, they fled the country. Let me tell you why.

When Ayatollah Khomeini overthrew the Shah of Iran, he took 52 of our countrymen hostage. He and his followers tormented this nation for a long time, and while we've gotten our people back, that will never be enough. Americans have long memories. There will be a payback.

However, as you will learn when Ali and Yousef take the stand, Khomeni's government also turned with a vengeance on some of its own people. Businessmen with a history of doing business with Americans were prime targets. And no one in Iran had a longer history of doing business with Americans than Ali and Yousef. Ali's dad had been working with American companies for 40 years, back to the fifties. Yousef not only had ties to American business, he graduated college here in the United States. He earned his engineering degree at Texas A&M. He put himself through school with summertime jobs in the United States, one summer laying out roads as a surveyor for the Texas Department of Transportation. Then, degree in hand, he returned to Iran and, after a couple years, set up a construction business with his boyhood friend Ali Ebrahimi. They had every reason to believe they would live in Iran the rest of their lives. The revolution changed all that.

In 1979, Ali was arrested twice. The second time he was beaten. Through their sources, the men learned Yousef was next. That was enough warning for both of them. Both families sneaked across the border, and if either had been caught, there is no telling what would have happened to them.

Once across the border, they made their way to America and never looked back. That's Ali's wife in the front row. Yousef's family is next to her. And this crowd back here includes other members of both families—uncles, aunts, and other relatives—that these two men have worked to bring over to this country.

It's an old story. Like millions of men and women before them, these two families fled oppression for the freedom of America. They came looking for freedom and found it. Recently, on what you will hear was the proudest day of his life, Ali became an American citizen. In four more months, Yousef will, too. For a long time now, they have been a part of the American family.

The judge allowed me real latitude in this opening, but even if I had been forced to intersperse formulations like "what I say is not evidence," or to cut back substantially on the story, the barest description of their flight from Iran would still have been compelling. If there is one thing true of all of us, it is that someone in our lineage, if not we, was once an immigrant, often fleeing from oppression in another land.

If possible, humanize your clients with facts that can be woven into the case itself. It's one thing for jurors to learn that crusty CEO is actually involved in his community, but that doesn't explain why he stiffed his customer. It's quite another for jurors to see a relationship between the facts that humanize your client and the central allegations in your case. My subtle message to the jurors in Ali's and Yousef's case was: You wouldn't expect a native-born American to be familiar with securities laws. Why would you expect anything more of two guys born in Iran? To underscore our clients' dependence on the defendant law firm, and to strike a chord with the jury, I drew an analogy to doctors and their patients:

> Lawyers are powerful people. They are educated in ways others are not, and that information and training is what makes them powerful. People go to them when they need help with something they cannot do themselves. It's the same as when you go to a doctor. They have education, training, and skills that we don't. They know about the very thing that matters most to all of us—our health. We put ourselves, and our loved ones, in their care. We trust them to do the right thing. Sometimes, like all of us, they make mistakes. When they do, as the saying goes, doctors can bury their mistakes.
>
> Ali and Yousef's lawyers made a terrible mistake, and, as you will learn, tried to bury it, but they got caught. In a series of secret meetings with several senior partners of the firm, they devised a plan to save their own skins and betrayed their own clients.

By telling the story of Ali and Yousef's immigration, and then tying that story into the facts of the case, we converted a liability—ethnicity—into an advantage. Nor did it hurt that we had hard evidence of the lawyer's betrayal, about which, more to come. (See p. 151, "Make the jury mad.")

B. Logos

Lest I slice Cicero's method for organizing argument too thin, even the appeal to logic, which sounds somewhat clinical, should stir emotions. Just let the evidence do the heavy lifting. Few jurors will remain impassive in the face of overwhelming proof. The weight of a damning chronology or a stack of bad documents will leave them staring at your opponent in disbelief.

1. Use your draft jury charge.

Organize your presentation of the evidence around the jury questions in your draft jury charge (as you will during closing—with the real thing). Jot down in bullet points, under each jury question, the arguments and evidence that support each answer that you want the jurors to give. Condition jurors to think about the case in your terms. Tell them, "I anticipate you will have to answer this question at the end of the trial. In fact, it is the very reason we are in the courtroom." Then launch into your best arguments with your best available evidence. For example, if you want jurors to find that the defendant, your client's former CEO, breached his fiduciary duty while employed by your client, show them your client's customer list that the former executive downloaded from his computer before he quit. Show them the invoices and other financial records that prove he did big business with your client's customers after leaving the company. Tell them that after hearing the evidence, you feel certain they will conclude that the answer to the question is "yes," that the man did in fact breach his fiduciary duty.

As anxious as you might be to win, be careful never to overpromise during opening. As you outline the evidence, limit yourself to a discussion of the rock-solid proof that you are certain is going to be admitted into the evidence during the course of the trial. When the jurors see and hear the evidence, they should feel that what you told them was true and that their first instincts about the case were correct.

2. Simplify the evidence.

Remember, this is opening. The last thing you want to do is bury your best themes under a mountain of complex evidence. All that does is leave jurors confused. Rather than engaging them, you will turn them off. Once that happens, it's hard to get them back.

It is a premise of this book that even highly technical commercial cases can be made interesting. But you won't interest anyone in anything if you try to explain in opening that your client's engineers and scientists didn't misrepresent the ability of heat-exchanging tubes in nuclear steam generators to withstand the effects of subatomic corrosion, or the relationship of that problem to proper water chemistry. That was the critical issue in the *Westinghouse* case, but not a fit subject for opening argument—not in that form at least. Instead, we avoided arguing the scientific issues, and reduced the case to its simplest terms: What did the plaintiff's (South Texas Nuclear Project) own scientists, engineers, and executives know about the potential for corrosion in the nuclear steam generators before buying the power plant? If they were informed about the potential problems, then they could hardly claim they'd been defrauded. Relying on documents discussing that issue from the plant's own files, I told the jury we would prove that this was not a case of "Elmer Fudd buys a nuclear power plant."

> Ladies and gentlemen, when an allegation of fraud is made, the defendant has a right to introduce evidence about the state of mind of the plaintiff. In this case, what did STP's executives, nuclear scientists and engineers, know about the possibility of corrosion in those tubes inside the steam generators, and when did they know it? STP claims that Westinghouse misled its employees about the potential for corrosion in those generators when they were negotiating to buy the power plant in the early seventies.
>
> However, before STP's executives made a decision to purchase the power plant, they hired the leading nuclear power consultants in America to help them. STP paid them millions of dollars to review the entire transaction from a scientific standpoint and advise them on whether to purchase the Westinghouse plant or a competitor's. The result was this 400-page report. One section is called "Potential for corrosion in the tubes." It warns of every single problem STP claims to be having now. In the words of that immortal song, "Who's zoomin' who?" How much clearer could it be that STP's engineers and executives knew about the potential problems before buying the plant? Do you think they paid millions of dollars for this report to ignore it?
>
> And would you look at this? This magazine, as you can see, is called *Corrosion Magazine*. STP engineers subscribed to this magazine. There are articles in it that predate STP's purchase of the plant that warn explicitly of the potential for corrosion in the tubes of *every* nuclear steam generator around the world.
>
> Ladies and gentlemen, Westinghouse didn't try to fool anyone. This was, and remains, a relatively new industry filled with risks that everyone in it knows about. STP knew those risks. That company had and has sophisticated nuclear scientists and engineers and hard-nosed businessmen who made a calculated decision to go into the nuclear power business. And, as you will see from their annual financial reports, it has paid off big time. STP was not defrauded. In fact, as I mentioned earlier, that plant was the leading producer of electricity in the world last month. If it ain't broke, folks, there's no need to fix it.

Throughout the trial, one piece of evidence after another supported our contention that Westinghouse did not hide the ball from STP. To our delight, a month after trial began, there was yet another front-page story in the local paper declaring that the power plant once more led the world in production of electricity. Newspapers aren't evidence, but I might as well have had that edition on the overhead projector. Every juror in that small community had to have read it.

3.   Make good on your promises.

Opening provides a perfect opportunity for you to deliver on the explicit and implicit promises you made during individual voir dire. For example, that question that you asked the panel about experiencing "betrayal" implied that your client was betrayed. During opening, the jury naturally expects you to make the implicit explicit. The only way to avoid letting them down is to back up your promises with hard evidence, at the earliest possible moment.

Recall that we represented Eric Fleisher and his company, Assist Sports Management, in a suit alleging that ASM's former president, whom we shall call Bob Johnson, improperly solicited away the firm's key players. (See, p. 94, "Linkage and your themes.") Within days of Johnson's resignation from ASM, the players began sending in letters terminating Eric and his agency, and just as quickly, every one of them hired Johnson to act as their agent.

I told the jury that a major aspect of ASM's business was to obtain endorsement agreements for their players, like Kevin Garnett's Nike shoe deal. Then I put a typical ASM marketing agreement on the screen, and explained how it worked. I pointed out precisely where the player signed the agreement. I showed them where in the contract it said that ASM was the player's marketing agent and would receive a commission from the fees the players earned. I had a reason for going into so much detail:

> In March 1999, the defendant took a marketing agreement just like the one I just showed you, out of the offices of Assist Sports Management, went to his home in New Jersey, and, later—in the dark of night—drove to a Kinko's and typed up a copy of the marketing agreement. I want to put one of the agreements that he typed up on the screen. If you look closely, you will see that it wasn't an exact copy. Instead of typing in "Assist Sports Management" on the line for the agent, Johnson typed in his own name. In fact, ASM's name doesn't appear anywhere in this document.
>
> Within 30 days, he negotiated endorsement deals for three of ASM's players. But he had them sign marketing agreements like this one, making him the agent, not ASM. At the time, he was still working as president of ASM. He still owed the company a duty of loyalty. ASM was the player's agent, not his.
>
> And guess what. He doesn't bill the players for commissions on fees they earned—commissions that should have gone to ASM. Why would he

do that? It was bait on the water, designed to lure these players to leave with him when he walked out on ASM. And they did. Every one of them.

How do we know the details of what happened? That he copied the contracts at night? That he copied them at Kinko's? That he signed those players to ASM marketing agreements with his name typed in? Because prior to trial, ladies and gentlemen, questioned under oath, Johnson admitted it is true.

I told the jury that Johnson came to work for Eric Fleisher as an intern, and that within a few years, when he was only 28, Eric had made him president of ASM—and paid him a six-figure salary. With that information, and the undisputed evidence about the marketing agreements, the jury understood why I asked during voir dire if any of them had been betrayed.

4.   Embrace and explain your own bad facts.

At every stage of trial, you must anticipate or respond to arguments (or cross-examination) about the worst facts in your case. That way, the impact of those arguments will be weakened or defused. The plaintiff, who goes first in open (and close), has the advantage—pulling the teeth out of your arguments before you open your mouth. As a result, you must be ready on defense with powerful rebuttal for each of those arguments. But either way, whether plaintiff or defendant, whether anticipating or responding, you must never ignore a damaging issue about your case. If you do, the jury will perceive your silence as an admission that your opponent has told the truth—and that you have no answer. On the other hand, your willingness to tackle bad facts head-on sends an unmistakable signal to the jurors that your case is strong.

The timing of your arguments about your own weaknesses is also critical. Starting off talking about them is too defensive, elevating them in importance, and giving them credibility. At the same time, you will be burying your lead. Instead, argue your strongest case first. If you are persuasive, the jury will be prepared psychologically to accept your explanation of the bad facts in your client's case. Once you have argued your strengths, grab whatever "smoking gun" document your opponent waved in front of the jury. Put it on an overhead or circulate it to the jurors. Stand his argument on its head:

If you recall, counsel showed you this document—an internal study of the materials Westinghouse used in the manufacture of its nuclear steam generators. He called it a "smoking gun" and showed you where an engineer named Bob Rigley wrote across the top, "what a tangled web we weave." He reminded you that the next line of that couplet is, "when first we practice to deceive." He says those words are proof of Westinghouse's fraud—that it intended to hide defects in its generators from STP so that it wouldn't lose the sale of its nuclear power plant. Ladies and gentlemen, that accusation is false, and Westinghouse will prove that it's false. Bob Rigley, the man who wrote those words, is a gifted nuclear engineer. He is seated right here, in the first row. Bob will take the stand to tell you precisely what he was talking about when he wrote those words. He will tell you that they related to an internal disagreement among the engineers at Westinghouse about using a material called Inconel 600 in the generators—and that STP's lead engineer knew about those results. How did he know? Because Bob told him. Bob will also tell you that when he wrote those words he thought he was helping solve a serious safety issue—and that he had no idea that 14 years later they would be twisted and used against him and his company.

Sometimes you need to do more than just embrace bad facts during opening. On the odd chance your client—say, a tobacco company—has actually done something wrong, you may have to apologize. And I don't mean one of those apologies my wife makes ("I'm sorry you're a jerk"). I mean a real apology, made first during depositions, and reiterated during opening. That very human act goes a long way toward defusing juror anger, minimizing damages, and most likely, knocking out punitives altogether.

I realize this is a tightrope for defense lawyers, who wonder: How much can I say without admitting liability? I have walked that tightrope myself, but in a case where a liability finding seems certain, there is little to lose and much to gain from a sincere apology and an expression of concern about a badly injured plaintiff—in any kind of case. Jurors are notoriously forgiving in the face of real contrition. They may still hit your client, but it is unlikely they will hit him or her as hard as the plaintiff requested—and, with the anger factor defused, even less likely they will award punitives.

5. Appeal to the leaders.

Tailor at least part of your argument about the evidence to the leaders on the jury. Who are they? Once you start looking for them, they will be easy to identify. In the first place, because both sides will have struck strong panelists who might lead the rest of the jury down an undesirable path, there will be only two or three leaders left on the jury. With that small number in mind, review the questionnaires and think about each panelist's reactions during voir dire. Who seemed self-assured? Who was anxious to speak up? Who staked out a clear position during the group discussion?

There are some other, fairly reliable predictors of who they will be. Leaders on juries tend to be the most highly educated—the professionals and businesspeople who supervise others and make decisions. If they occupy a position of authority at work, they will likely assume a position of authority on the jury. At the same time, don't restrict your search. A strong person who runs the show at home can easily take charge in the jury room.

If you can get the leaders on your side at the beginning, they will generally be there for you throughout the case. Even more beneficial, one of the strong jurors is likely to become foreperson of the jury and will exert a strong influence on the verdict. Just make sure your appeal to the influential panelists is subtle and smart. Stare at one of them too long, make the appeal too obvious, and you may patronize that juror into the arms of the enemy, and by your lack of interest, offend the rest.

Assume that you are trying a medical malpractice case. It appears to you that the three strongest jurors are a quality-control expert, the owner of a retail store, and a lay minister. Argue some part of the evidence that you know will hold special appeal for those jurors. Aim for their intellect. But all the better if you stir their hearts.

The quality-control expert, who lives by scrupulous standards, needs to learn during the plaintiff's opening that the defendant kept sloppy medical records and that his motive for making them so confusing was to cover up his negligence. On the defense side, counsel should argue that the doctor's records, while difficult to read, are organized and complete. Therefore, the records can be trusted to reveal the truth.

The retailer, a small businessman who fears getting sued himself, needs to learn from the defendant that this is the plaintiff's second lawsuit for personal injury in the past five years. The plaintiff's lawyer should bring up that difficult fact first and discuss the evidence that shows that *both* suits are legitimate.

The lay minister needs to know that as a result of the defendant's negligence, the plaintiff's work *and* charitable activities are severely curtailed. The defendant must counter that the doctor spends much of his waking hours helping others, including the plaintiff.

Build on your first impressions about the leaders during the remainder of the trial. Discreetly observe them at critical moments. That information will help you tailor not just your arguments, but your witnesses' testimony as well—focusing you throughout on the jurors who are with you, and those you must try hard to persuade. (See p. 237, "Tailor testimony (but rarely)"; see also p. 276, "Tailor arguments to the leaders.")

C. Pathos

Don't mistake Cicero's advice to conclude with an appeal to passion as an invitation to melodrama. There is nothing worse than a lawyer yelling or crying while the jury wonders whether he's a lunatic or just off his medicine. There are ways—and there are ways—to move jurors. When you argue with conviction and confidence, it doesn't take much. Something of what you feel will rub off on them.

1. Take your themes to the next level.

David McAtee and I knew we were in deep trouble as we sat in his office, staring at the Dallas skyline. The head of Akin, Gump, Strauss, Hauer & Feld's litigation section, McAtee begins every case by immersing himself in *Corpus Juris Secundum*—searching for ways to merge his most persuasive factual arguments into the fundamental elements of the law. I'm not saying he's a modern-day Cicero, but, trust me, he's as close as you'll find in Dallas.

We were defending a major corporation in an impossible case. The detailed facts don't matter. Suffice to say that they were awful and that we had inherited a mess. In fact, the $50-million dollar "verdict" I had just managed to get against us following a summary jury trial represented a vast improvement over the results of our two previous focus groups. The client, oddly enough, seemed unmoved by our progress. To cap a perfect day, the judge was mad at our side, and set the aging case for trial the following Monday.

As we watched the setting sun—the symbolism was not lost on either of us—McAtee put his finger on the problem: "Themes are often conventional—not enough depth," he observed. "In every antitrust case, the defense seizes on the public's cynicism about business, arguing that 'everyone does it this way.' Railroads rely on clichés, like 'She didn't stop, look, and listen.'" I started taking notes. "But jurors see themselves as the enforcers of the best of societal values. Our case has to be rooted in a deeper moral truth than themes can convey. They don't have enough depth. We have to get beyond themes."

David had done just that in one of our focus groups. Arguing against our client and for the plaintiff, he wrote several questions on butcher paper. Each created havoc with my defense. Pointing to each question, David asked the panelists, "Could it be that [the defendant] can repeatedly break its written promises—break its word—without getting into trouble with the law?" "Can [the defendant] steal the valuable property of another—sell it for $425 million—lie and deny it took the property and then refuse to pay for what it took?" "Or, will the law require [the defendant] to give back its unjust enrichment?" "How many times may its executives lie about this and not face punishment?"

He wasn't arguing. He wasn't pushing a theme. Instead, he was raising a profound moral truth: It is unacceptable in a civilized society to steal from other human beings and profit from what you've stolen. Those questions are not original with David. It was the way he asked them. Isolated in a corner of the "courtroom," speaking quietly, but with righteous indignation, he brought the focus group jurors to the edge of their seats.

Try as I might, I couldn't defeat those rhetorical questions. I knew they would be ringing in the ears of our panelists as they began their deliberations. Lest there be any doubt, split into two "juries," the panelists returned verdicts of $400 million and $350 million, respectively, in McAtee's favor.

As we pondered our next move in the comfort of his office, McAtee came up with one more fundamental truth: "We can't try this dog." The following Monday morning, we settled with the plaintiff as the jury panel assembled single-file outside the courtroom.

There is no case, no matter how complex, that can't be equated directly or indirectly with some enduring moral principle—without getting preachy. In opening argument, those truths emerge from the facts as you understand them going in, and in summation, from the trial testimony and the conduct of the lawyers in it. (See p. 279, "Start with the biggest theme.") Take care to find them, and the union of facts and principles will carry jurors along with you.

2. Make the jury mad.

In our legal malpractice case, we had facts aplenty to make the jury mad. I concluded my opening with a five-minute discussion of the transaction my clients alleged was mishandled by their former lawyers—and finished with powerful evidence that the lawyers had betrayed their clients.

In the early '80s, Ali and Yousef were approached by a New York real estate syndicator to block up land in the Houston area to be developed for housing. When that land was sold to builders, Ali and Yousef received commissions, which they then split with the syndicator. That was the sum total of their participation. For a couple of years, it proved to be a profitable arrangement.

To raise money to pay for the land Ali and Yousef located, the syndicator sent out this document—a Private Placement Memorandum, to potential investors nationwide. A "PPM," as it is called, is a kind of advertising brochure, which describes the proposed transaction and its risks. Its purpose is to attract and inform investors.

Ali and Yousef had never been involved in a transaction that involved a PPM or raising money from investors. So they sent a draft of the PPM to their law firm. A senior partner there, an expert in real estate transactions, told them in writing that since they were not identified as promoters in the PPM, they had no liability if things went wrong—that they should go ahead with the deal. [I put the letter on the overhead, and read the paragraph giving the clients the go-ahead to do the deal.] As our securities law expert will tell you, that was terrible advice. If things went wrong, Ali and Yousef, for a variety of reasons, would be subject to the securities laws of this country. In fact, when the real estate market fell apart in the late '80s, investors in the transaction sued everyone in sight, including Ali and Yousef.

The two men turned to the same law firm to defend them in the investor lawsuit. However, it soon became clear that the syndicator had made several false statements in the PPM. He had misled the investors. He had violated federal securities laws. A year after the suit was filed—and $200,000 in legal fees—the same lawyer who told Ali and Yousef to go forward with the deal suddenly did an about-face. He told Ali and Yousef that they were as responsible for those false statements as if they'd made them themselves. It didn't matter that they didn't know those statements were false. It didn't matter that they had nothing to do with the PPM. They had violated securities laws, too. As you will learn, the firm pushed hard for the men to settle the investors' suit—which they did, and it cost Ali and Yousef $3 million.

Those were the facts that led to the malpractice claim. Once the suit was filed against the law firm, a series of shocking facts began to emerge:

If you recall, Ali and Yousef sent the PPM to a lawyer at the firm who told them he'd reviewed it, and that they should go ahead with the deal—that even if it went bad, they would have no responsibility. That same lawyer testified under oath prior to coming to court that he never even read the PPM. He said he had seen a hundred of them and that 90 percent of what is in them is boilerplate—standard provisions. That was bad enough. But even if what he said was true—that a careful, seasoned real estate lawyer never bothered to read the main document in the transaction—the other 10 percent of the language in that PPM that wasn't boilerplate was a pack of lies—the syndicator's lies. And those lies cost Ali and Yousef $3 million.

As you will learn from the evidence, if these two men had been properly advised by their lawyers, even after the PPM was sent out, even after the investors put up their money, there were several things that they could have done to avoid even being sued, much less paying $3 million. Instead, they paid a fortune for the syndicator's dishonesty, and their own lawyers' negligence. And, as I am going to show you right now, they were betrayed by their own lawyers.

Then I put a computerized printout on the overhead, and explained that it was backup information for the firm's billing for July 1986—soon after the investors sued Ali and Yousef. Using a familiar example, I explained how law firms create the invoices they send to clients:

> Each month, the lawyers at the firm send a record of all the work they did to a person who records it—"inputs" it—on a software program that creates client invoices. For example, if a lawyer in the firm drafted a deed for a house, and spent an hour doing it, that information would be recorded on a computer sheet just like this one. The client would receive an invoice for one hour's services rendered, along with a brief notation on the bill describing what the lawyer did to earn the money—in this example, "drafting of deed."
>
> Now look at the three entries I've highlighted in Ali and Yousef's account for July. Those entries never made it to their invoice. Each entry reads: "Discussion of firm's exposure." Those are the defendants' words—not mine, not Ali's, not Yousef's. The lawyers whose names are listed on this backup information are all senior partners in the firm. They met to discuss their own exposure and how to avoid getting sued themselves—rather than admit to Ali and Yousef that they'd made a terrible error and help correct their mistake. They knew their partner's advice about the PPM was wrong—clearly negligent. But instead of pitching in with their clients to solve the problem, they betrayed them. The lawyers devised a plan to strong-arm Ali and Yousef into settling, in the hope that the whole thing would just go away.
>
> And by the way, if you are wondering: The law firm charged the time they spent planning their cover-up to Ali and Yousef, burying it in a bill for something else. And Ali and Yousef, not knowing what they were paying for, paid the bill.

That wasn't all the evidence we had of the lawyers' guile. One of the partners who pushed them hard to settle testified during his deposition that his reason for being so insistent was "because they are, you know, dark, swarthy, and that won't play well with a Texas jury." Without question, the clients' country of origin and skin color—and local attitudes—are legitimate factors to consider when evaluating any client's chances in front of a jury. However, this lawyer had no intention of ever trying the case. Given the lawyer's testimony, it made our jury the personification of the very jury he claimed to fear—bigots who couldn't rise higher than the lawyer's expectations. I told the jurors about that testimony—and that they would find that the lawyer was far more concerned with saving his own skin than the color of the clients'. Angry at the lawyers from day one, the jury returned an $18-million verdict including punitive damages. As one of them was quoted as saying in the *Houston Chronicle,* "Those lawyers really hung their clients out to dry."

While plaintiffs are usually in the best position to arouse the jury's furor, defendants need not surrender the emotional advantage to the other side. Vexatious litigation against a corporation can anger jurors just as much as misconduct by a corporation. Beyond that, the defense can make use of a very practical advantage: going second. If the plaintiff makes a significant misstatement during opening, the defendant can refute it immediately. (See p. 255, "Seamless transitions from opening arguments to the first witness.") This is especially effective if the defendant can hand the jurors a document or some other hard evidence that clearly refutes her opponent's statement—like those purloined marketing agreements in the Fleisher case. Deceit makes jurors very angry.

3. Know when to quit.

The last thing you should do at the end of your opening is to ramble, searching for a way to finish. Do something dramatic, like asking the sort of questions McAtee asked, and then sit down. A decisive ending creates drama. Even in courts that strictly limit argument in opening, leave the jurors with a sense of your resolve about the case. Remember the devices of public speaking. Fill the courtroom with your voice, or speak in a whisper. But when it comes time to stop, stop.

If both sides have delivered strong openings, the case, as you would imagine, generally starts out even, but that's not really as equal as it sounds. At this stage of the proceedings, given the emotional advantage that generally goes to the plaintiff, "even" is a great place for the defendant to be.

D. Fructose

In many ways, opening argument represents the culmination of your work, not the beginning. After all the time you have spent preparing, this is the moment when you can tell your story to the people who can do something about it. So, to Cicero's compelling trilogy of ethos, logos, and pathos, I add a fourth: fructose. Enjoy the fruits of your labors. You've been waiting for this moment for a long time. Wade right in. Center stage is yours, alone.

Killer Cross 6

I. THE IMPORTANCE OF CROSS-EXAMINATION

There are many rules of fly-fishing, but the essence of all of them is this: Listen to your instincts. They become more reliable each time you cast. Lay your line gently across the water, with the fly on the end of your tippet floating to rest near the trout. When you sense that he has struck, set the hook and let him run; wear him out and bring him to shore. If you miss that moment, the fish, most likely, will be gone forever.

So it is with cross-examination.[1] There are many rules of cross, but the essence of all of them is to listen to your instincts, setting your hook at just the right moment. That "right moment" may announce itself with no more than the slightest word or nod from the witness, like the delicate nibble of a rainbow trout at the end of your line. When it happens, set the hook, wear him out, and reel him in. The witness, and often the verdict, will be yours.

Cross-examination is an elusive art, predicated as it is (in part) on discovering the truth from human beings. It is the hardest thing we do. Yet the rules of cross-examination minimize its uncertainties. They dictate the questions that you should ask, predict the answers you will get, and how to respond if you don't. Follow the rules, and you will win more cases out of your opponents' mouths than you ever dreamed possible. Ignore them and you become a hostage of witnesses and their capacity for surprise.

II. THE GOALS OF CROSS-EXAMINATION

The first goal of cross is to control the witness, so that the witness never controls you. To accomplish this, you must be able to impeach witnesses consistently and force them to make damning admissions.

Contrary to what you might expect, witnesses who resist making such admissions are actually helping you. Nothing makes jurors madder than a witness who has to be pressured into telling the truth, and making jurors mad is the ultimate, but unsung, goal of cross. Once they get angry, jurors will not only lose faith in the witness, but in his entire side of the case.

---

1. Author's note: The more you know about effective cross-examination, the better you will be at presenting witnesses on direct and preparing them to testify (on direct and cross). For that reason, I have reversed the usual order of teaching these skills. (See chapter 7, p. 217, "Preparing and Presenting Witnesses.")

By skillfully cross-examining witness after witness, you keep things exciting for the jurors and earn their respect. They will come to regard you as "Mr. Fix-It," withholding judgment about a witness's veracity until you get a chance to set the record straight on cross.

III. THE FUNDAMENTALS OF CROSS-EXAMINATION

Without exception, the legendary trial lawyers have been skilled cross-examiners. Yet no one is born The Complete Angler or The Master Cross-Examiner. Instincts must be honed—and then trusted. But to hone those instincts you must first learn the fundamental rules, and there is no better place to start than in your local courthouse. There are courtroom stars in every jurisdiction in this country—perhaps one or two in your firm. Invest some time to watch them cross. If you can't afford the time (a false economy if there ever were one), wait for a good trial on "Court TV," tape it, and watch it at night.

Grab any chance that you get to question a witness under oath. Take as many depositions as you can. Don't be hesitant about getting into the courtroom. Work your way into any evidentiary hearings your firm conducts. Get appointed to some indigent cases. Trust me: You'll do at least as well as the lawyers who regularly represent indigents, and you'll gain invaluable experience in front of a jury.

Read classic works like *The Art of Cross-Examination*, Herbert Wellman's account of exciting cross in early twentieth-century cases. Study famous transcripts, such as the prosecutor's grilling of Oscar Wilde during his trial for sodomy. Do all this, and the path from journeyman to skilled cross-examiner will be shorter and smoother.

The rules of cross-examination are universal, applying to every kind of case and witness. None, however, is written in stone. Once you are comfortable with them, once they become instinctive, infuse your cross with your *self*. If you are funny, be funny. If you are smart, be smart. (If you are neither, consider the judiciary.)

A. The Gateway to Successful Cross

The most common mistake trial lawyers make on cross is failing to listen to the witness's answers. That is why the rules in this section are so critical. They teach you to respond to what the witness actually says, not what you expected or wanted her to say. If you learn no other rules, learn these. They are the gateway to every successful cross-examination.

1. Keep a calm mind.

Psychologists did a study of some of baseball's greatest hitters. DiMaggio, Mays, Mantle—all of them kept a "calm mind," reading the seams on the ball, waiting to swing until it was on top of them. A more contemporary example is the golfer Tiger Woods, who maintains a Zen-like calm as he buries the competition. So, too, should trial lawyers keep a calm mind, reading the seams on the testimony, never panicking regardless of what a witness says. Of course, that is easier said than done. Every trial lawyer you have ever known, including this one, has at some time lost his concentration, his mind sent reeling, by a witness's unexpected answer. Keep a calm mind and that is unlikely to happen. You will be able to think clearly, ask questions that matter, and show emotion only when you decide the time is right.

2. Listen to every answer.

One afternoon in the early 1980s, I sat down after cross-examining a government witness in a RICO case. Although I had done all right, I was dissatisfied. Richard "Racehorse" Haynes, who represented one of the co-defendants, cross-examined the same witness right after me. His questions and the witness's answers quickly assumed a rhythm most often associated with great music. He slaughtered the man.

That night, I asked Haynes what I had done wrong. Generous as usual, he said that I had done fine. But I was insistent. Finally, he drew on his pipe and said, "You weren't listening to the answers." (Of course, what I heard was, "What a loser. Get into pipefitting while there's still time.") He told me that the witness had admitted under *my* questioning that he, himself, disregarded certain Coast Guard rules—the case involved shipbuilders—yet he criticized our clients' failure to follow some of the same regulations.

I could have followed up, but I had no idea he had made that admission. As I thought about it that sleepless night, I realized that the deeper I got into cross, the less I listened, sometimes afraid of the answer, sometimes intent on asking a preplanned question. The next time I cross-examined, I actually focused on what the witness said, not on what I wanted to ask next. It was liberating. Each answer was a springboard to another question. I will never forget how powerful that felt.

3. Know your case cold.

In cross-examination, the old maxim is proven absolutely true: Knowledge is power. There is no greater confidence-builder than knowing more than the witness. That knowledge allows you to respond effectively to any answer he gives.

This advice applies to the basic facts of your case as well as to the most arcane corners of an expert's report. It takes commitment whether your case involves the simplest tort or a complex commercial case. But you will be amazed at how much solid-state physics you can learn with a tutor and a textbook. No matter how skilled an adverse witness, you can always learn enough to even the score.

4. Formulate follow-up.

I cannot urge you strongly enough to think through the cross-examination of every important witness you are about to face. It forces you to focus on what you need to prove with the witness, what you can prove, and how to use any documents or exhibits that can help to make your cross successful. If nothing else, you will reduce the anxiety that so often undermines lawyers during cross-examination.

Start by sitting at your computer and typing up the questions that you are most likely to ask. Then, with each one, type out how you will follow up if the response is "yes," "no," "I don't know," or any other logical answer. Do this a few times and you will seldom be surprised by what the witness says—or at a loss for what to ask next. Do it enough times and you will be able to anticipate even absurd and self-serving responses. As you will see, there is only a limited universe of unresponsive answers—although you need to be ready for all of them. (See p. 168, "Controlling Unresponsive Witnesses.")

Ironically, it is indisputable, or even undisputed, facts that witnesses often contest. Why would they deny something that is in black and white? Because those are the facts that kill them. Key witnesses have run from them in almost every case I've handled, at trial and during depositions. Pinpoint these bad facts beforehand and you will likely anticipate a major part of your cross.

In Westinghouse,[2] the plaintiff, the South Texas Project (STP), played word games with the nuclear steam generators' 40-year "design life," an engineering *goal* that it attempted to stretch into a 40-year *guarantee* of useful life. You didn't need an expert to tell you that had to be wrong. "Design

---

2. See p. 50, "Uncover compelling themes."

life" didn't even sound like a guarantee of how long the generators would be useful, any more than the 20-year design life of a Chevrolet means that each individual car will last 20 years. In fact, I would like to find a guarantee or warranty for anything that extends longer than ten years. I don't care what it is, I'll buy it.

In any event, if there was one indisputable fact in the Westinghouse case, it was that there was no 40-year guarantee written into the contract. Yet, when the power plant's former vice president took the stand, he insisted that there was such a guarantee. "I negotiated the contract," he testified. "The guarantee is in there. That is clearly what we intended." For at least two hours, I chased him around every relevant provision in the contract, demanding that he show me the guarantee. Finally, he blurted out, "Well, you just have to find it in a roundabout way."

Jim Quinn, my co-counsel, immediately stood up behind me, and politely asked the court reporter if she could "mark that spot in the transcript and get us a copy of that answer as soon as possible." I stood silently at the lectern, solemnly writing, "I can't believe he said that" on a legal pad. Then lest any juror missed the point, I asked the witness, "Do you mean to tell this jury you want them to return $800 million in damages against Westinghouse, and another $1.6 billion in punitives, for a promise that you can only find in a 'roundabout' way?"

When a witness denies the undeniable, whatever damage his case would have suffered from a straightforward admission is exacerbated by his evasions. In the instance of the Westinghouse case, "roundabout" became our refrain in questioning every key witness—and a brand-new theme for our case.

5. Never laminate your cross.

Some areas of your cross will be dictated by the witness's deposition testimony and documents—matters that you will ask him about whether he brought them up on direct or not. However, those preplanned questions are not to be confused with real cross-examination—which emanates from what the witness actually says on the stand. Always, the witness's testimony will be different in some degree from what you anticipated. A fact that she emphasized during depositions may be subtly shaded, or a claim or defense may disappear—any number of things will be said that materially affect your questioning. Despite that fact, many trial lawyers read one scripted question after another, regardless of the witness's answers. Instead of mixing it up, the witness and lawyer carry on two separate conversations that never quite make contact. Examinations like that have an absurd quality, like one of those Harold Pinter plays where the characters are always answering a question that was asked two questions ago. It may be great theater, but it's not great cross-examination.

If you want to be effective, never laminate your cross. Once the witness takes the stand, set those typed-up questions to one side. Mold your cross-examination from what the witness says on the stand, both on direct and in answer to your questions. If you are prepared, your best questions will be inside of you. The witness's answers—not those typed-up questions—bring them out.

Instead of a script, create a flow sheet, just like the one high school debaters use. Draw a line down the middle of the page of your legal pad. Take precise notes of the witness's most important testimony on the left-hand side, and make bullet-point reminders of questions to ask and documents to use on the right. The flow sheet will keep you on point and organized and will force you to respond head-on to the testimony the jury just heard. As you near the end of your cross, quickly scan those typed-up questions. Use them only as a reminder of any area of questioning you may have skipped.

If the case justifies the cost, real-time transcription is also helpful in organizing cross, and particularly helpful for impeaching. Just take your laptop up to the witness and show him the contradictory statement he made "just twenty minutes ago, sir—during your direct," or project the testimony onto a monitor. Still, keep a flowchart. Your notes will be more accurate than a court reporter's first draft.

6. Review evidence through trial eyes.

Reread the evidence in your case prior to trial or, if possible, on a break or overnight after you've heard the witness's direct testimony in court. You will be amazed at what you missed and what suddenly becomes significant. Trial pressure focuses you as never before.

A witness who denied knowing a particular company policy may have been copied on a document laying it out. Or, you may decide that you should be friendly toward an adverse witness whom you questioned harshly during his deposition. (See p. 183, "Befriend adverse witnesses (if you can).")

7. If you don't need to cross, don't cross.

The hardest thing for a trial lawyer to do is nothing at all. Yet, when a witness hasn't hurt you, and you have no reason to believe that he will help you, you'll only make matters worse if you cross-examine him. I still remember my associate telling me not to cross one of the witnesses in the Sakowitz case. He hadn't said a critical word about our client, despite a nasty disagreement they'd had. Undaunted, I waded in and managed to develop their feud with no effort at all. Since we won, it was no big deal, but I shouldn't have asked a single question. Ten years later, I'm down to thinking about it only once or twice a week.

B. Don't Forget the Jury

The following rules suggest ways to get and keep the jurors' attention, and ultimately, to enlist them psychologically on your side of the battle. They help even emotionally remote lawyers connect with the jury. All they require is courtesy and common sense.

1. Never bury your lead.

As the witness testifies, begin organizing your cross by subject matter. If you end up with ten areas you want to cover, put your most powerful impeachment first, the questions you are certain will draw blood. Never bury your lead: Nothing inflames jurors faster than a witness who has trouble telling the truth. The sooner you expose his dishonesty, the sooner the jury will turn against him.

If you decisively impeach the witness at the start, it won't be necessary to go over all ten areas of cross. Begin and end with your most forceful cross, eliminate the rest, and sit down. If, instead, you delay your most effective impeachment and conduct a needlessly long cross, the impact of your questioning will be lost.

2. Don't get ahead of jurors emotionally.

Starting out with your best impeachment doesn't mean hyperventilating. Cicero's warning against the impassioned onset during argument applies equally to cross-examination. It is off-putting, even silly, to jurors when the lawyer's emotions are out in front of theirs. Don't get emotional or aggressive before the jurors understand the reason for such a display, and even then, never become melodramatic.

In his book *Anatomy of a Verdict*, D. Graham Burnett, a Princeton historian, describes his experience as a jury foreman on a murder case in New

York City. He recounts the prosecutor's histrionics while questioning the defendant about the killing, arms flailing and voice rising. In contrast, the defendant remained composed, calmly answering each question. Burnett admits to a fleeting thought as he watched the performance that the prosecutor ought to lose. In fact, that's what happened. The jury acquitted the defendant. While it's clear that the jurors did a conscientious job sorting out the evidence, their distaste for the prosecutor's theatrics probably cost him the case. At least from my reading, the jurors explained away some fairly strong evidence against the defendant that they otherwise would not have.

3.   Stay under the witness emotionally.

This rule is of a single piece with the previous one. Staying under a witness emotionally sends all the right messages to jurors, including that you are in control of the cross—and of yourself. Some of the most effective cross-examination I have seen has come when the examiner remained calm and polite as the witness came undone. Cross-examination where the lawyer gets overly aggressive is effective only for the other side.

In 1994, I tried a medical malpractice case in which the doctor failed to diagnose my client's meningeal brain tumor. For two years, he repeatedly dismissed her debilitating symptoms as premenopausal. He never even ordered a CAT scan. By the time the tumor was diagnosed (by another doctor) and removed, it had grown to 9 centimeters, the size of an orange.

The defendant doctor practiced on the margins of medicine, advertising in *TV Guide,* and officing far away from any respected medical center. Luckily, my client had obtained a copy of her medical records before she left the doctor's care. He obviously didn't know that, because when he produced the records during discovery, they had been altered. Additionally, I got his expert to agree at trial that he had failed his patient "completely and utterly."

Nevertheless, the case didn't come out as I expected. One of the reasons was my client's strong recovery. In response to questions from my talented opponent, she actually did interest-rate calculations in her head—a feat not entirely consistent with our claim of brain damage. Equally important, I was too aggressive at the beginning of my cross of the doctor, a sad-looking fellow in his late 60s. As I got ready to question him, the doctor said, "Have at me, Mr. Berg." I failed to recognize in time that, with that one sentence, he'd warmed up the jury—and made me the heavy. After a while, I toned things down, but it was too late. They felt sorry for him. While the jury did find him negligent, their award of $500,000 was a bit less than the millions I'd asked for.

4. Let jurors know where you're headed next.

As you change subjects, tell jurors what you are going to cover next so that they can follow you. All you have to do is inform the witness, and thus the jury, of where you are headed. It can be as simple as this: "You said in your report that you found evidence that the tire had been punctured by a nail. Let me ask you a few questions about that."

5. Include jurors in your anger and indignation.

For this suggestion to work, your timing must be impeccable. If the witness has given a truly incredible answer, or is unmistakably on the run, look directly at the jury and ask the witness, skeptically, "Do you really mean to *tell us* . . . ?" Or, "Are you really telling these twelve people . . . ?" Metaphorically, the thirteen of you are teaming up to get at the truth—a powerful way to create a bond with jurors.

Of course, if you overdo it, a clever witness can make you look foolish. One of my closest friends since childhood, a radiologist and a very funny guy, did just that to a plaintiff's lawyer in a medical malpractice case, testifying as the defense expert. The plaintiff's lawyer, known in equal measure for his skill and arrogance, began his cross-examination with his hands on the jury rail, his back to my friend. "Dr. Gerson," he asked contemptuously, "you got ten thousand dollars for your testimony, didn't you?" The good doctor said nothing. "Doctor," the lawyer demanded, "did you get ten thousand dollars for your testimony or not?" Still no answer. He repeated the question even louder. "Excuse me," my friend finally replied, sounding like Robert De Niro in *Taxi Driver*, "Were you talking to *me?* You must be talking to me—but I'm over here." The jury thought that was pretty funny. The lawyer, who didn't have the sense to laugh, turned toward him and fairly shouted the question again. With the lawyer firmly under *his* control, Dr. Gerson acknowledged that he had received ten thousand dollars, adding that he had endorsed the check over to a camp he founded for kids with cancer. The lawyer nonsuited after lunch, and, in those days of easy venue, refiled in a different county. I love that story. It reminds me that trial talent isn't limited to trial lawyers.

6. Cross *about* documents, not *out* of them.

When I first started trying commercial cases, I had no particular idea about how to use the boxcars of documents that usually accompanied them. I just knew I hated crossing with them. They either slowed me down or interrupted my questioning entirely. In one case, in an effort to manage the problem, I supplied the jury with a notebook of ten "hot docs." We got through the first document just fine. It was when I referred to the second one that a confused murmur arose in the courtroom. A few of the jurors seemed content, but the rest were furiously turning the pages to catch up. It turned out that our paralegal had put the documents in a slightly different order in each notebook. To show she wasn't just playing around, some of them were also upside down.

I learned something valuable that day, including a little lesson about swearing under your breath and acoustics in a cavernous courtroom. I retrieved the notebooks, put them to one side, and started over. This time, I questioned the witness about the substance of a document, not the document itself. Instead of tying my questions to the documents ("Didn't you write on August 19th that you were opposed to the merger?"), I stuck to the subject matter in it. If the witness's answer was truthful, I moved on. If he said he didn't remember, I would pull out the document to refresh his memory. If he contradicted what he said in a document, I would use it to impeach him.

Equally important, I limited my questions to the contents of the very few documents that mattered—out of the ocean of documents that had been produced. Incidentally, in almost every case, there are rarely more than a few important documents, no matter the thousands of pages of evidence you've gathered.

The product of that difficult day is my personal guideline for cross-examination and documents: Cross *about* the document, and then *out* of it—but only if it becomes necessary for impeachment or some other purpose. That eliminates the potential for momentum-killing delays while the jurors flip through their "hot-doc" notebooks, or you fish around in a banker's box for a document that has disappeared.

7. Keep cross brief; or at least, keep it interesting.

You can bury powerful points under the weight of unnecessary cross. When you get everything that you need from a witness, quit. I don't care if it took just 15 minutes: Don't ask another question.

On the other hand, if you legitimately need more time to do a thorough cross, take it. Just don't drone on for no reason. And don't undermine the drama you've created by asking for "a moment to check with co-counsel" or "two minutes to check my notes" before wrapping up. Quickly scan those questions you typed up before trial. As soon as you are confident that you have finished, announce that you've got no further questions, and walk away from the lectern. The witness's admissions will linger like applause as you sit down.

The longest cross-examination I ever conducted took two and a half days. The witness was that STP power plant vice president with whom I played ring-around-the-contract until he finally admitted the alleged 40-year guarantee could be found in the contract only in a "roundabout" way. The jury was attentive the entire time—no small accomplishment considering that the subject matter was contract negotiations, with microscopic corrosion in a nuclear steam generator thrown in for good measure. What kept them interested was the witness's insistence on playing dodgeball with my questions. He could not give me a straight answer. It took a half-day of questioning before he admitted that there was no 40-year guarantee in the contract. He made other damaging admissions, but never without a fight. Had he been straightforward, the cross would have been over in a day, and its impact diminished. As it was, I never lost the jury's attention—thanks to the witness.

But there was at least one cross when, singularly pleased with the sound of my own voice, I stayed too long at the fair. During my questioning of a railroad grade-crossing expert in the MoPac case, my associate slipped me a note that delicately called my attention to the problem. It read: "Dear David: You have now proven you know more about grade crossings than anyone else in the world. No one cares. Please stop. Love, Tamera."

IV. BECOMING A MASTER

If Professor Wigmore is correct that cross-examination is the greatest engine ever devised for the discovery of truth, then the following rules are the ones that power that engine. They teach you how to control difficult witnesses, get the answers that you want, or prove that you are never going to get them, no matter how many times you try. Although I am not certain it was of concern to the good professor, these rules also teach you how to make boring cross interesting. Enormously effective, they are a key to becoming a master.

A. Controlling Unresponsive Witnesses

Unresponsive witnesses are dangerous. If you can't stop them, they take over your cross, arguing their case instead of answering your questions.

When you don't know how to control them, it's like getting caught in a hailstorm—you get pelted with answers from all directions. Yet, with experience, you realize that there is actually a limited universe of unresponsive answers. A witness who makes speeches is a witness who makes speeches. A witness who quibbles is a witness who quibbles. In time, you instinctively fire back with a particular kind of question to defeat a particular kind of unresponsive answer.

Once you learn to control these witnesses, you will welcome their unresponsiveness rather than run from it. As you will see, it is a great opportunity (perhaps your best opportunity) to turn the jury against the other side.

1. Insist on the answer to your question.

Ironically, as formidable as they may seem, the simple act of demanding and getting direct answers to your questions forces most combative witnesses into compliance. That transition is not lost on the jurors—and the benefit is incalculable. If you refuse to put up with the witness's game playing, demonstrating that he won't answer your questions, or that he won't answer them without a fight, you undermine the jury's faith in the witness *and* his side of the case. *Nothing* makes jurors madder than a witness who won't answer your questions, but answers his own lawyer's without hesitation. (See p. 243, "The most dangerous point in every trial.") Moreover, once your ability to control these witnesses becomes well-known, it will instill justifiable fear in your opponents. "Hell," Joe Jamail once comforted an adverse witness, who was literally shaking, "It's just a deposition. You ain't goin' to jail."

2. Never ignore an unresponsive answer.

Trial lawyers frequently ignore an unresponsive answer, blithely going on to their next question, as if it never happened. That is a terrible mistake. It creates the impression that the witness answered the question fully—that there's no more to the story. It also creates the impression that the witness answered the question that mattered, as opposed to the irrelevant one the lawyer asked. Predictably, once a witness realizes that he can run all over an examiner, he'll never stop. That means you must never ignore an unresponsive answer—not until you demonstrate that the witness will not give you a direct answer no matter what you do.

3. Five categories of unresponsive answers.

The chart that follows categorizes five types of unresponsive answers. In my experience, they are the ones that you will get most often:

Figure 6.1
Types of Unresponsive Answers

Unresponsive Answers

a. Evasions

b. Speeches

c. Recasting Questions

d. Quibbling

e. Offers to Explain

Note that the chart doesn't address whether the unresponsive answer is true or false. In fact, an unresponsive answer can be either, and at the proper time, you must respond to whatever the witness said. But the only thing that matters initially is that the witness did not answer your question. For that, the witness must pay.

4. Defeating the five categories of unresponsive answers.

The discussion that follows suggests effective methods (but not the only methods) for responding to answers in each category.

a. Evasions.

Most unresponsive answers are evasions—the witness's attempt to avoid admitting a simple but damaging fact. In this instance, however, I am referring to a specific kind of evasive answer—when the witness avoids your question to argue his case. You ask Mr. Jones if he *negotiated* the contract, and he answers, "Your client *tricked* me into signing it." Mr. Jones actually may be telling the truth, but since he didn't answer the question that you asked, he set himself up to be impeached. All you have to do is insist on the answer to the question that you asked before addressing the answer that he gave:

> Now, Mr. Jones, with due respect, all I asked you was, "Weren't you the one who negotiated the contract?" I didn't ask if you were tricked into signing it. And I promise, we will get to that. But for now, please answer "yes" or "no." Did you negotiate the contract?

If Mr. Jones persists in refusing to admit that he negotiated the contract, when it is perfectly clear that he did negotiate it, or even if he finally acknowledges it, his unresponsiveness itself becomes an *admission*—jurors will conclude that he has something to hide. Having waited to tackle his claim head-on, you will have nicked his credibility and bolstered your own, the perfect time to attack the substance of his unresponsive answer:

> Now, a moment ago, you claimed that my client tricked you into signing this contract. Let's explore that. You will at least admit, will you not, that you and your lawyer sat across the table from my client and negotiated each and every term of the contract for the sale of your business? That's true, isn't it?

Obviously, the problem is one of Mr. Jones's own making. If he had admitted immediately that he negotiated the contract, he would have avoided being impeached, and his candor would have created the latitude for him to explain how he was tricked into signing. But Mr. Jones, like many witnesses, recoiled at admitting even the slightest truth that might damage his case.

b. Speeches.

Witnesses who give speeches are generally evasive, too, but the greater problem is that they take over the case. You must stop them or lose control. The first rule, as always, is to get the answer to your question, or demonstrate that you're never going to get it. The second is that the only thing that stops some of these witnesses short of an admonishment from the court is brutal impeachment.

In the early 1990s I brought suit against Phil Donahue and his production company, alleging invasion of privacy for revealing a sordid family secret and harming a young boy badly by doing so. On one of Donahue's shows, it was disclosed that our teenage client's "sister," unknown to him, was actually his biological mother—and that she had been raped by the man he knew as his stepfather. The disclosure traumatized the boy, and subjected him to so much taunting from classmates that he had to transfer high schools. I decided against videotaping Donahue's deposition, on the assumption that no one would do better on camera. I was wrong. He was one of the worst witnesses I've ever examined. He insisted on making speeches in answer to the simplest questions, especially my attempt to get him to acknowledge something he'd already said publicly, that his competition was forcing him to put on increasingly provocative shows:

> A: I am on record as saying that this effort to draw a crowd in the day-time schedule, competing as I do with seminaked people rolling around on a bed, on soap operas, creates a certain pressure to entertain more than to inform. Having said that, it does not follow that I have buckled to that pressure. You will not call me self-serving to remind you and say for the record that during the time that we have felt this pressure, we have featured the loved ones of those who were killed in the Pan Am disaster, we have featured Nelson Mandela, we have featured Winnie Mandela, and the president of Nicaragua. We have featured Ariel Sharon and this only names a small portion of the programs we feature. We feature programs on violence in the home. We feature this program about which provokes this proceeding. All of these programs which can hardly be called entertaining, and I assure you that when we do these kinds of programs our interest is a noble one and that is to shed light on what are some very, very agonistic and tragic issues.

My son, Geoff, honestly thought he'd been drinking, and wanted me to ask if that were true, but I was certain it wasn't liquor talking. It was just Donahue's nature to enlighten the unlettered masses, meaning, in this instance, my son and me. At the end of a couple of his answers, I asked the classic, "Do you even remember my question?" Often, forcing the witness to acknowledge that he doesn't remember what you asked embarrasses him into ending the speeches. In the courtroom, you can even sit down at counsel table while the witness blathers on, conspicuously watching the clock on the courtroom wall. When he finally finishes, you can say something like, "That answer took four minutes. All I asked was if you were in the office when the contract was signed? Do you think you could answer yes or no?" Once you have demonstrated that a witness is not going to quit giving long-winded answers, you will have created a platform to impeach him about the subject matter of his speech, which, for Donahue, came very soon. Holding a book he'd written, I asked:

Q: Aren't you really telling me that in your business, tragedy is good business?

A: I disagree with your barroom generality and rather crass description of our business. I would not go so far as to say that tragedy is good business. And I didn't say that in my book. I said the greater the tragedy, the more compelling is the story, not only to those who cover it, but to those who watch it as well.

Q: If I understand your response, you object to my "barroom" and "crass" characterization that—

A: I really do, sir. "Good business."

Q: May I read something to you from your book? At page 121: "In the news business, tragedy is good business. The bloodier, the better." You did write those words, did you not?

Our point was made, and Donahue, finally, was humiliated into answering my questions. As a disappointing footnote, the district court dismissed the case on First Amendment grounds, and following an appeal, the U.S. Supreme Court denied our petition for certiorari. Donahue was lucky not to face a jury.

c. Recasting questions.

Some lawyers and forensic experts teach witnesses innocent-sounding ways to throw trial lawyers off track. One of the subtlest methods is to recast your question to one of their own liking: "With all due respect, Mr. Berg, I don't think you meant to ask the question exactly that way. I think you would want to know the *value* of the inventory, not its cost." Don't take the bait. If you change your question, you've acquiesced in the witness's ever-so-polite suggestion that you don't know what you're talking about. Instead, insist on your answer—and let the jury know what the witness is doing:

Let me be clear. I want to know the cost of the inventory first. Then I will get to the value. Everyone in this courtroom understands those are two completely different issues. So let me ask the question again, and if you will, please answer it this time. What is the cost of the inventory?

d.   Quibbling.

Frequently, witnesses quibble over the meaning of words, not to clarify what you have asked, but to avoid answering. The examiner's built-in advantage is that quibbling, by itself, can make a witness look evasive. The testimony of a former president comes to mind: "It all depends on what the meaning of the word 'is,' is. . . . If 'is' means is and never has been, that is not—that is not the only one thing. It means there is none. That was a completely true statement." Moreover, by taking on the quibbling directly, demonstrating on the spot that the witness is playing word games, you impeach the unresponsiveness *and* the answer the witness wants to give.

My favorite example of quibbling came during a patent infringement case. The number-two man in the company was trying to shield his boss, the CEO, from responsibility for the contents of a letter that the CEO himself had signed. It instructed the company's patent counsel to withhold critical information ("prior art") from the U.S. Patent Office, which, we argued, would have defeated the company's patent application had it been disclosed. The witness testified that he, not the CEO, drafted the letter, that he was not authorized to write what he had, and that he had stuck it under the busy CEO's nose for signature with a dozen other documents. I took a different view—that the CEO was a micromanager who kept his vice president on a short leash—even physically.

Q: Isn't your office next door to the CEO's?
A: What do you mean by "office?"
Q: You know, a place with a desk, a chair, and a phone that goes "ring, ring." Does that clear it up?

By the time the witness admitted the inevitable ("Yes, my office is next to his"), the quibbling became an admission that the two of them worked closely together. Why else would he try to avoid admitting the location of their offices? The witness's attempt to (literally) distance himself from the CEO left no doubt in anyone's mind (if anyone doubted it to begin with) that the CEO knew what was in the letter to patent counsel.

e.   (Never ignore) offers to explain.

It is not uncommon for a witness to respond, "May I explain?" rather than answer your question. That's no different from any other unresponsive answer, and you should proceed accordingly. However, once you get a direct answer, or the witness stupidly refuses to provide you one, you *must* allow him to give whatever explanation he has in mind.[3] Don't snap, "Explain it when your lawyer's up here," or simply ignore the witness's offer and go on to your next question. If you do, at a minimum, you will appear rude, or even worse, that you are afraid of what the witness is going to say. Not only does the witness score psychologically, but opposing counsel gets to belittle you on redirect: "Mr. Jones, for reasons best known to Mr. Berg, he cut you off when you tried to explain your answer. . . . Please tell the ladies and gentlemen of the jury what you were trying to say."

In fact, you may have reason to fear what the witness is going to say— especially if he answers your question honestly first, and only then offers to explain: "Yes, I did negotiate the contract, Mr. Berg, but may I please explain?" There's no opportunity to demand the answer to your question, because he just gave you one. Nor is there any percentage in cutting him off, because he's going to give the explanation during redirect, anyway, providing the jurors with the information that you wanted to hide from them. To maintain credibility, you *must* allow the witness to explain. Then, rebut whatever he says with the cross that you had planned all along.

On the other hand, *never* ignoring a witness's offer to explain doesn't mean *always* allowing him to explain. If the witness persists in offering explanations that just keep covering the same ground, you can safely cut him off. When your gut tells you that the jury has had enough, reject his offer. "Mr. Jones, with all due respect, I know you want to tell this jury yet again that you were tricked into signing the contract. But you've said the same thing three times by my count. So, I suggest you save it for when your lawyer gets up here. I'm moving on to something else." By then, the jury will think he's got it coming, and will silently cheer you for putting an end to their suffering.

---

3. Readers familiar with Irving Younger's Ten Commandments of Cross-Examination will recognize that this advice is contrary to his rule 7, "Do not permit the witness to explain." From what I have read, Professor Younger intended his advice for beginning trial lawyers. With the exception of Commandment 5, "Listen to the answer," which is essential, his rules are simply too rigid to create a powerful cross. So that you might compare my advice to those rules, his Ten Commandments are: (1) Be brief; (2) Short questions, plain words; (3) Ask only leading questions; (4) Never ask a question to which you do not already know the answer; (5) Listen to the answer; (6) Do not quarrel with the witness; (7) Do not permit the witness to explain; (8) Do not ask the witness to repeat the testimony he gave on direct; (9) Avoid one question too many; (10) Save the explanation for summation.

5. Enlist the judge.

When it is clear that a witness isn't going to give you a direct answer no matter how you ask the question, consider objecting. Most likely, the judge's first response will be a calm instruction to the witness to "just answer the question the lawyer asks." If the witness persists, and the judge gets mad, it will be like having another member on your trial team: this one, the most influential person in the courtroom. (See p. 260, "When the judge gets mad.")

B. Breathe Life into Responsive Cross

Unresponsive witnesses are dangerous; responsive witnesses are usually boring, which is almost as bad. This section offers advice—some of it counter to conventional wisdom—on how to liven up responsive cross.

1. The paradox of responsive answers.

Irving Younger's Third Commandment is to "ask only leading questions." His Fourth Commandment is to "never ask a question to which you do not already know the answer." That advice has influenced a generation of trial lawyers. Its virtue is that it disciplines lawyers to be careful about how they ask their questions. You don't ask Mr. Jones *why* he signed the contract, because that invites him to answer responsively that he was tricked into signing it. Instead, you load up your questions with undeniable facts that tell your story and prevent the witness from telling his: "Mr. Jones, you negotiated this contract, didn't you?" Jones is forced to admit the truth or face certain impeachment. The vice is, if all you ever do is what Younger teaches, you will never learn to cross-examine. While the technique is safe, it sacrifices confrontation for control. As a result, there is no drama, no moral blame, and often, no point.

I started thinking about this issue years ago while representing one of two men accused of bank fraud. A young colleague, representing the co-defendant, cross-examined a bank examiner who had testified on direct about irregularities in the loan documents. He placed a stack of loan files in front of the witness, and asked her questions that could only be answered by verifying information contained in them: "On June 6, 1986, you received a loan application, didn't you?" "On June 8, the loan went to committee?" Pinned down, the witness could never stray, her answers confined to, "yes," "no," or "the document doesn't say." It was a classic cross that compelled expected answers and admissions, and in the end, was a nonevent. He had missed the opportunity to rip the government's case.

The irony is that my colleague did exactly what young lawyers are taught to do. He followed Irving Younger to the letter. He elicited answers that were entirely predictable. The witness also followed conventional wisdom. She was completely responsive, answering questions directly and succinctly. The problem is that when these two approaches converge, nothing happens. The witness does no harm, but the lawyer does no good. In such a situation, the tie goes to the witness, because jurors tend to believe people who answer directly even if they are lying.

2. Defeating the paradox.

I've struggled to pinpoint why the classic cross is so often ineffective. The closest I can come is this: To win the heavyweight championship, you can't just dance around the ring the entire fight; at some point you have to mix it up. The same is true at trial. To win, you have to engage witnesses on cross. To the extent possible, you must try to make the most predictable answers and admissions as meaningful as the ones you fight for. To do this, you must open up your cross in ways you were taught to avoid.

a.   Ask open-ended questions (like "why?").

During voir dire, you ask open-ended questions to elicit good *or* bad answers, because either response helps you. During cross, you ask open-ended questions only when the answer will help you *and* damage your opponent—badly. You just have to pick your spot.

It is not possible to describe every situation that presents the right opportunity for such questioning, but the most common is absolutely bulletproof. It occurs when a witness admits that *something important was done that should not have been done,* or the opposite, *that something important wasn't done that should have been done.* It's a lot less complicated than it sounds. Let me illustrate with a medical malpractice case I handled in 1994.

In the case, an 11-year-old girl had complained of abdominal pain, including in the lower right quadrant—a dead giveaway of appendicitis. The child's mother called her pediatrician several times over a five-day period to describe her daughter's escalating symptoms. On two occasions, the mother specifically asked if her daughter might have appendicitis. Both times, the answer came back from the doctor, through his nurse: "No."

The doctor also saw the girl in his office twice during the same week, the second time on Christmas Eve morning, just before he closed his office for the holiday. At that time, her eyes were sunken and dark, indicating severe dehydration. She had been vomiting and complained of nausea and dizziness. The pain in her abdomen persisted. Nevertheless, the doctor failed to order a Complete Blood Count ("CBC"), a quick pin-prick test that would have pointed to appendicitis immediately—a classic example of *something important that should have been done but wasn't.* Instead, he hurried her and her mother out of the office with the same diagnosis of gastroenteritis that he'd made all week. The doctor then took off for a family skiing vacation. The girl died the next day as her parents drove her to the hospital. The cause of death was sepsis, a wholesale poisoning of the body, caused by a ruptured appendix.

Venue was in Galveston, home of the University of Texas Medical School. The area is heavily dependent on the medical community and juries are very protective of doctors. Perhaps that is why the doctor's partner was designated as his expert. The defense lawyer probably thought that he couldn't lose in that jurisdiction, despite his expert's obvious bias.

After doing some research about appendicitis in the medical school's library, I took the partner's deposition. As it turned out, he hadn't been provided the child's entire file to review. He was surprised when I handed him copies of the mother's call slips containing a shorthand rendition of her reports about her daughter's symptoms and her concerns about appendicitis. The witness quickly conceded that if he had been confronted with all that information, he would have ordered a CBC:

Q: In fact, Doctor, it's just a little pin prick test, isn't it? Can't you do that right in your office, and get the results in a few minutes' time?
A: Yes.
Q: You agree, I take it, that a CBC is an *important* test in the diagnosis of appendicitis?
A: Yes, it is.

When a witness admits the *importance of something that should have been done but wasn't,* in this case, the CBC, always follow up with the question you're taught never to ask:

Q: *Why* is the CBC important?
A: Well, if her white cell count was elevated, that would tell you, especially with pain in her lower right abdomen, that appendicitis was part of the differential diagnosis.
Q: Doctor, her white cell count was more than 200,000 the next day, when she died. Your partner would have found an elevated white cell count if he'd done the CBC when he saw her in the office? True?

A: It would have been elevated.

Q: Her white cells would have been way above normal limits?

A: I think so, yes.

Q: So, had your partner performed the CBC and found the white cell count elevated, that would have eliminated gastroenteritis from his differential diagnosis, wouldn't it?

A: Yes.

Q: Would it have left standing as the most reasonable diagnosis that the child had appendicitis?

A: Yes.

This form of "friendly fire" forces witnesses to kill their own kith and kin. Under these circumstances—the failure to do a CBC that should have been done—there was no credible "bad answer" to the wide-eyed "why" question. No matter what the witness said, he was trapped into harming his own side of the case.

When you think about it, almost every case includes a situation in which something wasn't done but should have been—or the opposite. For example, the CEO in that patent infringement case—the one with the vice president who didn't know what "office" meant—admitted on the stand that he had failed to include in his company's patent application the prior art referred to in his letter to his patent lawyer. As an acclaimed solid-state physicist in his native Japan, and the holder of 1,200 American patents, the CEO knew better. He had no choice but to admit that he owed a duty of candor to the U.S. Patent Office—a legal obligation to disclose material that could potentially defeat his own company's patent application. But he had not done so. Rather than launch into the scientific issues raised by the omitted prior art, I set him up for a "why" question: "Was it important to include that material in your patent application even if it prevented you from getting the patent?" To which he replied, through an interpreter, "It would have been more polite to include it." I saw no necessity to ask him "why" it would have been more polite. The answer seemed pretty clear. Shortly thereafter, the judge invalidated his company's patent, the one he'd asserted had been infringed, and politely dismissed the case.

b.   Ask one too many questions ("seal off the exits").

As soon as you get an admission, the common wisdom (and Irving Younger's Ninth Commandment) is to take it and run–to an entirely different area of cross. The fear is that if you ask one too many questions you will give the witness an opportunity to backpedal on his admission. I think that is a mistake. When a witness like that doctor in the med mal case is as close as he was to admitting that his partner was negligent, there is no point in stopping with half a loaf, scooping up all your information and tying it together in summation. Trial lawyers must be opportunists, seizing every chance to nail down witnesses before they get a chance to think things over and recant or alter their admissions. If you get a significant admission and there is any escape hatch, assume that the witness will slip through it, and seal off those exits. The only way I know to effectively do that is to ask "one too many questions." There is an additional benefit: Boxing in a witness also makes for compelling theater, commanding the jury's attention.

Given the expert's damaging testimony, I would have no better opportunity to get him to admit that his partner deviated from the standard of care—but only if I first sealed off the exits. I started at the back door, certain that the doctor would have to agree that almost no one in America dies from a ruptured appendix—its very rarity an indictment of his partner's negligence:

Q: People with access to competent medical care just don't die any more from a ruptured appendix, do they?
A: Well, I don't know.
Q: Doctor, have you ever had a patient die of a ruptured appendix?
A: No, that hasn't happened.
Q: How long have you practiced?
A: I've been in private practice for 21 years.
Q: Would you agree with me that the incidence of death from a ruptured appendix is statistically meaningless in the United States?
A: I don't know for certain, but I'd have to say that's probably right.
Q: Outside of this case, have you ever heard of it happening in Galveston since you've been in practice?
A: Well, no.
Q: Did your partner diagnose appendicitis in Sandy?
A: No.
Q: Was missing that diagnosis the cause of her death?
A: Well, yes. But he wasn't negligent. Not from my review of the medical records.
Q: But, doctor, that's not supposed to happen, is it? If she receives competent medical care, she is not supposed to die of a ruptured appendix, is she?

Before getting to his actual answer, let me raise a red flag. It is true that the last three open-ended questions are a step removed from the bulletproof "why" question in the previous section. The witness could have seized on any one of them to attempt to undo the damage he'd done: "Well, Mr. Berg, no one planned for the girl to die. No one, least of all my partner, wanted it to happen. It was a terrible tragedy. But he didn't cause it." You have to be prepared to respond, undaunted by the truth or the emotional appeal of what the witness says, by pointing out that his answer is irrelevant to the issue:

> Doctor, let me be clear. No one contends that [the defendant] intended to harm this child, or wanted it to happen. No one doubts that your partner is a good doctor. My only question is, if he properly diagnosed appendicitis, would this little girl have lived? Now, please just answer that question.

On the other hand, an honest answer to either of the last two questions pushes the expert even closer to admitting the defendant's liability. In fact, admitting that his partner missed the diagnosis *sounds* like an admission of liability. Even so, given his prior admissions, what else could the witness say that was credible? With the exits sealed, the doctor agreed that the patient is "not supposed to" die from a ruptured appendix. The only thing left to do was to close the circle on malpractice:

> Q: Was [your partner's] failure to take a blood test a deviation from the standard of care, given these facts and circumstances?
> A: It would be a deviation from *my* standard of care, yes, sir.
> Q: Well, you don't practice any differently from other pediatricians in Galveston, do you?
> A: No.
> Q: So, would [the failure to take a blood test] be a deviation from the standard of care for all physicians who practice pediatric medicine?
> A: Probably.

"Probably" isn't good enough—not when you're that close to an unequivocal admission:

> Q: All right, sir. Given [that she died], and the cause of her death was sepsis, secondary to her ruptured appendix, isn't it within reasonable medical probability that either a blood count, or a urinalysis, or perhaps a KUB, a flat x-ray—just one of those tests—would have alerted you that something was wrong and that something was probably appendicitis?
> A: Considering the degree of her illness, it should.
> Q: All right, can we say that the doctor missed the diagnosis of a ruptured appendix?

A: I think retrospectively, yes, we can say that he missed the diagnosis.

Q: Well, retrospectively, we can also agree that he missed the diagnosis because he didn't perform any tests that might have tipped him off to what was going on—which deviates from the standard of care. True?

A: Yes, sir.

In all candor, that was an easy cross. I had the sense the doctor was relieved to admit what he did, even about his own partner. The case settled soon after that.

Most witnesses aren't nearly as honest as that doctor, and will head for the exits the minute they see a chance to undo the damage they have done. My son Gabriel recently took the deposition of an executive accused by our client of sexual harassment. During discovery, the executive had produced two computer-generated memos that appeared to have been created by his assistants, our client's former co-workers. The memos supported the executive's version of events and criticized our client. After a long cross, the executive admitted that he had composed both memos himself, on his own computer. Not an hour later—after a lunch break—he decided that he had "misspoken," that he had only typed up the memos, not composed them. In between the admission and the atonement, however, Gabe had asked a few questions "too many," and sealed off most of the witness's exits. To do so, Gabe figured out the various ways that the executive might try to backpedal, and, to the extent possible, denied him those possibilities. For example, the executive could claim that it was a natural mistake to represent the memos as being written by his assistants because the memos merely summarized what they told him. Under pressure, the assistants might have backed up their boss when they testified. Knowing all that, and the kind of man he was dealing with, Gabe sealed off as many exits as he could:

Q: Those were your words in the memos, not your assistants'?

A: Yes. But I did talk to them first.

Q: Did you tell either of them there was going to be a memo made of your conversation with them?

A: No, we didn't discuss that.

Q: Then I take it your testimony will be that you summarized what they told you and typed it up?

A: Yes, that's exactly what I did.

Q: And that neither of them reviewed the contents?

A: That's right.

Q: I notice you composed those memos the week after my client filed her complaint with the EEOC. Did you mention that fact when you had the conversation with your assistants?

A: I don't remember.

Those questions did not create an airtight seal, because they couldn't. Gabe was never going to get the man to admit that he'd made up the memos out of whole cloth. But, at a minimum, his claim that he only typed up what his assistants told him was not credible.

Obviously, you don't have to wait for the admission to seal off the exits. Nail the witness down tightly on the predicate facts, and he will have no choice but to give you the admission that you want when you finally ask "one too many" questions. For example, getting members of the MoPac train crew to admit that they frequently traveled through the crossing where Mrs. Lemon was killed, robbed them of the ability to deny later that they were aware of the dangerous conditions at the crossing. It's not the same as sealing off the exit *after* you get an admission, but the effect is identical. The witness has nowhere to run.

Knowing when to ask "one too many questions" and when to stop with the admission you already have is a judgment call. It is a tough one to make. Other than evaluating the various avenues of escape, and sealing them off, the decision depends on your experience and instinct about whether the witness can credibly back off from what she has admitted. Unfortunately, about the only way a young lawyer can learn is to get burned a few times, but it is pain worth enduring. You never want to lose the impact of an admission to a quick-witted witness or her lawyer.

c.   Befriend adverse witnesses (if you can).

Even with the caveat about not letting admissions get lost in a sea of civility,[4] cross-examination does not have to be confrontational to be destructive, or to hold the jurors' attention. An adverse witness who is supposed to kill you, but instead becomes a friend, makes the jury sit up and take notice. It's like a disputed call in a sandlot baseball game, where a player says his own teammate was out at the plate. As soon as someone shouts, "Your own man says so," the argument is over.

---

4. See p. 176, "The paradox of responsive answers."

Before you adopt a confrontational attitude toward an adverse witness, ask yourself if he truly benefits from agreeing with his own side's position. In commercial cases, especially, loyalties within a company can shift overnight. An employee may be unwilling to cover up for a co-worker, or it may be in his interest to unload on someone else. Better still is the employee who has left the company—which is exactly what happened with a major witness the plaintiff called in the Westinghouse trial.

STP's nuclear power plant had taken 17 years, thousands of workers, a lawsuit against a third-party contractor, and a tough new vice president to get it up and running. In rereading my deposition of the vice president the night before his trial testimony, I realized that I had been too confrontational. A Ph.D. in physics, he was a man of enormous intellect and an ego to match. He wasn't about to admit anyone put anything over on him—and certainly not that Westinghouse stuck him with $800 million worth of defective nuclear steam generators. Moreover, he had left the South Texas Project to become president of one of the largest utility companies in the nation. What was he going to say: that he got his new job because he performed badly in his old one? I decided to build my cross around the vice-president's obvious stake in his own reputation:

Q: Surely the utility company did some checking up on you to make certain you were the right man for the job?

A: I'm sure they were thorough. I know they checked down here at STP.

Q: You must have done something right at STP to get that big a job?

A: Well, it went fine here. Yes.

Q: You must be very proud of getting this plant built and then having it perform so well.

A: I had a lot of help.

Q: You are a modest man. You must be proud of the number of jobs that plant created here in Bay City, in fact, in this entire region.

A: Like I say, I had a great team.

Q: That team included Westinghouse, too, didn't it?

A: Absolutely. They had the expertise.

Q: And when you called on them to help, they responded.

A: Yes. I asked for their help often.

* * * *

Q: Will you accept my representation that the company has repeatedly said in its annual reports to shareholders, that production of electricity at the nuclear power plant has been outstanding—and my further representation that in August of this year, STP was the leading producer of electricity in the world?

A: I have no knowledge to dispute it. I'll—let's assume you're right.

Q: Now, assuming the truth of what I have said, that, in fact, the power plant is an outstanding producer of electricity—would that be consistent or inconsistent with your view that these are one-of-a-kind steam generator units, that this is one-of-a-kind nuclear power plant?

A: It's not inconsistent.

Q: Well, that makes it consistent, doesn't it?

A: Yes.

Q: Would you agree with me, then, that as far as those steam generators are concerned, they have been fit for use?

A: Up to the present time, they appear to be. So far, so good.

That last answer was a home run for my client. Westinghouse's warranty on the steam generators guaranteed replacement if the generators (actually, the energy-producing tubes within them) were not "fit for use." His answer that the generators had been fit up to that point had a huge impact on the jury—especially coming from a Ph.D. in physics. And I never asked a single contentious question.

You may worry that by befriending the adverse witness, you are precluded from impeaching him should he begin to evade or lie. That's a fallacy. You can have it both ways. All you have to do is avoid giving the jury the impression that you want them to believe the adverse witness when he helps you, but disbelieve him when he hurts you. To do so, your questioning should convey the message that the witness told the truth until it started to hurt his friends. For example, suppose that the former vice president had a change of heart following a break, and that as soon as he got back on the stand, he said, "Mr. Berg, I misspoke. Just because the plant is producing, doesn't mean the steam generators aren't corroding and don't need replacing." When something like that happens, you can't pass up the opportunity to do a "We heard you the first time" cross: "Let me understand. We take a 15-minute break, you confer with those lawyers over there, and you now change your sworn testimony?" "Don't tell me what was said, but you were talking to them about your testimony, weren't you?" Then you can finish him off. "Let me review the annual reports first and see if you agree or disagree with all the bragging the company has done on the power plant."

d. Make cross memorable.

Your questions should be phrased to convey your themes and arguments, which can make a predictable cross exciting. It would have been a waste of time to ask the conductor in the MoPac case tepid questions, like, "Your train collided with Mrs. Lemon's car at 8:30 P.M., didn't it?" Everyone knows the train hit her car or you wouldn't be in the courtroom. Instead, infuse your questions with context and passion. "You still don't think that terrible moment—when she looked down the track and saw death was seconds away—could have been avoided?" "You don't think that if your railroad had installed an automatic gate at the crossing, Mrs. Lemon would be alive and with her family today?" Let the questions vividly remind the jurors that the railroad was indifferent to human suffering; that the cost of an automatic gate was more important than a human life.

Many judges, who are often former trial lawyers, will let you argue a bit during cross, especially while winding up your examination. However, if an objection is sustained that you are arguing, make your opponent pay a price. Ask questions that are unargumentative, but stark and chilling: "You have crossed this intersection hundreds of times?" "At that hour the intersection is deserted except for an occasional car, true?" "It is very dark out there, isn't it?" "There is no gate, no flashing lights—not even a street light, true?" "I take it her car appeared suddenly?" "Can you tell us, in those final moments, could you see Sharon's face?" Once you have questioned like this a few times, you will almost instinctively question in a way that creates vivid impressions.

These questions are not intended solely to persuade jurors. They wreak havoc on witnesses' psyches, vividly reminding them of their role in something they'd rather forget. As a consequence, they can be incited to admissions, emotions, and other responses that will make their testimony as memorable as the questions themselves.

Remember, too, that emotion and empathy are not the special province of plaintiffs. If you were defending the railroad, you could try to create the same effect by turning the questions around. "When you first saw Mrs. Lemon's car, did she still have time to stop?" "When did you realize she wasn't going to stop?" "Did it appear to you she was trying to beat the train across the track?" "Were you still hoping she would get off the track?"

"How fast was she going?" "How did you feel when you realized the train was going to hit her?"

C. Cross Like a Criminal Lawyer ("Blind Cross")

Bullfighters and boxers are sissies compared to criminal lawyers. With no depositions, and few, if any, documents, they are forced to cross-examine in the blind—armed only with whatever they can put together after the witness takes the stand. There are no picadors to soften up the prey. No one rings a bell every three minutes for a rest. It's just the lawyer, mano a mano with the witness, pitting his considerable skills at cross-examination against the witness's aptitude for ruinous answers. Fortunately, those skills—developed to compensate for the lack of discovery—translate beautifully to civil trials.

1. Cross the whole person.

This is one of the most effective techniques of cross-examination, designed to impeach a witness's alleged lack of memory or knowledge with little hard evidence. All you need is resume-type information about the witness, which you can develop while she is on the stand. To show that the witness's forgetfulness or ignorance is just a ruse, juxtapose her background against her claim that she doesn't know or doesn't remember something.

In my career, I have used this technique against a CEO who testified that he didn't understand financial statements ("Let's see, you went to Harvard, got an M.B.A., took accounting courses, have run two major companies, and you don't understand financial statements?") and against an equally experienced businessman who testified that he couldn't remember whether a bank note he signed was for $10,000, $100,000, or $1 million ("I am not a businessman, so excuse my abysmal ignorance, but is your point that the amount of a bank note doesn't matter?"). But, for sheer gall, nothing matches the testimony of the CEO and sole owner of a large collection agency, in a racial discrimination case we brought on behalf of African-American employees.

The collection agency was huge. More to the point, it did more than $1 billion a year in government contracts, had hundreds of employees, and yet had never had a single African-American executive. At his deposition, the CEO testified that he had neither read his company's hiring policies nor been consulted by his employees about them. With all that government business, you would think he'd know at least a little something about the regulations of the Equal Employment Opportunity Commission, but he also claimed that he'd never discussed his company's minority hiring policy with any government agency, either. When an adverse witness weds himself to the party line, it gets easier and easier for him to lie, and you should not stand in his way. Given his claim that he didn't know about federal regs related to minority hiring, I asked the CEO if he knew whether the EEOC considered African-Americans minorities. He smiled benignly into the camera and said, "I have no idea." Distancing yourself is one thing, but living on another planet is quite another.

At that point, I began contrasting his background with his feigned ignorance about minority matters. First, as the company's founder and sole shareholder, he was deeply involved in company policy. He brought in all the government business personally. While he admitted attending regular Monday morning planning meetings with his regional vice-presidents for at least ten years, he was quick to point out that the subject of race had "never once" come up in any of those meetings. Mind you, it wasn't just race as it related to hiring policies that the group hadn't discussed. It was the subject of race itself.

Given his ignorance of all things racial, I would have bet money on the answer to my next question. "Your secretary makes more money than your highest-paid black employees, even though some are college-educated and have been with the company longer than she has. Yet, you have never had an African-American executive in your company. Why?" He didn't hesitate. "We can't find any qualified blacks." Had the case not settled, a jury would have come over the rail after him.

2. Take extreme positions to their extremes.

The night my client, Sharon Lemon, was killed, MoPac had illegally parked a row of tank cars a half-mile long on the tracks closest to the road where she entered the crossing. I argued that those cars blocked her view of the oncoming train, and since the parked cars weren't visible in the dark, made it appear that the tracks were clear. The railroad argued that the accident was completely Sharon's fault. The conductor of the train even insisted that "nothing" could have made the crossing safer. Instead of pouncing immediately, I asked the conductor a series of questions designed to show that he would take any position, no matter how extreme, to avoid admitting that the crossing could have been made safer:

Q: Well, [not being able to make that crossing safer] puzzles me. I may just be dense about this, but isn't it fair to say that if those tank cars had been moved farther down the track, you'd have seen a much broader view of the intersection?

A: I wouldn't, I wouldn't say that, you know.

Q: If those tank cars were just gone—parked somewhere else . . . and that would have allowed you to see her sooner, would that have been better for your job as a conductor?

A: Would that have been better? No.

Q: Would it have been better if the train had been stopped so a flagman could light some fuses at the intersection?

A: No.

Q: Wouldn't have made it any safer?

A: No.

Q: Would it have been better or safer for anyone out there—Mrs. Lemon or a member of the crew—to have had an automatic gate at the crossing?

A: No.

Q: Would it have been safer if you had stopped the train and just waved her across, said "Come on, Mrs. Lemon, go on across." Would that have been safer?

A: No.

Note the idea behind this approach. As soon as the witness commits to an extreme position—which he will cling to in order to avoid impugning his original answer—make him apply it to more and more outlandish situations. You don't need a shred of additional evidence. Just a ready reserve of adjectives, in this case, in a range from "safer" to "better." Accept each answer rather than fight it, and keep riding the original proposition. In the example above, the more ridiculous I made the scenario, including stopping the train and waving Mrs. Lemon across the tracks, the sillier the witness looked. Every person in that courtroom except the conductor would have agreed that a gate would have made the crossing safer, and almost certainly, would have saved Mrs. Lemon's life. Conceding such an obvious point was the only smart move, but the conductor staked out an extreme position and stuck with it until he had no credibility left.

Sometimes, all it takes is a single question to expose the absurdity of a proposition. The *New York Times* described a brilliant one-question cross-examination that Ron Fischetti, a well-known Manhattan criminal defense lawyer, conducted on a government expert. In the case, the defendant was accused of selling a stolen painting to an auction gallery. The evidence showed that the defendant provided his own name to the gallery when he sold it. The *Times* reported:

> An expert for the prosecution then delivered damaging testimony that art thieves commonly gave such auction houses their own names. But Mr. Fischetti's question deflated the expert entirely. "What," he asked, "do innocent people do?"

Extraordinary. Without depos or documents, and using only five words, Fischetti exposed the expert's *Catch-22*.

3. Use gestures and silence.

When you have no other weapons, you can still control the witness, or at least minimize the damage, by using gestures and silence. When a witness starts rambling, try raising both hands, palms toward him, and glare at him wordlessly. Almost invariably, he will stop talking. Because the gesture is humiliating—like being silenced by a teacher in front of the class—he will think twice before running on you again. But, for that same reason, be careful. Use this kind of tactic only if the answer is genuinely unresponsive. Otherwise, you risk creating jury sympathy by belittling the witness.

4. Ask questions when you don't know the answer.

There will be times when you will have no idea what the answer to your question is going to be, but the temptation and possible rewards of asking it are too great to resist. One excellent opportunity arises when your opponent fails to ask his own witness a significant question that he should have asked, but didn't. You would be right to worry that your adversary may have laid a trap, spring-loading the witness to unload on you when you ask the omitted question. This tactic is not without its risks. But the greater likelihood is that the lawyer or the witness, once in front of the jury, decided against pursuing what may have been a tenuous or untruthful testimony. That's why it's worth a roll of the dice. You ask the questions the lawyer should have asked, but didn't.

In the Westinghouse case, the plaintiff called one my client's former employees—always a cause for concern. Ex-employees may be disgruntled, but if they have documents and details in admissible form, they are also dangerous. Worse, this one had not been deposed. STP had designated more than 400 people as having knowledge of relevant facts, and Westinghouse could not depose them all. However, this witness had nothing to do with the sale of the South Texas plant, and in more than 200 depositions, his name never came up. The only reason to put him on would be to testify that he had been told to misrepresent something about the power plant that he did help sell—classic 404(b) evidence of similar acts—but that wasn't true, and the witness had a reputation as an honest guy. Nevertheless, we couldn't figure any other reason to put him on the stand.

His testimony was puzzling, but a relief. Counsel never asked him a single question about the sale of nuclear power plants, other than to develop that he'd been involved in that one sale, in another state. In fact, I can't remember a single thing he said that hurt us. That created a perfect opportunity for me to ask the questions I was certain opposing counsel would ask, but didn't:

Q: During the nine years you were at Westinghouse you sold all sorts of products, including a nuclear power plant in another state?

A: Yes. That's correct.

Q: During the entire time, you were never told to misrepresent the life of those plants, true?

A: That was never suggested to me.

Q: You were never told to misrepresent any Westinghouse product you sold, were you?

A: No, sir.

Q: In fact, your bosses insisted that the sales force keep in touch with the technical side at Westinghouse, so that they would understand what they could and couldn't promise. That's true isn't it?

A: They did. We had joint meetings at least once a month to discuss all the products we were selling.

Once he proved friendly, I asked him a few more questions. I did not know what his answers would be, but under the circumstances, they could only help:

Q: I take it you discussed your testimony with opposing counsel prior to taking the stand today.

A: Yes. We met this morning for about a half-hour.

Q: Did you talk to him by phone prior to coming here? I assume he wouldn't have brought you without talking to you first?

A: Yes, four or five times. The longest was about 20 minutes.

Q: During all that time, did you tell him what you just told the jury? You know, that Westinghouse never told you to misrepresent anything in selling a product.

A: Well, we never got around to that.

Q: He didn't bother asking you about that?

A: No, sir.

The few times I have used this tactic in my career have all worked out well. Nevertheless, I concede that you could get sandbagged, so be ready with a backup cross if the witness turns on you. If the former salesman had answered my question that he *had* been instructed to make misrepresentations about the life of the power plant that he'd helped sell, I could have demonstrated that he'd waited a curiously long time to disclose his "burning" secret. "Let me see, you worked for Westinghouse for nine years, you were told to lie about the life span of a nuclear power plant, and you never reported this to anyone at all, ever. True?" "There were safety issues involved and you never reported them to the Nuclear Regulatory Agency or the United States Attorney or any government agency?" "What kept you from that? Were you more concerned about the safety of the folks who live near a nuclear power plant or the safety of your paycheck?"

D. *Gore the Witness When You've Got the Goods*

The easiest impeachment comes from prior statements, documents, and physical facts that contradict the witness's trial testimony. Armed with that kind of ammunition, your cross should be easy. The goal is to make it powerful.

1. Set the stage for prior inconsistent statements.

There is no more effective impeachment than with a witness's prior inconsistent statement made during a deposition. However, you must convey to the jurors that the witness has done more than just give conflicting testimony. It's too easy for them to forgive the contradiction, because "anyone can make a mistake." You must let them know that the witness has done something terribly wrong. There are several steps involved.[5]

First, make the impeachment inescapable. On cross, ask the witness the *identical* question that you asked him during his deposition. Otherwise, he can slip through the net ("That's not what you asked me at my deposition") and you will be vulnerable to an indignant objection ("That is misleading, Your Honor"). Misstating the question that you asked or the answer the witness gave, no matter how innocent, can also make you look dishonest. If that happens—as it sometimes does in the heat of trial—immediately acknowledge that you were wrong. A prompt correction—and a bit of humility—go a long way toward altering the impression that you were

---

5. The questions in this section also fulfill typical foundation requirements for impeachment with prior inconsistent statements, in those jurisdictions where one is required.

doing something underhanded. Note, also, that to impeach a witness's current answer with a prior inconsistent one, the contradiction need not be explicit. It is sufficient if the essence of the two answers is contradictory. For example, assume the witness testifies at trial that he has "no idea" about the date of a particular meeting, but testifies on his deposition that he believed the meeting was just before his vacation in August. That is contradictory enough to impeach.

Next, before using deposition testimony to impeach the witness, question him in a way that explains to the jury what depositions are—and the solemn circumstances under which they are taken. This is the curtain-raiser on impeachment. Done skillfully, it creates a sense of drama and backs the witness into an embarrassing corner: "Do you recall giving your deposition on February 20th, 2002, in your lawyer's office?" "Before you began your deposition, you took an oath, just like you did before beginning your testimony today in this courtroom?" "You raised your right hand and swore to tell the truth?" "I told you that your testimony that day was the same as sitting in this courtroom in front of this jury?" "I warned you about the penalty for not telling the truth, didn't I?" "Just like now, your lawyer was with you the entire time?" "You recall that I told you to stop me if I asked a question you didn't understand, tell me what wasn't clear, and I'd clear it up?" "I also warned you that if you said something different in court than at your deposition, I was going to pull out the transcript and let the jury know?" Not only will jurors understand the importance of deposition testimony, and pay more attention, these questions will show them how fair you were—even warning the witness you would contradict him with his own words if he didn't tell the truth.

Then, standing next to the witness, his deposition in hand, state the page and line number of the testimony you are going to read, to avoid being interrupted for that information by opposing counsel. You don't want anything to disrupt your momentum. Point the witness to the contradictory testimony and tell him, "Correct me if I misread a single word." Then, *you* read the colloquy to the jury. *Never* allow the witness to do it for you, or the drama of the moment will be lost as he mumbles his prior testimony into the microphone. Instead, read it with the inflection that conveys the meaning of what you asked, and what the witness said: "Do you recall that I asked you, 'Did you negotiate the contract?' and you answered, on the next line, 'Yes.' You didn't say anything else, Mr. Jones. Just 'yes.' Do you recall giving that answer?" If he admits making the statement, don't stop. Demand that he acknowledge that the two statements are contradictory. Force him to admit that he changed his testimony on the stand because his prior testimony was so harmful. The point is, to the extent permitted by the court, don't just impeach the witness; gore him.

If the witness denies the meaning of his testimony or claims that he misspoke—not an uncommon response—use him to explain errata sheets to the jury. "Weren't you given 30 days to review your deposition and change or correct any answer?" "Let me show the jury the pages provided for corrections, here at the back. There are no changes or corrections, are there?" "In fact, you didn't change the answer from your deposition until you sat down in that witness chair, did you?" On the other hand, if he changed his testimony in the errata sheets, you can use that to impeach him, too, by showing that he made the change only when he realized he had admitted something that he shouldn't have. "You never asked me to explain or repeat the question during that deposition, did you?" "Now you say you didn't understand the question?" "All I asked you was whether you learned about the improvement to your source code from my client. You answered, without hesitation, 'yes.' What part of that question did you fail to understand? Or is it that you now understand how badly your admission hurts you in this case?"

Of course, not all prior inconsistent statements are made under oath. But no matter the source, don't fail to explain the context in which they were made: "You wrote this letter to your shareholders?" "You are required by your position to write this letter?" "You have what is called a fiduciary duty to those stockholders?" "That means you have to put their interests above yours?" "So you must have been careful in this letter to tell them the truth?" Once you've explained the meaning of the document, impeach the witness as you would with any other prior inconsistent statement.

As soon as you impeach the witness, zero in while he's still reeling. It's the perfect time to extract critical admissions. The witness will be in no mood to be humiliated again. Because the need for approval runs deep, some witnesses may even be anxious to demonstrate their honesty—a good person after all.

Finally, no matter how good you are at impeachment, nothing is more effective than an excerpt of an inconsistent statement taken from a videotaped deposition. (See p. 38, "Let Them Eat Tape.") You can either barcode the entire videotape (which allows you to go to the testimony you want instantaneously), or create brief excerpts from the areas of testimony the witness is likely to lie about. If the witness contradicts his prior testimony even once on the stand, hit the "play" button, sit back, and let the tape do your work for you.

2. Ask questions when you know the answers (sometimes).

When you have documents and discovery from which the witness cannot escape, simply follow Irving Younger's advice: Ask questions loaded with information that you are certain is true. That forces answers and admissions mandated by the evidence and all but eliminates unresponsiveness, even with dangerous witnesses anxious to slip something harmful into the record. However, as discussed, when your tightly controlled cross begins to sound like direct, open things up. (See p. 176, "The paradox of responsive answers.") Solicit answers that aren't always 100-percent predictable. That's when cross really starts to count.

3. Demand every document that the witness reviewed.

This is not a method of impeaching witnesses, but a means of obtaining additional ammunition to do so. At some point early in your cross, ask the witness to tell you every document that he reviewed to prepare for his testimony. Often, witnesses will be forewarned and will have stashed their notes somewhere other than in the courtroom, or deny that they reviewed any at all. Keep a watchful eye out for clues. When you've got a good-faith basis, rather than ask the witness if he reviewed anything to refresh his memory for testimony, confront him as if that fact is a given: "Mr. Witness, as you were sitting in the hallway this morning, just before you took the stand, I could not help but see you reviewing some notes for your testimony—which you stuck in your briefcase. Isn't that your briefcase over there?"

If the witness admits he reviewed anything related to his testimony, he must produce them to you immediately, subject to an opponent's right to have the judge review them *in camera,* and to redact irrelevant portions. If you get lucky, the material the witness turns over will contain some notes in his own handwriting. For reasons I have never understood, witnesses write down the most damning comments, like the one I found scribbled in the margin of a document I got years ago, which said, "don't admit that." I can't remember what "that" was anymore, but I can't imagine it helped the witness.

V. CROSS-EXAMINING EXPERTS

A. There Is Rarely an Expert You Can't Impeach

While President of Yale, Kingman Brewster said that the best minds of each generation go into the law. I believe he is right. Although trial lawyers can't learn everything about an expert's field, most can learn enough to conduct a highly effective cross, no matter how esoteric the subject matter. It doesn't take genius—just curiosity, a reasonable intellect, and an obsessive desire to win.

The major difficulty in crossing experts is not their professional expertise but their skill at testifying. If an expert senses that you are in over your head, he won't stop making speeches. However, if you quickly demonstrate that you are prepared to engage him on a very high level, in the language of his field, and that you are a skillful cross-examiner, the speech-making will stop. If it doesn't, the jury will turn on him with a vengeance.

In *Westinghouse,* I hired an engineering professor who had worked at a nuclear power plant to tutor me. It cost $400 and about eight hours of my time. That modest effort made a big difference in my case. I was able to cross-examine STP's witnesses on my own turf, refusing to relinquish my main point—that its executives and scientists knew the risks when they purchased a nuclear power plant—to their claims of ignorance of problems of corrosion in nuclear steam generators. I was also able to keep my cross on a plane that jurors would understand—simplifying complex scientific issues into language anyone could comprehend. Racehorse Haynes once defended a murder case in which the prosecution expert planned to testify that the odds were 999,999 in one million that a hair found on the deceased came from the head of the defendant. That single strand of hair was the only physical evidence tying the defendant to the crime. Haynes took a course in probability at the University of Houston, which enabled him to destroy the expert's opinion during a hearing on a motion to suppress that hair. It's been many years, and I don't recall precisely Haynes's demonstration of how the expert's methodology was flawed, but it had something to do with the odds against a two-headed goat being born (it happens). In any event, the point is Haynes's extra effort. The motion was granted. With no other evidence, the defendant was acquitted.

Not everyone agrees with aggressively cross-examining experts, especially about their own field of expertise. During my cross of a solid-state physicist in a patent infringement case, the judge pointedly interrupted me. He said that when he was in private practice, he told young lawyers not to cross-examine experts about their field of expertise. Instead, the judge said to impeach an expert with an expert. Taking note of my contrary approach, the judge said, "Apparently you feel you can win cases out of the [opposing] expert's mouth."

He was right. I do think you can win cases out of an opposing expert's mouth. If you fail to cross-examine *any* witness, including an expert, about his most important testimony, you concede that it is trustworthy. No matter how persuasive, your expert—who will almost certainly testify days or even weeks later—cannot destroy the opposing expert's easily won credibility. The real product of a "do-no-harm" cross-examination of an adverse expert is that the expert wins.

On the other hand, when you successfully cross-examine an adverse expert, jurors are more likely to be influenced by your expert's opinions. Judges are not all that different. In his order, the federal judge who criticized my approach to cross-examining experts held that the plaintiff's patent was unenforceable and dismissed the case. His ruling relied in part on admissions made by the expert I was cross-examining when he interrupted me. To top it off, the judge's decision was affirmed on appeal.

B. Build Your Cross around the Expert Pyramid

If you were to diagram the structure of an expert cross, it would look like a pyramid, beginning with the expert's credentials at the bottom and moving through her opinion at the top.

If you are able to impeach an expert effectively at any level of the pyramid, the opinion collapses. Of course, if you can impeach the opinion itself, you won't have to claw your way through all that sand and mortar. Just head straight for the top. But most often, you have to cross-examine from the bottom up. The discussion below follows that path.

Figure 6.2
The Pyramid of Expert Cross

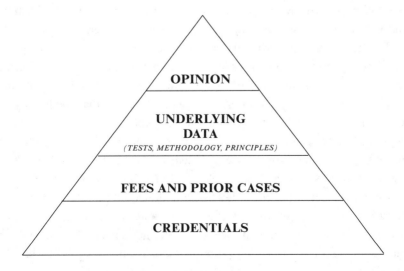

C. Attack the Expert's Credentials

It's not often that you will be able to disqualify an expert because his credentials are somehow lacking. But you can undermine his qualifications so dramatically that his opinions won't matter.

1. Take the expert witness on voir dire.

When your opponent finishes developing the expert's qualifications, or, as is still the practice in some jurisdictions, tenders him as an expert to the court, stand up. Tell the judge you want to take him on voir dire. If you can impeach his credentials because (1) he has misrepresented something on his resume, or (2) his area of expertise does not apply to the facts of your case, the jurors will write him off before he begins.

a. Never take an expert's resume at face value.

Verify every item on an expert's *vita,* even items that no one in their right mind would lie about. I don't care if he claims he won the Nobel Peace Prize, call Oslo and make sure it's true. Experts frequently misrepresent their credentials. Between phone calls, online research, and discovery, you should be able to confirm every significant entry on a resume.

In the mid-1990s, I represented the principal owner of a Houston S&L, who was part of a group that bought United Press International out of bankruptcy. He borrowed the money for his investment from a friend's bank, also located in Houston. About the same time, he made a loan to the same banker-friend from his own S&L. The government alleged that the loans were "illegally linked," that neither man was creditworthy, and that each had pressured his own institution to approve the other's application. Both men were indicted for bank fraud, and tried together.

The government led with its expert, a former banker. We had interviewed her in the U.S. Attorney's office only a few days before trial. During the interview, she mentioned that she had left her job at Irving Bank and Trust Company in 1981. However, her resume indicated that she left a year later, in 1982. I casually asked about the discrepancy as we were leaving. She looked at her resume, and with a demure, "Oh, my," said that she had neglected to include a job as vice president at the First Woman's Bank of New York—a position she held in 1981, after leaving Irving B and T.

I spent the better part of a day tracking down the expert's former boss, who was in Brazil. Even then, 15 years later and on vacation, she was so anxious to criticize her ex-employee, I couldn't get her off the phone. As a practical matter, it was too late to subpoena documents to support what she told me, but the details I got were pretty compelling. As it turned out, the government's expert had been fired by First Woman's Bank.

At trial, after the prosecutor developed her credentials, I took the expert on voir dire. She readily agreed that if borrowers misrepresented anything significant on a loan application, it was a "red flag" for a bank's loan committee. All the while, her own resume loomed in the background, blown up on poster board, bigger than Dallas.

> Q: Now, your own resume says that from 1969 to 1982, you worked for Irving Bank and Trust Company in New York. That's not true, is it?
> A: No, that's a mistake.
> Q: What you have omitted is that in 1981, you left Irving Bank and went to work for the First Woman's Bank of New York, didn't you?
> A: That's correct, sir.
> Q: That information was not contained in the resume you provided to this court and to me, was it?
> A. No, sir.
> Q: And the only way I found that out was to ask you that question last Monday in the prosecutor's office, true?
> A: Yes, sir.
> Q: Now, there came a time in December, 1981, that your immediate superior at First Woman's Bank, Judith Thompson, went to Japan. That's true, isn't it?
> A: Yes, sir.
> Q: And during that time, you approved a lease deal.
> A: It was a purchase money lease, yes, sir.
> Q: And it was funded in your boss's absence?
> A: Yes, sir.
> Q: And you failed to get the title to the collateral?

Confronted with detailed knowledge about a specific event in her life, the expert's options were to attempt to bluff, or, just in case her former boss might be on call to testify, admit the truth. She chose the latter option:

> A: Yes, sir. The collateral for the loan never came in. And when we called the borrowers they admitted they had not used the loan proceeds for the purpose intended.

* * * *

Q: And when your boss got back, she said to you, "You didn't get the collateral, you didn't do due diligence. We've lost $200,000. You're fired." Didn't she?

A: No, sir.

Q: She did not fire you?

A: She asked me to resign, but she did not say because I did not do the due diligence. [S]he fired me, quote-unquote, because I was not a team player.

Q: Is it your testimony under oath today that your firing had nothing to do with that $200,000 loan you funded without getting the collateral?

A: When she asked me to resign she did not refer to any loan that I had approved or not approved.

Q: Forgive me. Perhaps it was the way I asked my question. Is it your testimony that you were not fired over a loan that you approved and funded at First Woman's Bank?

A: Again, I say she made no reference to a loan upon my firing.

Q: I'm not talking about what she made reference to when she fired you. I'm asking if your firing had anything at all to do with that loan.

A: No, I did not understand that, sir.

Q: Let's move on. I take it from your answers that you concede you were, in fact, fired?

A: I will concede that I was asked to resign, same thing.

Q: And you never got another job in banking, did you?

A: I never applied for another job in banking.

Q: Whether you applied for one or not, will you concede you never worked again in banking?

A: I never again worked in banking, yes, sir.

* * * *

Q: Now, can you see why, since your resume says that you worked in '82 at Irving Bank and Trust, but that is not true, that you were fired from a different bank in '82, that one could conclude that you were trying to misrepresent your credentials?

A: One could conclude that, yes, sir.

During the rest of my examination, the expert sat slumped in her chair, occasionally rousing herself to demand more tea for the sudden onset of a sore throat. But that was about it for her. During her cross she even admitted the defendants' loans were not linked. Had I pressed, she probably would have confessed to the Manson murders.

b. Show the expert lacks the relevant expertise.

An expert's credentials, no matter how impressive, must be relevant to the facts of the case. Otherwise, the expert is not qualified to testify. If you have any running room at all, it is always worth it to challenge an expert's credentials. Even if a disparity doesn't result in the expert's testimony being excluded or limited by the judge, the expert's questionable *bona fides* will still weigh on the jurors' minds.

In the *Fleisher* trial, our damage expert testified to the loss in value our client's agency, Assist Sports Management (ASM), suffered after ASM's former president stole key players. The defense brought an expert in business valuations who was there to criticize our expert's methodology. Immediately after counsel tendered him as an expert, I took the witness on voir dire:

Q: Sir, is it true that you have never evaluated a sports agency, isn't it?

A: Yes, that is correct.

Q: Now, you were sitting right over there when our expert testified that he had actually put a dollar value on Wayne Gretzky as a player, because his team wanted to use him as collateral for a loan. Do you remember that?

A: Yes, sir.

Q: But you've never done that either, have you? You've never valued an athlete as an asset?

A: No, sir.

The judge sustained my objection, precluding the defense expert from providing any testimony about our expert's opinion. She did allow him to discuss general methods of valuing businesses. For 45 minutes, he rambled on about the time-value of money, earnings multiples, and other topics guaranteed to thrill and delight a jury. But he never got to say a word about our damages. The jury ultimately awarded Fleisher and his agency $4.6 million.

Nothing in a trial should occur in a vacuum, so when you know from pretrial discovery that the other side's expert may lack relevant experience, plant a seed in the minds of potential jurors during jury selection. For example, ask, "If you were selected for this jury, Mr. Johnson, based on what you have heard so far, would you expect an expert on sports agencies to testify? Would you *want* such an expert to testify?" Of course, someone is going to say yes, because it is logical. When you take the expert on voir dire, your eyebrows raised in disbelief about his lack of relevant experience ("You mean to say that you have *never* in your career evaluated a sports agency?"), the seed you planted with the jury will bloom. They will be ready to dismiss whatever opinions the unqualified expert may offer.

D. Attack the Expert's Objectivity

There are opinions aplenty about the impact expert witnesses really have. Conventional wisdom holds that jurors automatically disregard their testimony because it is bought and paid for. Jurors also frequently say that the experts neutralized each other. Don't believe it. Comments like those are more cliché than true. When you ask jurors to identify specific factors that influenced their verdict, they invariably cite some part of an expert's testimony, although they often forget that the testimony came from an expert.

1. Spotlight excessive fees.

In the Westinghouse/STP case, the plaintiff's expert, a metallurgist, had been paid $650,000 for his testimony—more than many of the jurors would earn in a lifetime. That obscene fee, and the expert's arrogance, did him in. Nor is it just the bottom line that matters. Doctors at Baylor Medical School in Houston charge as much as $1,000 per hour for expert testimony—guaranteed to rob them of credibility with jurors, and instituted by the school's administration to dissuade plaintiffs' lawyers from retaining them. Although I've had to make exceptions, my personal rule of thumb is to pay an expert no more than $350 per hour, and that's stretching it.

To reduce the sting of an expert's rate and total fee, you must be upfront about both—and be ready to stand behind the witness's billings. Never leave it to your opponent to tell the jury how much you are paying an expert. In a case against Tenneco in the early 1990s, defense counsel failed to mention the fees paid to his damage expert. It was the plaintiff lawyer's first question on cross: "Mr. Williams, with all these numbers you discussed, did you forget this one?" He pointed to a blackboard, on which he'd written "$500,000." "That's the amount you've been paid for your testimony, isn't it?" The jury returned a $625 million verdict against the defendant. The magnitude of those fees, and the defense's failure to disclose them, had to have played an important part.

Of course, with jurors already skeptical of experts, don't do anything that could give them more reason to doubt. Make certain your expert is paid up to date when she gets on the stand. Otherwise, your adversary will turn the balance due into a contingency fee, payable only if her testimony is emphatic enough for his side to win the case. "Now, doctor, you are owed $14,000 for your testimony. Tell me the truth: Aren't you the least bit concerned that if the plaintiff loses, you won't get paid?"

2. Reveal the expert as a captive witness.

Some experts testify only for one side or the other, while others are retained repeatedly by the same law firm or client. Show the jury that these experts are really captive witnesses, or, as we call them in my firm, "utility witnesses" —willing to take any position they are assigned.

However glossy their credentials, such experts are very vulnerable on cross. Jurors don't trust experts who make up their minds before they know what a case is about. Demonstrate that the expert derives a high percentage of his income by doing repeat business for your opponent. Show that he consistently adopts the same position, case after case, regardless of the facts. Turnabout being fair play, the jurors will disbelieve his opinion even before they hear it.

E. Attack Reliability and Relevance

The 1990s brought a sea change in the standards of admissibility for expert testimony, and with it, heightened awareness of the ways to attack it. The Supreme Court's decisions in *Daubert*, *Joiner*, and *Kumho Tire* make district judges gatekeepers at the door of all expert testimony, with vastly expanded power to determine its admissibility.[6] Whether you agree with those holdings, or even practice in jurisdictions that follow them,[7] they provide a roadmap for an excellent cross, and suggest questions that we should ask of all experts.

---

6. *See* Daubert v. Merrill Dow Pharm., 509 U.S. 579 (1993) (scientific opinion not admissible unless the principles and methodology from which it was derived are both relevant and reliable); General Elec. v. Joiner, 522 U.S. 136 (1997) (expanding the power of district courts to exclude expert testimony if the opinion itself is not reliable or relevant—not just the methodology and principles that produced it; and holding that the standard of review on appeal is abuse of discretion); Kumho Tire Co. v. Carmichael, 526 U.S. 137 (1999) (extending *Daubert* to all expert testimony, not just scientific).

7. Twenty-six jurisdictions have adopted the *Daubert* standards in whole or in part. Sixteen jurisdictions continue to follow the *Frye* rule, which bases admissibility of scientific testimony on "general acceptance" of its reliability in the "relevant scientific community." Frye v. United States, 293 F. 1013, 1014. Six states apply *Daubert* but have not totally rejected *Frye*. Four states have created their own standards. See Appendix A, table of *Daubert* jurisdictions.

1. Get experts under oath as often as possible.

In the post-*Daubert* world, a pretrial evidentiary hearing on a motion to exclude expert testimony is as critical to a civil case as a hearing on a motion to suppress evidence is to a criminal one, and not just for the obvious reason that you might actually succeed in excluding the testimony. Criminal lawyers push for hearings on a motion to suppress on the theory that the police officer or federal agent won't be able to tell the same story twice—and, therefore, will contradict himself when he takes the stand at trial. Civil lawyers have an even greater advantage. Having already deposed the expert, a *Daubert* hearing allows them to get the witness under oath a second time. If her testimony survives the motion to exclude, she will be testifying at trial for the third time. Few witnesses, including experts, can tell the same story three times in a row.

2. Undermine the underpinnings—and the opinion itself.

In *Daubert*, the Court suggested four areas of inquiry that are relevant to determine the admissibility of expert scientific testimony: (1) Whether a theory or technique can be (and has been) tested; (2) Whether it has been subjected to peer review and publication; (3) Whether, for a particular technique, there is a high "known or potential rate of error" and whether there are "standards controlling the technique's operation"; and (4) Whether the theory or technique enjoys "general acceptance" within the relevant scientific community.

As the Court later clarified, these standards are neither rigid nor exclusive; they are "meant to be helpful, not definitive." *Kumho Tire*, 526 U.S. at 151. They also apply to all expert testimony, not just scientific testimony. *Id.* Those four areas of inquiry are a good starting point in planning your cross. Thoroughly develop each one into a series of questions tailored to your case, with an eye toward undermining the reliability and relevance of the expert's methodology, testing, and principles, and, ultimately, the opinion itself.

In addition to extending the district judge's gatekeeping role to all expert testimony, the Court in *Kumho* held that, where possible, the expert's conclusions must be independently verifiable, based on objective principles. The more objective the tests, principles, or theories underlying an expert's opinion, the less likely the testimony will be excluded. If an opinion is predicated on the First Law of Thermodynamics, it's coming in. On the other hand, as Justice Breyer pointed out in *Kumho Tire*, the scientific method frequently involves subjective analysis—an area of expert testimony that has always been vulnerable on cross. Whenever an opinion rests on an expert's observations, your goal should be to reduce it to no more than a guess.

In addition to the important goal of persuading a judge to exclude (or admit) expert testimony,[8] there is the equally important matter of convincing a jury to dismiss (or give weight to) an expert's opinion. The discussion that follows addresses that concern, including in ways suggested by the *Daubert* line of cases.

a. Let the air out of subjective determinations.

The best example of undermining an opinion by attacking the subjective determinations underlying it comes from *Kumho Tire* itself, where the defense lawyer's cross destroyed the expert's opinion. In that case, no one questioned his qualifications. He was a mechanical engineer, worked for Michelin for ten years, and had experience as a tire-failure consultant in tort cases. He was prepared to testify that the fatal accident that was the subject of the litigation was caused by a design defect in a blown-out tire. What undid his opinion was that his subjective determinations were totally unreliable, which was made clear by an obviously amused Justice Breyer:

> Among other things, the expert could not say whether the tire had traveled more than 10, or 20, or 30, or 40, or 50 thousand miles, adding that 6,000 miles was "about how far" he could "say with any certainty." The court could reasonably have wondered about the reliability of a method of visual and tactile inspection sufficiently precise to ascertain with some certainty the abuse-related significance of minute shoulder/center relative tread wear differences, but insufficiently precise to tell "with any certainty" from the tread wear whether a tire had traveled less than 10,000 or more than 50,000 miles. And these concerns might have been augmented by [the expert's] repeated reliance on the "subjective[ness]" of his mode of analysis in response to questions seeking specific information regarding how he could differentiate between a tire that actually had been overdeflected and a tire that merely looked as though it had been. They would have been further augmented by the fact that [the expert] said he had inspected the tire itself for the first time the morning of his first deposition, and then only for a few hours.[9] (citations omitted)

Consider the effect of *Kumho* on a cross of a CPA in the post–Enron/ Arthur Andersen world. While the CPA's treatment of a transaction for tax

---

8. For an excellent outline of specific questions for a pretrial *Daubert* hearing to exclude expert testimony, *see* THOMAS A. MAUET, TRIAL TECHNIQUES 332–33 (5th ed. 2000).

9. *Kumho Tire,* at 154–155.

or financial-statement purposes may be perfectly reasonable under Generally Accepted Accounting Principles, jurors are going to be highly skeptical of any judgment calls the CPA makes. Given the public predisposition against that once-respected profession—in fact, against all financial types— it is preferable to put the company's self-trained bookkeeper on the stand, rather than its outside auditor. Short of that, one of those retired FBI agents who do financial analysis would make a better choice than the regular outside accounting firm.

b.   Garbage in, garbage out.

When experts make even innocent mistakes about the "facts and data" underlying their opinions, neither they nor the case can survive cross. That is especially true when the mistakes are slightly more sinister, or can be made to appear so. As the saying goes, garbage in, garbage out.

There are many ways to undermine the underpinnings of expert testimony. One of them—demonstrating that the expert ignored important data—leaves her vulnerable to a brutal cross: "Are you serious? You have never seen these lab tests before?" "So you only read the material those lawyers spoon-fed you—just what they wanted you to see?" If the data is truly essential, the witness faces a classic Hobson's choice. She can either admit her mistake and undermine her own opinion, or stick with her story and lose all credibility: "Now that you've taken the time to read that lab report, you have to change your opinion about the validity of the plaintiff's patent, don't you?"

You should scrupulously avoid making this type of mistake with your own experts—in fact, with all your witnesses. Keep them educated about their part of the case during discovery and update them on relevant testimony during trial. (See p. 37, "Educate witnesses about their part of the case.")

c.   "Would that mine enemy had written a book."

When it comes to expert testimony, that old adage should be amended to include, "given a speech, uttered a single word under oath, or sent one relevant e-mail." One of the surest ways to destroy an expert's opinion is to quote his own impeaching words back to him. When you do that, the jury will conclude very quickly that the expert's opinions are for sale, and that your opponent is his most recent customer. All you have to do is invest an afternoon at the library, online, or ensconced with his prior depositions, and almost certainly you will find some contradictory comment.

The Lemon/MoPac wrongful death case didn't require that I learn rocket science, but it did involve some complex issues related to the design and safety of grade crossings. The railroad's expert had published numerous articles on the subject, including one that he'd written 15 years before, describing ways to improve safety at unmarked grade crossings.

I mentioned in an earlier chapter an ugly incident in which an expert all but came across the table for me—the trial lawyer's dream. The railroad's crossing expert was that witness—and I had it on videotape. What led up to it was my asking him if certain improvements would have made the crossing where Mrs. Lemon was killed safer. I didn't tell him that the ideas came from one of his own articles. He rejected each of them as unwarranted, cost-prohibitive, or, in one case, "silly." When I finally showed him that the ideas came from his article, he erupted: "Well, can you remember what you wrote 15 years ago, sir?" Actually, I have trouble remembering what I did an hour ago, so that would not have been a half-bad response had he not also been yelling, tugging at his tie, and clearly contemplating the consequences of punching me out.

Inconsistent statements made by an expert under oath in a deposition—including those made in a different lawsuit—are especially valuable for undermining an expert's testimony. Noncaptive witnesses often are fertile targets. Having testified for both sides of the bar, they appear to be evenhanded, but they frequently leave a trail of contradictory testimony. And every expert caught contradicting his own sworn testimony is, in the vernacular, toast.

d. Nail down every opinion.

It is critical that you identify and explore as precisely as possible each and every one of the expert's opinions. The last thing you want is to hear a new one at trial. When you try to block an opinion's admissibility on grounds of surprise, the first thing the judge will want to know is if you had any notice of it, even indirectly. Inevitably, opposing counsel will claim that the contested opinion was mentioned in the expert's report, albeit indirectly or obliquely, but that you never asked about it during his deposition. Unless you can demonstrate that you did all you could to flush out the opinion, it's coming in. Therefore, if an expert vacillates at all at his deposition ("I am waiting on further records. . . . "), demand that he supplement his written report. If there is a change or addition of consequence, and you need to question him further before trial, notice him for deposition again.

It is equally critical that you determine the basis for each opinion. Sometimes, you will discover something untenable and the opinion will crumble. Occasionally, you will discover that the expert is goofy and the opinion will crumble. Sometimes, you will discover both at once, which brings up a perfect example. I received an odd damage report from a Ph.D. economist in a medical malpractice case. In the case, the doctor had missed the diagnosis of a client's brain tumor. I read the economist's report several times because he appeared to be rendering medical opinions, which I confirmed during his deposition:

> Q: Do you have any quibble or disagreement with the proposition that Mrs. Khajavi is not able to return to teaching school?
>
> A: I'll give you my opinions about her ability to teach. One is her letter of resignation, which does not say that she is unable to teach. She says she is resigning to join her husband in Saudi Arabia. So from that document, one cannot draw the conclusion that she's unable to teach. However, in subsequent documents the lady notes she is unable to teach due to her loss of memory. Noting for the record that I'm not a physician nor do I have any medical training, I have read many depositions in my career and, in hers, she is able to remember characteristics regarding her brothers and sisters, when and where they were born and their education, which I cannot remember for my only sibling, thereby leading me to conclude that her memory is not as bad as she says because it is impossible for her to remember all that information if she has a bad memory. Combining those two facts together as an economist leads me to conclude that she is not 100 percent disabled.

You're not misreading it. That's a verbatim quote. He thought she was a malingerer, a fairly jaundiced view to take toward someone who's had a brain tumor—even for an economist.

> Q: Now, sir, is there anything else? Any other basis for your opinion?
>
> A: Other than the neurophysiological [sic] evaluation, no.
>
> Q: I noticed that among your many and admirable degrees [four of them] that you do not have a degree in psychology. Am I correct?
>
> A: That is correct.
>
> Q: Do you make any claim to expertise as a psychologist?
>
> A: No, sir.

Q: Are you in any way qualified to interpret the results of a neuropsychological test?

A: No, sir.

Q: So what you have done is conclude with no expertise at all that the neuropsychologist is wrong, that my client is not disabled and could return to teaching?

A: With one exception. I do have another expertise. Since September, approximately, of 1985 until the present, I have been an adjunct professor, to my credit, educated approximately 1,200 individuals between the ages of 20 and 35, blending race, religious creeds, national origin, and sex. It is my opinion, based upon an observation of a random 1,200 individuals, that Mrs. Khajavi, with two master's degrees in engineering and a rather good memory, from her deposition, of April 10, 1991, would fall somewhere in the range of those 1,200 individuals, and most, if not all of them, including some people you might know personally in the community, including Alan Rubenstein's son, earn $24,000 or more. This lady could do the same. So, I basically disagree with the fact that she is 100 percent incapable of doing anything but being a vegetable.

Q: So you are estimating that your students' IQs mirror hers, guessing they have jobs making $24,000 a year, and concluding Mrs. Khajavi should, too?

A: Easily, yes, and that includes my observations about truck drivers, waitresses, salesclerks, and others in an administrative-support capacity.

Q: Do you have any other reason why you believe she can return to her work as a teacher? If so, what is it?

A: Based upon my reading of her deposition and my experience in the educational system both in the State of New York as a graduate assistant for New York University, a librarian, assistant librarian, for New York University Hospital, Hope Library, and an adjunct professor at the University of Houston for the last seven years, that lady could get a position, obtain a position in some administrative educational support role, including kindergarten for tots, to earn approximately $24,000 a year with promotions, and thereby suffer *de minimis* loss in relation to her job.

Q: Now, are you holding yourself out also, then, as an expert for the requirements of teaching in the public schools?

A: I'm relying upon the documents presented, namely—

Q: Forgive me. Perhaps it was the way I asked my question. Are you an expert in, for instance, the qualifications for teaching in elementary schools in the Houston Independent School District?

A: It depends on what you call an expert. I have been called upon by the University of Houston to help evaluate doctoral candidates—

Q: Forgive me. Perhaps it was the way I asked my question. Do you know, sir, what is required of a person to be able to teach a classroom of kindergarten students that you mentioned?

A: No.

Q: Yet, you are advancing the opinion that she is perfectly capable of getting a job teaching, in some sort of capacity such as teaching kindergarten, is that true?

A: Yes.

Q: She could be a teacher right now?

A: I believe, without being argumentative, she could get an equivalency position of $24,000 a year based upon her deposition, the economy, the level of compensation, her Texas teaching certificate, and that neuro-something-or-other report.

Q: You told me she could teach, she could teach kindergarten. Do you have any qualification that allows you to reach that conclusion?

A: Partly.

Q: What is that qualification?

A: I'm an adjunct professor who has been compensated by the University of Houston for the last seven and a half years.

Q: Having taught, that allows you to conclude that Mrs. Khajavi could teach at the present time?

A: I don't understand what you mean by "teach." I don't understand the question.

Q: Are you telling me you don't know what the word "teach" means?

A: I am telling you I know what I mean by "teach." I don't know what you mean by "teach."

Q: Let me ask it this way. Have you ever taken a single course in how to teach? Have you ever even read a textbook on teaching?

A: Twenty-two years ago, Mr. Berg, maybe.

Q: Your answer is that you don't know either way?

A: I'm like Mrs. Khajavi: I don't remember.

Q: How are you like Mrs. Khajavi?

A: Well, she claims to have a loss of memory when it's convenient.

Q: I see. I like it that you have finally told me what you really believe here, and I'm not being facetious. You've told me that you believe that she has a convenient memory loss? That you reject the doctor's findings about memory loss?

A: I am just giving you my opinion as an educator, graduate school educator, and an economist and a citizen of this nation.

* * * *

Q: Given your testimony, why do you think she should be compensated at all?

A: That $24,000 would be what I would consider a dismissal fee so we don't tie up the Judicial District Court forever over matters of a questionable nature.

Q: So what you're saying is that since this lawsuit is, in your mind, hokey, that she's making up her memory loss, she ought to be paid some nuisance value just not to clog up the courts?

A: That is my opinion as a citizen, not as an expert. I do pay taxes in this state and country.

Watch Tim Russert on "Meet the Press." He is one of the best cross-examiners I've ever seen. He knows instinctively when he's gotten all he's going to get from an unresponsive guest. Once his point is made by an admission or, as is more frequently the case, by the guest tap-dancing around the truth, he moves to another subject. I'm not Russert, but I sensed I'd just about milked this witness's testimony dry. There was nothing reliable or relevant about his opinions or how he arrived at them. When I played this excerpt for the jury, opposing counsel confided how strange it was to have a jury laughing three days into a trial about a brain tumor. You will not be surprised to learn this was the same economist I mentioned in an earlier chapter—the one who counted to eight on his fingers.

VI. CROSS-EXAMINATION CHECKLIST

This checklist, like the one for voir dire, is organized chronologically, with the rules within each division listed roughly in order of importance.

A. **The Gateway to All Successful Cross-Examination**
   1. Keep a calm mind.
   2. Listen to every answer.
   3. Know the case cold.

    4. Formulate follow-up.

    5. Never laminate your cross.

    6. Review evidence through trial eyes.

    7. If you don't need to cross, don't cross.

B. **Don't Forget the Jurors (Not Even When Taking Depositions)**

    1. Never bury your lead.

    2. Don't get ahead of jurors emotionally.

    3. Stay under the witness emotionally.

    4. Let jurors know where you're headed next.

    5. Include jurors in your anger and indignation.

    6. Cross *about* documents, not *out* of them.

    7. Keep cross brief; or at least, keep it interesting.

C. **Control unresponsive witnesses.**

    1. Insist on the answer to your question.

    2. Never ignore an unresponsive answer.

    3. Five categories of unresponsive answers

        a. Evasions.

        b. Speeches.

        c. Recasting your questions.

        d. Quibbling.

        e. (Never ignore) Offers to explain.

    4. Enlist the judge.

D. **Breathe Life into Responsive Cross**

    1. Defeat the paradox of responsive answers.

        a. Ask open-ended questions (like "why?").

        b. Ask one too many questions ("seal off the exits").

        c. Befriend adverse witnesses (if you can).

        d. Make cross memorable.

E. **Cross like a Criminal Lawyer ("Blind Cross")**

    1. Cross the whole person.

    2. Take extreme positions to their extremes.

    3. Use gestures and silence.

    4. Ask questions when you don't know the answer.

F. **Gore the Witness When You've Got the Goods**.

    1. Set the stage for prior inconsistent statements.

    2. Ask questions when you know the answers (sometimes).

    3. Demand every document that the witness reviewed.

G. **Build Your Cross around the Expert Pyramid**

    1. Attack the expert's credentials.

    a.   Take the expert on voir dire.

        i.   Never take an expert's resume at face value.

        ii. Show the expert lacks the relevant expertise.

2. Attack the expert's objectivity.

    a.   Spotlight excessive fees.

    b.   Reveal the expert as a captive witness.

3. Attack reliability and relevance.

    a.   Get experts under oath as often as possible.

    b.   Undermine the underpinnings—and the opinion itself.

        i.   Let the air out of subjective determinations.

        ii. Garbage in, garbage out.

        iii. "Would that mine enemy had written a book."

        iv. Nail down every opinion.

APPENDIX A

Table of Daubert *Jurisdictions*

Jurisdiction	Follows *Daubert* or has created similar test.	Continues to follow *Frye*.	Applies *Daubert* factors but has not totally rejected *Frye*.	Has created its own standards.
Federal	X			
Alabama			X	
Alaska	X			
Arizona		X		
Arkansas	X			
California		X		
Colorado	X			
Connecticut	X			
Delaware	X			
District of Columbia		X		
Florida		X		
Georgia				X
Hawaii			X	
Idaho	X			
Illinois		X		
Indiana	X			
Iowa	X			
Kansas		X		
Kentucky	X			
Louisiana	X			
Maine	X			
Maryland		X		
Massachusetts			X	
Michigan		X		
Minnesota		X		
Mississippi		X		
Missouri		X		
Montana	X			

Jurisdiction	Follows *Daubert* or has created similar test.	Continues to follow *Frye*.	Applies *Daubert* factors but has not totally rejected *Frye*.	Has created its own standards.
Nebraska	X			
Nevada			X	
New Hampshire			X	
New Jersey			X	
New Mexico	X			
New York		X		
North Carolina	X			
North Dakota		X		
Ohio	X			
Oklahoma	X			
Oregon	X			
Pennsylvania		X		
Rhode Island	X			
South Carolina	X			
South Dakota	X			
Tennessee	X			
Texas	X			
Utah				X
Vermont	X			
Virginia				X
Washington		X		
West Virginia	X			
Wisconsin				X
Wyoming	X			

Preparing and Presenting Witnesses

7

I. THE IMPORTANCE OF EFFECTIVE WITNESSES

You had a great voir dire. Your opening was charming and persuasive, while opposing counsel's sounded like a Gregorian chant. You are ahead, but you no longer get to tell the story—the witnesses do, a sobering thought for any trial lawyer even casually interested in winning. That is not meant to be snide, but as recognition of an absolutely crucial truth: No matter how well things have gone, no matter how well you have performed, if the jury doesn't believe your client and key witnesses, you will lose.

II. GOALS FOR WITNESSES AND LAWYERS ON DIRECT AND CROSS

The goal of witnesses on direct is to tell their stories as convincingly as possible. Their goal on cross is to advance that story, answering directly and politely, but insisting on the truth of their testimony on direct. By the time your witness steps down, jurors should not only believe her story but also believe *in* it, and that her side deserves to win.

That won't happen without teamwork. If you have established a good relationship with your client and other witnesses, that will influence everyone else in the courtroom. Direct will automatically go better, and your mutual trust will rub off on the jury. Most important, by your comfortable dialogue during direct, the two of you will make an effective cross-examination far less likely.

III. PREPARING WITNESSES (AND LAWYERS) FOR DIRECT

A. *Witnesses*[1]

When a witness testifies badly at trial, there can be a variety of reasons. When she does well, you can be assured of at least one: She was well prepared. That means that every witness you put on the stand must take a trip to the woodshed, no matter how much time you spent preparing her for her deposition, or how well she did when she gave it. The pressure will be far greater testifying before a judge and jury. So find a deserted courtroom and put your witness in the dock. Take command and teach her how to testify.

---

1. To avoid constantly distinguishing between clients and witnesses, I have referred primarily to witnesses in this chapter. Except where indicated, the rules apply equally to each.

1. Put witnesses at ease.

Seasoned lawyers get nervous before trial, so imagine how your clients and their witnesses feel, especially when a great deal is riding on their performance. Take time to put them at ease. Your toughest-talking client will need reassurance that he will do well on the stand.

Put their task into perspective. Tell witnesses that if you boil it all down, testifying is only about one thing: answering questions in a way that satisfies jurors that they are telling the truth. That is different from simply telling the truth which, by itself, is insufficient in a trial. A witness can be honest, but a talented cross-examiner can still make him look like a liar. Or, a witness may be honest, but unconvincing. To be effective, the witnesses must accept that there is more than one way to tell the truth—and that the two of you will find the most credible way to tell it.

At this point, enthusiastic witnesses may be tempted, and so you must make one thing clear: You will never ask them to testify to anything untrue. That may come as a disappointment to some ("Look, I can always say I wasn't even there. . . . "), but you didn't take the case to risk your ticket. So perjury, tell them, is a bad idea.

2. Let them be themselves.

There's a thin line between preparation and over-coaching, and it usually comes at the point at which witnesses cease to sound like themselves. You want the witness to give specific testimony, but you want it delivered by a real person, not a windup doll. In my career, one person stands out as the perfect witness: Robert Sakowitz's regal mother, Ann. Her testimony reminds us that there are things we cannot teach, intangibles that touch jurors deeply if we just let witnesses be themselves.

It was in her kitchen, over meatloaf she made for us, that I learned about her remarkable life. For half a century, her family had been central to Houston's business and cultural growth. Now, a victim of the bust in the oil business in the 1980s, their upscale department stores were first bankrupt, and now, gone.

The lawsuit against her son forced Ann to make a kind of *Sophie's Choice*. She was close to both her children, but her daughter, Lynn Wyatt, had made the lawsuit possible. Lynn transferred her rights as an heir under her father's will to her son, Douglas, who in turn, brought suit against Robert as trustee of his father's estate, for breach of fiduciary duty. The publicity surrounding the suit had harmed Robert immeasurably.

Ann sat next to Robert and his wife during opening arguments. Afterward, the plaintiff's lawyer wisely invoked the rule that requires witnesses to wait outside the court before testifying. When she finally walked back in to testify two weeks later, the courtroom was completely silent. As she sat in the witness chair, I moved my own chair directly between her and the plaintiff's table. I hadn't intended the symbolism, but it did look as if I was protecting her from the other side.

Her story was as riveting to the jury as it had been to me. Ann let them into her world. She told them that she and her late husband wanted Robert to invest outside their family business, that they encouraged the so-called "secret side deals" her grandson claimed were not disclosed. "Bernard [her husband] felt we had run a huge risk, putting all our eggs in one basket—the stores," she said and added with a sly grin, "I guess we were right about that." The jury was smiling, too; Sakowitz Bros. had been in bankruptcy for four years. "We wanted Robert to have more security than that. After all, our daughter was already fixed for life," a welcome reminder of the Wyatt family's wealth. Lynn's husband, Oscar Wyatt, is one of America's richest men. Ann explained that she also served on the Sakowitz board and, along with her daughter and other members, approved each of Robert's "secret" deals. "I love my daughter but she was just too distracted to pay attention."

Cross was a disaster for my talented opponent. He started by trying to demonstrate how generous Lynn and her husband were with Ann. "Didn't they give you $10,000 apiece last year?" he asked. "Yes, and I needed it so much," she replied but, before he could ask another question, she turned to the jury and added, confidentially, "I used it all for legal fees."

The lawyer kept going, this time to show what a good friend Lynn's husband, Oscar, had been to Robert. "Well, wasn't Oscar Wyatt your son's best man at his first wedding?" "Yes," Ann said, and then, as if dying to get something off her chest, added, "But you know, I didn't like that wedding." She waited for the laughter to subside, and then said, "I never liked that daughter-in-law." She smiled at Robert's current wife, seated at counsel's table. "This one, I do." The jury roared.

I think I might have quit were I in opposing counsel's shoes, but he plodded ahead. He wanted Ann to admit that her strained financial condition was Robert's fault. "You need money just to get by now, don't you?" She admitted, "Things are not like they once were." Then, in answer to his next question, Ann acknowledged that she owned a large ranch in East

Texas. "Robert won't let you sell it, will he? He wants to inherit it." Ann looked stunned. The lawyer persisted, "Robert blocked you from selling it, didn't he?" She turned her head toward the jury, tears streaming down her cheeks, answering almost inaudibly, "No, *I* won't sell it. It's all I have left of my husband." There was no reason for redirect.

Jurors later told us that they took 30 minutes to exonerate Robert. They spent the remainder of the time, about three hours, reading and rereading the jury charge to figure out if they could make the plaintiff (Ann's grandson) pay her living expenses. She wasn't even a party to the lawsuit.

Few witnesses are naturals like Ann, and what's more, the basic elements of her credibility can't be taught. Her calm manner and gentle humor put everyone at ease. The emotion she shared was real and she spoke from the heart. She told the truth and was easy to believe. There's rarely a witness who combines all those characteristics. On the other hand, there's rarely a witness who doesn't have some good quality that the jury should see—even the most difficult people you put on the stand.

3.   Dig deep with difficult people.

With difficult people, do your best to teach them to testify, but resist the urge to make them something they are not. Like more natural witnesses, they will do best if you let them be themselves—the jury will understand quirky but honest people. In the *Westinghouse* case, involving the nuclear power plant, I presented a retired vice president, a distinguished nuclear physicist and a member of the National Academy of Sciences. He wasn't greedy. He wasn't unprincipled. He was just old and cranky. For added measure, he hated lawyers. When we practiced his direct, it sounded like cross-examination.

I thought a dozen times about not calling him, but his name had come up too frequently during trial. If I failed to put him on, the jury would have drawn a negative inference from his absence. That, I thought, might actually be preferable to the negative inference they'd draw from his actually being there, but my colleagues prevailed.

Sometimes, we get lucky with witnesses. They inexplicably do better on the stand than during rehearsal, like a basketball team that peaks during the playoffs. Mine, however, did not seem likely to turn in a clutch performance. Once he was sworn and seated, he took pains to scowl, first at the jury, then at me.

However, while he was telling the jury that he studied physics at Princeton in the early 1950s, I remembered something. "Doctor, wasn't Albert Einstein there then?" The scientist looked surprised, probably by the fact that I had actually heard of Einstein. Then, he smiled broadly. "Yes. I met him once. I went over to his house one Sunday with a group of physics students and knocked on his door. His housekeeper checked with Professor Einstein, and he came to the door and let us in. We spent all morning around his kitchen table, eating bagels and talking about the theory of relativity."

The transformation was remarkable. The jury caught a glimpse of the aging scientist as the awestruck student, thrilled to be in Einstein's presence. No matter how brief his meeting had been, it was an encounter he remembered vividly 44 years later. The scientist's story drew them in and, given even that brief encounter, created credibility. After all, how wrong can an expert be about nuclear energy, when he's eaten bagels with Einstein?

By the time I asked him to step down to a model of the power plant to explain its operations, he was ready to teach, and the jury was ready to listen. His commitment to his profession and confidence in his opinions were apparent in everything he said. On cross, he was unshakable. By the time he finished, I had the feeling he was having a good time.

What I took from his testimony was that relationships and experiences that will mean something to jurors sometimes lie buried at the bottom of a witness's memories—and that you have to dig deep to uncover them. Granted, in this case it was an encounter with Einstein. But in others, it's simply been a story about a witness's favorite teacher or coach, the kind of relationship many jurors have experienced themselves, and a way to create common ground.

4.   Explain the essentials of nonverbal communication.

Although witnesses don't need to become experts on nonverbal communication, they must be familiar with a few of the essentials. If it's a problem, teach your witness to look confident. Start by having her walk to the stand, head held high. Once seated, tell her to lean forward, hands folded in front of her. That keeps her from sitting slumped in her seat or making disconcerting gestures, which leave a poor impression.

One question the witness will ask is when to turn to the jury to answer questions. That's critical. She has to appear confident to them, but she won't create that impression if her head is swiveling back and forth with each question, like she's watching a ping-pong game. To get her acclimated, put a couple of colleagues in the box. Tell her to turn to the jury *only* when her answer is significant—to think of it as underlining. As you rehearse her on direct and cross, tell her when you think she should turn. Let her practice until she feels comfortable, and looks natural, turning her head from you to the "jurors" and back again. Insist that she maintain eye contact with them until she finishes her answer completely. Make certain she understands to follow the same procedure while opposing counsel cross-examines her.

It is also important that a witness not appear impetuous, as if nothing asked of her requires thought. Tell her to take time before answering significant questions. Some lawyers advise witnesses to count silently to ten before answering, even when they already know what they are going to say. She can also ask to review any document she's questioned about, to make certain that she has seen it before, and that the lawyer quoted or paraphrased it accurately. Even if it's not entirely necessary for her to review the document before answering, she will appear thoughtful, and serious about being accurate. But warn your witness not to play games. Spending an inordinate amount of time going over a one-paragraph memo that she authored wastes everyone's time and gives the appearance of stalling.

As for clothing, which sends signals all its own, witnesses, as lawyers, should dress conservatively. To me, that means, most often, dark suits and ties for men, and suits or skirts and blouses for women. Although it always seems out of place in a courtroom, I can't argue against a client wearing a flannel shirt and pressed khakis in front of a working class jury. It stands to reason that they will find it easier to identify with him than someone wearing a suit. But don't do that with someone the jurors know doesn't ordinarily wear casual clothes. Flannel shirts and work boots didn't work for Jimmy Carter when he was president, and they won't work for most senior executives either.

Of course, make sure you and your witnesses remove expensive jewelry before trial begins. Think of the calamitous interview given by Linda Lay, wife of former Enron CEO and Chairman of the Board, Ken Lay, on NBC's "Today Show." Her effort to elicit sympathy and to claim near-bankruptcy, while sporting very large diamonds, subjected her to ridicule nationwide.

Nonverbal communication is a two-way street, so you must watch the jury as they are watching the witness. If they believe what she is saying, they will say so with their eyes and relaxed posture. If instead they tense up, look puzzled, or just look away, try to take a break and help her correct whatever is causing the problem. If you can't take a break or are prohibited from talking to the witness about her testimony until counsel passes her, don't worry about faking a heart attack to stop the carnage on the stand. If it's bad enough, you won't have to fake anything.

B. Lawyers

Direct testimony is best when it's a comfortable dialogue between lawyer and witness, and better yet if it doesn't sound rehearsed. Walk her through her story a couple times, but don't overdo it. Once she's on the stand, in the best of all worlds, your role will be muted while the witness tells her story. But, as every trial lawyer knows, that can't always be the case. The following rules address that problem, and the things that you must do to help make a witness credible. The first step is to make her story understandable.

1. Simplify the story.

Good storytellers know that you can occupy center stage too long. If you keep direct short and simple, the impact is greater. Moreover, with less to question, the cross-examination generally is not as effective.

To develop that "short and sweet" direct, you must first give the witness sufficient time to tell you everything—the encyclopedic version of events. Once you are confident you have the full story, ask yourself these questions: When this witness steps down from the stand, what do I want her to have accomplished? What can be accomplished? How can I reach the critical points in her story in the quickest, clearest, and most compelling way possible? When you have these answers, you can amplify the points that matter, eliminate those that don't, and disclose some things the witness did not realize were important.

2. Substitute relationships for details.

Simplifying a witness's story does not mean sacrificing essential facts. If you do, the witness's story, lacking context, won't make sense. However, having said that, there are ways to eliminate a mountain of evidence and, nevertheless, tell the story completely. The more cases I try, the more I believe that you can replace details and documents with stories of relationships. Let me illustrate what I mean.

In the *Sakowitz* case,[2] I spent only a modest amount of time talking to Robert Sakowitz about his family history, especially about his relationship

---

2. See p. 41, note 5, The Sakowitz family tree.

with his dad, and I knew I had a key to winning his case. What he told me explained his "reckless expansion and risk-taking," one of his nephew's major allegations. On the stand, Robert told the jury about the first Sakowitz store, located on the seawall in Galveston, and how it had been destroyed by a devastating hurricane in 1900. Basically broke, his family rallied 'round, moved 45 miles north to Houston, where his grandfather already had opened a small store, and gradually built a merchandising empire. Their history was entwined with Houston's. The jurors, picked to include many longtime residents, were spellbound.

Years later, the Sakowitzes were among the first retailers in the nation to expand into the suburbs, a speculative move at the time. "I was in high school when we opened the Post Oak store. Before dad made a final decision, he and I went out to where the store was going to be located. It was a cow pasture back then. We counted cars for three days, from 9:00 A.M. until 9 P.M.—store hours. I held a counter and clicked off each car." Robert created a word picture about a father and son the jury would not forget—and, important to our case, insight about his dad's business philosophy. "There really wasn't as much traffic as dad would have liked, but he decided to open Post Oak anyway, and it became our most successful store."

By the time he testified about his own decision to expand, following his father's death, Robert sounded anything but reckless. He sounded like his father and grandfather. He had followed the route of the oil boom of the 1970s, expanding into Dallas, Midland, and Tulsa. "Macy's had come to town and they were killing us. We had to expand or we were going out of business. Dad always said that you either grow or die." Risk-taking was in his blood—a necessity to stay alive.

All the while Robert testified, I stood near rows of banker's boxes containing all the financial documents and feasibility studies he'd done prior to making a decision about each new store. Instead of boring the jurors with the details, he pointed to the boxes and generally described what was in them. Knowing his history, the jurors didn't doubt that Robert had "counted the cars" before expanding. "I did my homework," he said, and they obviously believed him, returning a unanimous verdict in his favor.

Stories of relationships—some quite moving—are there to be told in even the most complex commercial cases. They not only simplify presentations but often are the key to making dull or unlikable witnesses better. (See p. 222, "Dig deep with difficult people.")

3. Disappear on direct (when you can).

As with any conversation, there are times in direct testimony when one person will talk more than the other. If possible, the primary talker should be the witness—not you. If your client (or a key witness) is capable of telling the story himself, let him do it. While preparing him to testify, you can suggest a different word here and there, work through difficult answers, remind him of things he's forgotten, and fashion his testimony to reflect the themes of your case. But that's all you should do. If you program his testimony, you will undermine his effectiveness. The courtroom is nerve-wracking enough without his having to edit himself as he testifies, worried that he isn't following your script. Besides, jurors see through overcoached witnesses every time. "His lawyer told him to say that" wafts unspoken over the courtroom with each over-rehearsed answer.

Once the witness is on the stand, guide him through his story with simple, open-ended questions like "What happened next?" and "What are you asking the jury to do?" That invites the client to tell his story—not you. For instance, in a case alleging a doctor's failure to warn of surgical complications, just ask, "What did the surgeon tell you before your operation?" If you ask instead, "Didn't the doctor tell you just before surgery not to worry about the risks that appeared on the consent form, that he had never punctured a bowel, and that wasn't going to happen now?"—you leave jurors wondering why the client bothered to accompany you to court at all. Remember: It was his bowel that got nicked, not yours. There's not a lot to be gained by your suggesting the most critical answers in the case.

Actually, saying little magnifies your role when you do say something, especially if your remarks are accompanied by an occasional display of honest emotion. But make sure it's genuine; there's no place in modern trials for melodrama. Restrained concern in your voice and eyes are the subtle things that move jurors. Overacting is off-putting and can make you look ridiculous.

4. Dominate direct (when you have to).

Sometimes, a witness can't tell the story by himself. The material may be too dense. The witness may be too dense. Other times, the witness may lose focus, making mistakes and testifying without conviction. When that happens, you have to do a little testifying, as they say in Texas, your own self. By summarizing a faltering witness's answers into mini-arguments, asking cleverly worded questions, and using inflection in your voice, you can make his testimony more persuasive.

One of the most memorable directs that I ever saw came in the *Westinghouse* case, conducted by the plaintiff's lead lawyer, Daryl Bristow, of his star witness, a metallurgical engineer. The facts in that case spanned two decades, from the inception of the South Texas Project's (STP's) negotiations for the purchase of a nuclear power plant from Westinghouse in 1971, to the plant's going online (after years of delays) in the late '80s, to the date of trial in '95. There were at least a million pages of documents, including Westinghouse's internal memoranda and the results of its scientific testing. To prove one of STP's main allegations—that Westinghouse misrepresented the life expectancy of the nuclear steam generators—Bristow and the expert, Dr. Singh, had to boil down all those years of difficult science and complex events into bite-sized pieces.

The expert did an excellent job. For a full day he educated the jury about the fundamentals of nuclear science, and kept it interesting. He explained that there were thousands of tubes in the generators and that radioactive water ran through them, creating the power that drove the turbines and created electricity. But he added that those tubes were leaking radioactive water because they were corroding—and that the leaks could not be stopped even by changing the chemistry in the water. That, he concluded, threatened the life span of the steam generators, necessitating their replacement with new ones. If the jury agreed with his assessment, the cost to Westinghouse would be $800 million for the replacement generators and, possibly, some multiple of that amount in punitive damages.

The next day, Bristow took over, making straightforward little speeches interrupted by the occasional question—downloading the nuclear science to English. Even then, very few people in that courtroom could have understood it all. That's where Bristow's sincerity and gravity made so much difference. At one point a young associate leaned over and whined, "Can't you make him stop?" Actually, we couldn't. Because Bristow was nearing the end, the judge had quit sustaining any objections. Here is one brief example of the direct:

Q: Dr. Singh, I want you to assume with me that in 1973, in the effort to sell its steam generators and a nuclear power system to the South Texas Project, Westinghouse represented to [STP] that the cause of failures in other nuclear steam generators it had sold had been determined.

And Westinghouse represented that after a careful investigation by its engineers and scientists, they had concluded that the cause of those prior failures was poor water chemistry in the tubes, and that all you had to do was use the proper chemical compounds in the right amount, and there would be no tube failures.

Tell me, first, based on your review of Westinghouse's internal documentation, is there scientific documentation to support those statements?

A: No, sir, there isn't.

Q: Is the documentation within Westinghouse inconsistent with those statements?

A: Yes, sir, it is.

Q: Now, if Westinghouse puts in writing internally in this report from its investigative committee that there's no way to determine the cause of those leaks in the steam generators, what justification can there be technically for a public statement that the chemistry control prevents leaks?

A: I can't see any.

Q: Look at Exhibit 51, Westinghouse's internal report on the investigation we were just talking about. It goes on to say, "The technology regarding steam generator leaks is not well enough understood to be stated in the specification." If that is the state of affairs for the steam generator Westinghouse sold to the nuclear project, would you tell me where it was at that time in terms of its being a commercially acceptable product?

A: Well, this indicates to me that the product was in a state of grave uncertainty.

That went on for about two hours. Singh disappeared into the scenery as Bristow organized a potentially rambling presentation into a fluid, convincing performance. Even using two dozen documents and charts, there was barely a pause between Bristow's questions and Singh's (brief) answers— nothing to break the momentum. Although it seemed anything but rehearsed, it was clear to the lawyers that the two men had spent a great deal of time making the testimony go smoothly. It was a four-star performance and you could hear the "attaboys" from across the courtroom when Singh stepped down from the stand. Yet, there is something to be said for ignoring those glowing, early reviews. Singh still had to be cross-examined, about which, more will be said. (See p. 243, "The most dangerous point in every trial.")

5. Humanize witnesses.

As soon as the witness begins testifying, develop those things about their personal lives calculated to turn the stranger on the stand into a real person that the jurors can identify with and believe. If she lights up talking about her family, or the Little League team she coaches, or some special experience in her life, like that cranky nuclear physicist's breakfast with Einstein, the jury needs to see that, too. Developing that the CEO of a Fortune 500 company loves fishing with his granddaughter may not strike you as relevant, but it is important that you get it in. If you marry the CEO's sense of devotion to his family to the way he runs his company, the case will take a decidedly humane turn. Moreover, while the jury gets to know him, the witness can get comfortable talking about the things that matter most to him. How can you make such personal information relevant? And not be obvious? Some judges will just allow it. In less generous courts information like that can come in as part of the witness's story about the case itself. For instance, that CEO may have missed an important meeting. Asked why he didn't attend, it may be that he took his granddaughter fishing on her birthday.

To the extent possible, develop the witness's history chronologically, weaving what might otherwise be disjointed data points into a more interesting story. "My wife and I were classmates in college. That's where I met her. We got married the year we graduated. That was '75. Then, we had our first child in '78, the year before I graduated medical school." If he's been married a long time or has worked at the same job for years, emphasize the point. Stability translates into credibility—even with jurors who aren't stable themselves. There's something innately trustworthy about a guy who sticks.

It is unlikely that you can learn the little things about clients and key witnesses that make such a big difference with jurors—unless you spend some time relaxing with them over dinner or drinks. (See p. 10, "Get to Know the Clients.") They don't always know what about their lives will matter in trial, and there's no better time to pull it out of them than when you're away from the office. Often, an opportunity to humanize a witness will fall into your lap. In the trial involving the sports agent Eric Fleisher, opposing counsel was reading into the record the deposition of a basketball player who terminated Fleisher's agency, to show the player wanted to leave, as opposed to our allegation that he'd been solicited improperly to join a new sports agency. However, when the lawyer hit some testimony that humanized my client, he skipped over it. I objected immediately and was allowed to read the remainder of the colloquy. In it, the player mentioned how much he missed playing one-on-one with Eric and his sons in the Fleishers' back yard. The "litigant" I represented suddenly became a real-life father—and an agent who included his players in his family life. And the player, rather than fleeing Eric as the defendants insisted, missed him, instead.

There are opportunities like that in every trial if you are alert to them. They transform hard-driving executives like Eric Fleisher into regular guys. They also surprise jurors by showing them the ordinary things in the lives of others, no matter how rich or successful, that mirror their own—common ground that closes the gap.

6. Humanize unpopular witnesses.

Humanizing witnesses usually is not difficult. Sometimes, however, your client will have been demonized—pilloried daily in the press and on TV. Sometimes, he will have deserved it, and sometimes, not. In either event, if you can show that the vilified client has good qualities, the shock value can help turn the tide, or at least help to hold it back. For example, given the press he received, you wouldn't think Ken Lay, former board chairman and CEO of Enron, would have a prayer with any jury, civil or criminal. But I know from living in Houston that, should he ever stand trial, his personal story could change the outcome. His lawyers would almost certainly develop testimony along these lines:

Q: What is your relationship with the NAACP?

A: I have been a supporter for some time.

Q: Can you be more specific?

A: In '91, Howard Jefferson, the president of the local chapter, came to see me with a problem. He needed $250,000 to bring the national convention to Houston. They were broke. So we underwrote it at Enron.

Q: Who approved the contribution?

A: I did.

Q: What was your position at the time?

A: I was president and CEO of Enron.

Q: Did you take it to your board?

A: Yes. But reluctantly.

Q: Why?

A: They were always too concerned about the money. They always fought me when I put up money for charitable events.

Q: How much did Enron finally put up?

A: The full amount—$250,000.

Q: And you? How much did you put up out of your own pocket?

A $25,000.

Q: Did you do anything else? Did you send out a fund-raising letter?

A: Yes, and Howard and I spent hours on the phone, following up.

Q: Did it cause you problems with the board?

A: Yes. But so what? The business was doing great.

Q: So, Enron was Ken Lay's company back then?

A: Absolutely. Back *then*. Then, things changed.

With such testimony, Lay would merge his values with "his" Enron, and in turn, foreshadow the defense that he had lost control of the company by the time dishonest or inept decisions were made.

I can think of several arguments that would get this sort of testimony admitted, but even if not, consider the impact on the jury if all you were allowed to develop was that he received the NAACP's Humanitarian Award. With Houston's diverse population the jury would be comprised of at least 25 to 30 percent minorities, if not more. That would create some loyal jurors, especially among African-Americans. Maybe that's oversimplified; maybe his friends on the jury would turn against him if they heard stories of personal corruption. But Lay, who apparently was nice to people on the way up, will get help in a trial, on the way back down.

7. Pull the teeth out of cross.

No one with trial experience doubts the wisdom of pulling the teeth out of an opponent's cross. By asking your own witness your adversary's best questions, you can minimize the impact of cross-examination, or defuse it altogether. If you fail to ask the hard questions first, when you had the opportunity, the result can be disastrous. When he's cross-examined, jurors will feel shocked by the revelation of his bad behavior and betrayed by your silence on the subject. You also leave your witness open to needless humiliation: "Let's see. You just testified for two hours on direct. Yet, neither you nor your lawyer mentioned this letter that you wrote about the pipeline. . . . There's a reason you didn't bring it up, isn't there?" It isn't the letter itself that will do your witness in—it is your failure to cushion the blow.

No matter how effective anticipating cross is, I know from experience that it is difficult psychologically to bring up issues that could prove fatal to your chances. Yet that is exactly what you must do in every case—bring them up, embrace them, or credibly explain them away. In that regard, let me offer a rash suggestion: Ask the witness what happened, and why he said or did whatever it was. The truth often is not so bad, and it may be something a jury can excuse—like a lie told under pressure, something each of them has done themselves. It still surprises me just how much bad behavior jurors are willing to forgive—if the witness is candid.

The best example I know of that sort of "defanging" came in a breach-of-contract case against Tenneco in the early 1990s. Apparently, the plaintiff lied throughout his deposition. Houston personal injury specialist John O'Quinn inherited the case after the depositions were taken. Toward the end of his client's direct, O'Quinn asked if he agreed that his deposition was awful. The client agreed that it was. "Some of your answers were ridiculous. Totally unbelievable. What were you thinking to say such stupid things?" The witness said he wasn't thinking, that he was just mad about the way the defense lawyer was treating him that day.

At that point O'Quinn passed his client and wished him well. Smiling broadly, he added, "This is going to be a bumpy ride. Nobody cross-examines better than Mr. Milam. Good luck." Then, every time Mr. Milam pulled out the witness's deposition to impeach him, the plaintiff grinned sheepishly and said something like, "You don't need to read it to the jury. I said the opposite during my deposition. I just wasn't telling the truth." There is pretty good evidence that the plaintiff persuaded the jury his repentance was genuine. Maybe I'm jumping to conclusions, but a $625-million verdict in his favor sounds a lot like forgiveness to me.

Granted, this case is an extreme example. The teeth you have to pull on direct are seldom that sharp. Nonetheless, if it takes pointing out your own client's dishonesty to clear the air, you have to do it.

8. Don't overreact.

As crucial as it is to defuse an opponent's best cross, you can overdo it. For instance, you can pull the teeth on a cross that never even occurred to your adversary—at least until she heard your questions. Or you can come across as too defensive, rather than simply explaining a weakness. Or you can explain to the point of straining credibility. On that point, let me offer a little confession.

In 1969, I tried one of my first cases, a misdemeanor DWI. The defendant was my secretary's father. After discussing the events surrounding his arrest, I concluded that a series of physical ailments explained his uncanny resemblance that night to a falling-down drunk.

Once on the stand, my client did just fine as he wended his way through painful bunions and loose dentures. It was while explaining his inability to touch his finger to his nose during the field sobriety test that the defense seemed to unravel. He explained that he had lost his eye in combat during World War II. As he was relating the story—I believe he was about a third of the way up Omaha Beach at the time—he pulled a handkerchief from his pocket, popped his glass eye out its socket, and then watched sullenly as it squirted a foot and a half onto the floor, slowly rolling to a stop near my feet. Even now, I cannot forget the way that eyeball looked, staring up accusingly at me.

I'm always preaching about including jurors in everything, but this was not exactly what I have in mind. Their own eyes, all twelve of them, were locked in what could only be described as a fixed stare. The most compassionate judge in the courthouse, Joe Guarino, slapped his hand over his mouth, whirled around in his chair, and faced the wall. There, despite his best efforts to stifle it, he could be heard laughing, one might say, convulsively.

Later, her father safely convicted and on probation, the defendant's daughter explained that popping out his eyeball was one of her dad's favorite conversation starters. From then on, I made it a point not to over-explain, and to this day I caution witnesses against impromptu demonstrations, especially if they wear prosthetic devices.

9. Ask questions the witness doesn't know are coming.

As you approach the end of direct, ask witnesses questions that are calculated to touch them deeply—but don't tell them in advance that is what you are going to do. Learn to cull those questions from casual comments they make about the case, and to make mental notes of what they've said without acknowledging the importance. You will know when they have revealed something about themselves that a jury should hear.

The easiest example is in a wrongful death case, where the testimony of the widow is almost too painful to hear. At the end of her testimony, ask her, "What is life like now, with your husband gone?" or even more specifically, "I know the two of you loved fishing. Do you take your boat out any more?" Remembering, her change of expression alone will convey volumes. Jurors are often left crying. It also puts your adversary in the unenviable position of beginning cross at the worst conceivable time—when the plaintiff's case has reached an emotional peak.

It's a lot harder to create emotion in a commercial case, which makes it all the more powerful when you do: No one will see it coming. Not only that, but it also shows jurors that your client is not there just for the money, an impression you must avoid in any kind of case, but certainly in commercial litigation.

In the *Samsung* case, my client alleged that Texas Instruments charged its Japanese competitors less for microchips than it charged Samsung, in violation of the agreement between the two companies. (See p. 136, "Analogize.") That provision, commonly referred to as a most favored nation (MFN) clause, was critical to Samsung. Its executives would never have approved an agreement that allowed a Japanese company to be treated better than its own—based on Japan's historical treatment of the Korean people. That explained to me why Samsung's patent counsel was so angry about the breach. The deal was his baby. He had vouched for TI's integrity. When I asked him on the stand about the negotiations leading to the agreement, I realized from the way he spoke and how animated he'd become that it was time to ask him some questions that he didn't know were coming:

Q: Do recall the point at which you finally reached agreement?

A: Yes, we were in a conference room at the Willard Hotel in Washington. It was after midnight and TI finally agreed to the most favored nation clause.

Q: You had reached an agreement?

A: Yes. Ted Wilson [TI's corporate rep] and I shook hands. Then we had a glass of wine to celebrate and everyone went home.

Q: You've told us about how difficult it was to negotiate the MFN, how important it was to your bosses in Korea. Can you remember where you were when you first learned TI had reneged on the deal?

A: I know exactly where I was. I was at my desk in Washington. I had just come back from a trip to Korea. I hadn't even opened my mail yet.

Q: How did you find out?

A: A guy in the accounting department just ran some numbers he found in a TI filing with the SEC. It was right there.

Q: You'd just been to the home office in Seoul?

A: Yes.

Q: So, your bosses must have been very much on your mind when you heard?

A: I couldn't believe it. I knew they were going to be very upset.

Q: How'd you feel?

A: Awful. I felt sucker-punched. And I dreaded telling my bosses in Korea because I was the one who got the company into the deal.

Recalling the moment brought back the emotion the jury needed to see. Every juror worked for someone else; each could identify with his concern about telling his bosses. Still, it was necessary to explain why the witness was *that* upset, lest they wonder why a grown man was so moved by the price of Dynamic Random Access Memory chips:

A: I have known Ted Wilson [TI's corporate rep] for years, mainly from patent law circles. We were good friends. Our families even took a vacation together once. I really trusted him. But looking back, I don't think he ever intended to honor this agreement. I don't think TI would let him. They just didn't think Samsung would find out.

Developing that theme was certain to have a greater effect than a purely commercial argument. The case, which started out being about the difference in prices TI charged to the Japanese companies and those charged to Samsung, ended up primarily about the relationship between the two men. That testimony created the emotional climate we needed to get an excellent settlement.

The testimony of a genuinely surprised witness can be very moving, even if the subject matter is a (mind-numbing) most favored nation clause. However, ask questions about matters that you are certain the witness cares about, and be doubly certain you know what the answer will be. Otherwise, there's always the potential for the startled widow to respond that she likes it just fine with Henry dead, since it's easier to date with him gone. But that's rare.

10. Tailor testimony (but rarely).

During opening and closing arguments, you are in control of what is said. You can fine-tune an argument so that it subtly appeals to a particular juror without that juror or any other realizing what you are doing. Trying to tailor a witness's testimony is far different. You can rehearse a witness's response over and over, but once she's on the stand, the answer may not come out as you planned. I am always mindful of a story about a client of Joe Jamail's, who was dumber, as they say, than a bucket of hair. Joe told him that when he took the stand, he would be asked four questions, and that the answer to each was "yes." He did fine on the first three, but when he got to the fourth, he stared blankly at Jamail for quite some time, and finally said, "I don't understand the question."

Even with a more nimble witness, the risk is great that tailored testimony will appear patronizing or obsequious. Use the tactic rarely, only when you have facts unique to your client and a particular juror—so much so that you'd be foolish not to bring them up. If you do decide that there is a juror you want to reach, help your witness introduce the facts in a subtle, if not offhand way.

Years ago, I tried a criminal case in rural Texas. The best we could hope for was a hung jury. There were two African-Americans on the jury, one of them a graduate of Prairie View A&M, a local black college. That juror seemed our best candidate to hang it. My client, a white, conservative businessman, had served on Prairie View's Board of Regents, and helped nurse the college through rough times. In developing his background, I asked him to tell us about his volunteer work. He mentioned in passing that he had served on the board at Prairie View A&M—and didn't mention it again. Not just the graduate, but both African-American jurors responded, with surprised smiles. The lesson is plain: If you make an appeal to a juror, choose one that is strong enough to make a difference in the verdict. And make certain the appeal you make matters to that person. In fact, you must try to identify and relate to the jury's leaders throughout the trial. (See p. 148, "Appeal to the leaders."; see also p. 276, "Tailor arguments to the leaders.") In my experience, there will be clues large and small who they are.

Often, the leaders are the ones who question the judge and bailiff about scheduling during trial, because they are asked to do so by their fellow jurors. In jurisdictions where the jury is allowed to separate during breaks, they often lead several of the jurors to lunch or coffee. Sometimes, you will notice a juror who just appears self-assured—a quality you can spot even if you never hear her speak. Some people strut sitting down.

Once you have a good idea of who the leaders are, try to determine where they stand. Are they for you? Against you? Undecided? If you have (discreetly) observed them during trial, you should be able to answer some essential questions: How do the jurors react when you are on your feet? Love you? Hate you? What do your colleagues think? Same questions about your opponent.

How do they respond to critical testimony? Do they relax after the witness explains a crucial fact, satisfied with the answer? Or are they as puzzled or unhappy as before?

Sound like an idle exercise? Not at all. Knowing where you stand pays off at every stage of trial, but especially when your opponent starts talking settlement.

C. Experts.

Everything you need to impress on fact witnesses about testifying applies doubly to experts. If you don't take control of your relationship from day one, they are the ones most likely to harm your case. And, as they are sinking your boat by being argumentative on the stand, you get to overpay for the experience.

1. Experts must cooperate.

If an expert won't agree in advance to give you the time you need to get him ready, or tells you that he doesn't need any help, retain someone else. Even when he agrees to cooperate, stay vigilant. Remind him of that agreement before depositions and prior to trial. If he becomes unresponsive or arrogant on the stand, and if you are allowed to talk to him before cross is over, tell him at the first break that he is ruining your client's chances. Every once in a while, that may actually work.

2. Experts must communicate.

In an age of complex litigation, you must help your expert convert the most esoteric principles to everyday language, or find one who can do it on his own. That is never truer than in science-laden intellectual property cases.

In 1998, I defended Samsung in a patent infringement suit, brought by a physicist who claimed the company was using his "discovery" in the manufacture of laptop computer screens—a billion-dollar-a-year line of business to my client that he sought to shut down. The language of the plaintiff's patent was turgid, but basically, it set out the level of impurities the million-plus transistors in laptop computer screens can tolerate before the transmission deteriorates, and the picture becomes blurry.

We felt certain Samsung could defeat the claim. We had any number of experts who could beat back the challenge—were the jury made up of say, 12 solid-state physicists who spoke as they did, which is to say, with all due respect, unintelligibly, except to one another.

Luckily for us, prior to demanding that Samsung license his patent, the plaintiff had made the same demand on IBM, which also turned him down. While at IBM, he met with Dr. Bernie Meyerson, a brilliant solid-state physicist, and more important to us, the same Dr. Meyerson who taught "Physics for Poets" to nursing students at City College of New York (CCNY) before joining the company. All I had to hear was the name of the course, and I knew that we had our lead witness for an upcoming evidentiary hearing. It was important to us to convince the judge how obvious the scientist's "discovery" was to anyone in that field, and, therefore, why our "prior-art" (virtually identical findings about impurity levels published years before the plaintiff's "discovery"), should invalidate his patent. Enter Dr. Meyerson, who testified, right off the bat, "When you were a kid, your mother would tell you, 'Don't put dirt in your food.' Why would you want to eat food with dirt in it? It would taste awful. It's the same with transistors. Too high a level of impurities—they don't work right." Citing Dr. Meyerson's testimony (albeit without referring to the dirt-in-the-food analogy), the judge invalidated the patent and threw out the case.

Of course, at some point, you must introduce the scientific evidence, no matter how complex, to have a complete record. But Dr. Meyerson's testimony is a great example of reducing complex scientific principles to a memorable example in everyday language. The closer to home those analogies—references to dirt in food and mothers—the more likely they are to make a lasting impression on jurors. If our case had gone to trial, I feel certain that the jurors would have loved Dr. Meyerson's plainspoken ways.

3. Experts must not advocate.

Given the widespread skepticism about expert testimony, you'd think they would do all they can to establish their own objectivity and to earn the jurors' trust. But once on the stand, experts often lapse into advocacy—a terrible mistake when they confront trial lawyers who know how to cross-examine. (See p. 195, "Cross-Examining Experts.")

There's nothing novel about their tactics. Experts try to lose the lawyer in a hail of scientific or technical razzle-dazzle, defaulting into the language of their specialty. If the lawyer is prepared to fight it out on the witness's own turf, the only thing the expert will lose is the jury. Sometimes experts refuse to answer a hypothetical to demonstrate their contempt for the (silly) question—and the lawyer. That is, until the expert is forced to answer, either by further questioning ("Humor me, doctor. Answer the question.") or by the judge's order. But most frequently, the expert as advocate answers unasked questions—rambling on until she is impeached. Even then, there's no assurance that she will stop.

Why experts do these things is beyond me. To overcome the jurors' skepticism, all they have to do is answer questions directly—and to admit the obvious, no matter where it leads: "Of course, if my assumption about the water chemistry is wrong, my opinion would be wrong. However, if I may, let me explain why I believe it is correct." Yet experts fight with you even when you are killing them, oblivious to the damage they do to their side of the case.

That doesn't mean that experts should be pushovers. As any witness, they must insist on the truth of their testimony when challenged. If the examiner's hypothetical truly is irrelevant, the expert can point out why— but still try to answer the question. If the witness is pushed, he can push back. But in explaining all that to the expert, emphasize as strongly as you can that he is not there to argue the case. As I recall, and the jury understands, that is your job, not his.

IV. PREPARING WITNESSES FOR CROSS-EXAMINATION.

A. Witnesses Should Do More Than Survive

Most witnesses justifiably dread cross-examination.[3] They must run a gauntlet of difficult questions, answer in a way that satisfies jurors that they

---

3. The rules for preparing a witness for cross-examination apply equally to preparing a witness for deposition. For that reason, I have not written a separate section on deposition preparation. There are, however, a few special considerations that apply only when the deposition is videotaped. At the risk of redundancy, let me emphasize: Unlike a deposition with no camera present, there is nothing you can do to undo the damage captured on tape. If your witness comes across poorly, you can be sure you will see some part of her lousy performance again—at trial, with the jury as the audience, either as impeachment or, when the rules allow, during your opponent's case in chief. To avert disaster, remind her that her only audience is that judge and jury who may be at the other

are telling the truth, and do so in an unfamiliar setting governed by rules of evidence they don't understand. As a result, they sometimes feel helpless—completely at the mercy of the cross-examiner.

Allay your witness's concerns. Tell him that opposing counsel is worried about the same thing—that she won't be able to control *him* on cross. Add that the lawyer has good reason to worry—that you are going to teach him how to answer in a way that insulates him from a brutal cross. By learning to avoid the common traps that destroy credibility—really, just a handful of commonsense rules—he will do more than just survive her cross. He may well triumph, and if not, tell him that he will still do just fine.

1. Rehearsal should be rough.

Ultimately, after a practice session, you have to be reassuring. At the end of day, I hope you can honestly tell the witness that he did well. But rehearsing on cross is no time to be nice. You don't want him to be humiliated in the courtroom because you pulled punches. So, make rehearsal as rough as possible. Figure out your opponent's best cross. Add in the questions that she'd ask if she knew everything that you do. Then, cross-examine your witness as if he were your own worst enemy, never hesitating to impeach him if he gives an evasive or incorrect answer. Hopefully, the real cross will come as a relief.

2. Witnesses must know their part of the case.

If one of your witnesses shows up unprepared, tell him the jury won't trust him. Demonstrate why. Tear his testimony apart. Go over the

---

end of that lens one day. Tell her to dress conservatively, sit still, and, when an answer is important, to underline it—by looking straight into the camera while answering. (See p. 223, "Explain the essentials of nonverbal communication.") Most important, remind her to remain even-tempered, critical advice that applies throughout her testimony, but always on cross. If she is hostile toward opposing counsel, that will cause *serious* damage, especially on tape. Finally, warn her that she must never grimace, roll her eyes, or look toward you for an answer, which destroys credibility. She should look only at the questioner or the camera. (See p. 245, "Witnesses are on their own on cross.") There are some steps you must take at the deposition to make certain that your witness sounds *and* looks credible. Before the deposition begins, remove everything from in front of her—no cigarettes, coffee, or candy. Place a dark curtain behind her, to make certain the imagery is serious, and that she doesn't wash out against a light wall or Venetian blinds. Check the way she looks through the videographer's lens before you begin, and check her on the monitor throughout. If you need to take a break to make an adjustment, especially if her eyes are wandering or she appears fidgety, take it.

relevant documents and deposition testimony that you've sent him (or should have) until he "gets it." Like you, the more knowledgeable the witness, the better he will perform.

Because the "last live pleadings," the parties' final allegations and defenses, might not appear as important as deposition testimony and documents, you must make certain to review them with your witness. Parties and experts especially must know them cold. Parties, because they are asking a lot of the jury. If they don't know what they are asking the jury to do, or why, or if they contradict their own allegations or defenses while on the stand, they look awful. ("So you disagree with your own lawyer?") Experts, because their role is to opine about the essential allegations and defenses raised by the pleadings. Those opinions won't be worth much to jurors if the expert isn't familiar with what they are. ("Well, doctor, would you be surprised to learn that the man who hired you doesn't agree with your assumption?")

3. Witnesses must answer directly.

The human mind needs direct answers to be satisfied that they are honest ones, especially when they come from a stranger sitting on the stand. In court or out, an evasive answer is a dead giveaway of deceit. Out of court, people might get away with it. In court, with a good cross-examiner, it is a disaster.

To be effective during cross, witnesses must listen carefully to every question. Then, if the question is clear and doesn't contain unfair assumptions, the witness should answer "yes," "no," "I don't know," or whatever he must say to be straightforward, honest—and succinct. Only after such a response should the witness offer to explain his answer—and then, only sparingly. Done in reverse, explaining before answering directly, the witness will sound evasive.

The problem is that talented trial lawyers can make even innocent evasions sound like the cover-up of some awful truth. Recall that hypothetical exchange in the chapter on cross-examination[4] in which the defendant, Mr. Jones, was asked if he negotiated a contract, and answered, instead, that he was tricked into signing it. By not answering directly, Mr. Jones made himself an easy target on cross. But what if he *was* telling the truth? What if he was tricked? To avoid the impeachment, all he had to do was to admit that he negotiated the contract. Instead, he appeared to have something to hide when he really didn't. Moreover, had he answered directly first, he would

---

4. See p. 170, "Evasions."

created the kind of latitude that would have allowed him to explain why he felt that he'd been tricked.

Answering directly is a simple formula for successful testimony. Even people who don't answer that way naturally can be trained to get in the habit. Try the old trick of asking your witness if he has a watch. When he responds, "It's 2:30," tell him that if you wanted to know the time, you'd have asked him *that* question. It may be old hat to you but it gets their attention every time. During rehearsal, each time the witness fails to respond directly to your question, slam your hand down hard. Tell him that you didn't ask him what time it was. Most witnesses catch on real fast.

As beneficial as it is for witnesses to be direct, they are coached all the time to make the lawyer "work for every answer," a practice mostly of defense counsel, whose clients generally have more to hide. If the case settles, and the plaintiff's lawyer was unable to ferret out the right answers during depositions, the strategy works. If the plaintiff's lawyer is any good at all, it won't. The more cross is like pulling eyeteeth, the longer it takes to get the truth, the worse the witness does. Moreover, if the case goes to trial, when the witness smugly explains why he didn't give the answer during his depo that he's just given on direct ("You didn't ask me *that* question at my deposition")—talented trial counsel will whip out the depo and quickly demonstrate *that* question, or a similar one, was asked. The witness's arrogance and game-playing look awful to the jury. On the other hand, direct, succinct answers during depositions and at trial create little fodder for cross and insulate the witness from brutal questioning.

4. The most dangerous point in every trial.

The most dangerous point in any trial is when you pass a witness from direct to cross. If the witness suddenly changes his demeanor from cooperative and straightforward to angry and unresponsive, the jury will hate him. Following direct, jurors want answers. The examiner is trying to get those answers, and out of fairness, jurors think he—and they—ought to have them. Only the suddenly petulant witness stands in the way. The unprovoked switch from being amiable to having a chip on his shoulder tells the jury that the witness hasn't been telling the truth.

Nor is it just jurors who get angry at the sudden change. Like all people, judges, too, value consistency and cooperation, which is another reason why this point in the trial is so dangerous. When the judge sustains an objection for unresponsiveness, and orders the witness to "just answer the question," her tone of voice alone can convey a verdict on his credibility.

The phenomenon of the chameleon witness is well-known to trial lawyers. It happens in every trial and jurors are turned off by it every time. Which brings us back to the South Texas Nuclear Project's star witness, Dr. Singh. (See p. 227, "Dominate direct (when you have to).") The minute Bristow passed him, he changed. He was no longer the evenhanded scientist. He suddenly became an angry advocate. Jim Quinn crossed him.

> Q: Dr. Singh, you just admitted you have been paid $650,000 for your testimony. Did you just say that amount of money doesn't mean much to you? Come on, you didn't say *that*, did you?
>
> A: I said that my business sometimes does that much in a single day.
>
> Q: I understand. But didn't you mean to say by that you couldn't be influenced in your testimony by the money you were being paid, that it really wasn't that much to you?
>
> A: That's right. That is a drop in the bucket.

Singh answered flippantly for the most part of an hour. Then, there was this exchange:

> Q: Dr. Singh, you are here criticizing scientific conclusions Westinghouse reached 20 years ago. Is it possible that 20 years from now someone could prove what you are saying to be wrong?
>
> A: Not in 20 years, not in 200 years, not in 2,000 years.

On redirect, Bristow did exactly what he should have. He immediately lit into his own witness, "Dr. Singh, why did you say you thought you could never be wrong about your conclusions, not for 2,000 years or whatever it was?" The answer the witness was supposed to give, one imagines, was, "I apologize for the way I answered that, but I feel strongly about this issue. Of course I could be wrong in 20 years or two years. I just don't believe so." However, what he did say was, "Because I am right." The jurors told us that an hour into the expert's cross, they hated him.

Sometimes, it doesn't even take a dazzling cross to demonstrate that a witness is not being straightforward. Very little escapes jurors, especially not witnesses who forget where they are—and who's watching them. I learned that years ago in a case in which I conducted not one, but two distinct cross-examinations of the same witness, the first of which was the worst in the history of western civilization. Unable to pin him down, the witness ran all over me—stomped me like a vat of Italian grapes for about an hour, until the judge recessed for the day. I spent a sleepless night plotting my comeback. The next morning, I pinned the witness down, impeached him several times, and having avenged my poor performance, passed him. After the trial, however, the jurors told me that they hated the witness from the start of my cross-examination. "He would answer his lawyer like this," one of them said, snapping his fingers, "but he wouldn't give you a direct answer to anything."

Although that comment was reassuring—I felt awful about my first cross—I'm not suggesting you take a free pass on impeaching unresponsive witnesses. You can't depend on all jurors to have that much insight. But what they said has stuck with me all these years. When a witness is genuinely unresponsive, keep working relentlessly to impeach him. You'll have plenty of people—jurors and judges alike—pulling for you to pin him down.

5. Witnesses are on their own on cross.

Your witness must *never* look at you for an answer during cross-examination. In an instant, he will go from witness to puppet. Justifiably, your opponent will point it out: "Mr. Jones, rather than look at Mr. Berg every time I ask a question, would you rather have him sworn in?" The only two places that he should look while answering are at the lawyer who asked the question, or at the jury.

6. Being honest doesn't mean being passive.

Being honest doesn't mean a witness must be passive, absorbing body blows without fighting back. If a lawyer tries to put words in her mouth, makes unfair assumptions in his questions, or misstates her prior testimony, she can point out the errors. During rehearsal, ask her a couple of trick questions: "What part of the prospectus did you find misleading?" Encourage her to stand her ground: "I never received the prospectus. My broker recommended that I make the investment. I have told you that several times." Nor should a witness (or you) put up with unwarranted impeachment.[5] If counsel misstates her prior statement, she should feel free to insist "that's not what I said." Correcting a lawyer about a significant matter takes a toll, often leaving him subdued, concerned about being embarrassed again. However, tell witnesses to be careful about correcting a lawyer. His mistakes have to be serious and the misrepresentations, real. If not, the witness will appear petty. I can still remember a client of mine telling opposing counsel that he had misspelled an architect's name on a chart. "Earle has an 'e' on the end of it. Or didn't you bother to read his

---

5. See p. 257, "Make Objections That Matter."

signature?" I can't remember the relevance. But I remember the case, and the name, Earle, with an "e" on the end, a decade later.

B. Witnesses Should Be Opportunists

Good witnesses, like good lawyers, should pounce on every reasonable opportunity they get to tell their story. They just have to be patient—never volunteering a persuasive little speech until it's invited.

1. Adverse witnesses must get the defendant's story told.

By definition, it is the defendant's witnesses, and not the plaintiff's, who get called adverse, 99 percent of the time. By the time the plaintiff rests, the defense is lucky to have any significant witnesses of its own to call, much less adverse ones. Smart plaintiffs lawyers will have called all of them adverse during their own case, and, of course, all of their own witnesses who really matter.

Being called adverse can put defense witnesses at a huge disadvantage. They don't get a chance to get comfortable on the stand or to warm up the jury, by answering friendly questions from a friendly lawyer. Instead, they get cross-examined immediately about the worst facts in the case. That's a tough way to start. By the time the defense lawyer asks them a single question, their credibility can be shot.

On the other hand, adverse witnesses, as other witnesses on cross, aren't punching bags. The rules of engagement are the same. They should be direct and polite, but they should also insist on the truth of their testimony and correct any mistakes or false assumptions in counsel's questions. Most important, they should lie in wait, unleashing the defendant's story the first time the plaintiff's lawyer asks an overbroad question.

Once the plaintiff's lawyer passes the witness (for your direct examination), you must make a decision: Do you do direct right then and there? Or do you reserve your questions and call the witness back during your case-in-chief? Many defense lawyers will disagree, but I think it's a mistake to wait. In the first place, if your witness has done well on adverse cross, you can bet she will do even better on direct, and just fine during whatever re-cross your questions generate. Developing the defense story uninterrupted, immediately after her good showing on adverse cross, creates the kind of momentum that it takes to win. The plaintiff will be put on the defensive, recovering from the damage rather than running up the score. However, if you wait to put her on during your case, which can be days or weeks, you break that momentum and give the plaintiff time to recover. "Never," said the noted philosopher W. C. Fields, "give a sucker an even break."

Even when your witness does badly during adverse cross, immediately developing her direct will be your best strategy for overcoming the damage she's done, before her bad impression sets like concrete. She may even tell her story well. But, in my experience, once a bad witness, always a bad witness, an even more compelling reason to get her testimony over with. Calling her back during your case-in-chief will only remind jurors of her earlier, bad testimony—even if she miraculously does well. So, when your opponent completes his cross, do her direct, get her off the stand, and out of the courthouse. The passage of time and other witnesses are your strongest allies for reversing the harm she's done to your case—not her second trip to the stand.

2. All witnesses must lie in wait.

Actually, the advice for adverse witnesses to lie in wait for overbroad questions applies to all witnesses during cross. Sooner or later, trial lawyers, no matter how good they are, get going and "open the door" to an unwanted answer. In fact, trial lawyers don't come much better than my friend Rusty Hardin, of Arthur Andersen fame, who tells this story on himself. While still a prosecutor, he tried a woman for killing her husband. She claimed that the man beat her repeatedly, and that on the night of the shooting, she had acted in self-defense. During trial, her lawyer called the dead man's first wife as a witness, who testified that he beat her, too. "Yet, despite all those beatings," Hardin demanded, "you never took a gun and shot him to death, did you?" She walked right through the door Hardin opened: "In my heart I did, Mr. Hardin, a thousand times." Hardin, who won more than a hundred consecutive prosecutions, says that one almost broke his string.

3. Witnesses should not anticipate questions.

This is one opportunity the witness should forego. Some witnesses lie in wait for the lawyer, anticipating her questions so that they can show how much smarter they are than she. When it works, it pulls the teeth out of what was going to be the examiner's next questions. The problem is that it usually doesn't. The witness whose answer says, "I know where you are going, and you're not going to trap me," is courting disaster. There is always the outside chance the lawyer is not only marginally bright, but has traveled this road before, and will feast on the witness's arrogance.

For instance, had Mr. Jones (from chapter 6, "Killer Cross," p. 170, "Evasions.") been coached to anticipate the next question, when asked if he negotiated the contract, he might have answered, "Well, yes, I signed it, but if by that question you mean I signed the contract fully informed about your client's true financial condition, you know that is not true. I was tricked into signing." That answer may be daunting to some lawyers, but, if counsel is talented, Mr. Jones's triumph will be short-lived: "Mr. Jones, you have anticipated my next question. You sent in a team of lawyers and accountants to comb my client's financial records. They were in my client's office for weeks. You admit they had free rein over his records. Yet, you want this jury to believe you were tricked into signing because you got hoodwinked about the financials? Let's talk about that." Delivered with a "give me a break" tone of voice, this simple cross-examination turns the tables on the witness. Moreover, instead of defusing the lawyer's questioning by anticipating it, the witness has telegraphed his greatest concern—that the due diligence he did undermines his claim of being tricked.

I also worry that when a witness anticipates questions, even correctly, it puts him at odds with the advice to answer directly. By answering a question that he thinks is coming, and not concentrating on the one that was asked, a witness can ramble on about a topic that isn't on the table—leaving him vulnerable to the ever-humiliating question: "Mr. Jones, do you even remember the question?" Rather than seek the minimal gains achieved by anticipating a lawyer's cross, insist that your witness listen carefully to each question, and answer them, one at a time.

V. REDIRECT

A. Come Out Smokin'

There are few things that stir a trial lawyer more than a misleading cross-examination. When that happens, don't take a break when your opponent finishes. Get on your feet immediately. Unleash a redirect that sounds like cross-examination, with the focal point the misleading lawyer who just sat down. First, direct the jury to the misleading cross: "Do you recall being asked a series of questions by counsel concerning the second day of negotiations, when you left the room several times to call your boss in Korea?" "Do you recall that counsel implied you never really made those calls at all? That you came back and lied about your boss telling you to walk out if you didn't get that concession in the contract?"

Having set the stage, lay waste to each false impression counsel created. If you have documents, use them. Throw the client's phone bill up on a screen. Ask questions like these: "Is this what you wanted to explain when he wouldn't let you talk? That you made seven calls to Seoul on February 9—the ones on this phone bill?" "Now, this very phone bill was provided to opposing counsel last year, wasn't it?" "Yet, counsel never mentioned this invoice to this jury, did he?" "Okay, let's explain why he didn't. Tell us what your boss said that day."

When a lawyer overreaches on cross, the entire courtroom seems to be on your side. Even judges seem more tolerant of a little leading during a passionate redirect. It is the perfect time to take up for your client, take on your opponent, and set the record straight. As the great blues singer John Lee Hooker puts it, "This is *it*, pretty baby." You won't have the chance again.

B. Quit While You're Ahead. Quit While You're Behind.

Just like cross-examination, the most effective redirect can be none at all. Saying contentedly, "I have no further questions," is a great way to underscore how well you believed your witness fared against your opponent's cross. If there's no real reason to do redirect, quit while you're ahead.

On the other hand, if your witness cratered on the stand—was so bad it's doubtful redirect can help her—quit while you're behind. Ask a few questions if you have to, but add nothing new to stir up significant recross. Other factors may offset the damage she did; the jury may be conditioned to rationalize her bad answers, or another witness may be able to repair the damage.

If you let yourself get into one of those situations when neither you nor opposing counsel can quit—five crosses and six redirects—the witness on the stand is invariably the loser. Usually, the exchange means she has done badly and that her lawyer is desperate to undo the damage—while each recross only makes her looks worse. That sort of seesaw battle should never happen. Let her go. Fight out the issue on some other front.

VI. TIPS, TACTICS, AND STRATEGIES

A. The Order of Witnesses

While the order of witnesses is crucial, the number of witnesses you put on, and the length of their testimony, are too. I've seen too many cases lost because a party overstayed his welcome, boring the jury with minutiae, and giving the other side a chance to battle back by impeaching unnecessary witnesses. So figure out your batting order, cut down the lineup, and then simplify and shorten their testimony. In trials, less is always more.

1. The plaintiff's order.

Given the potential impact of the first witness, which can be immense,[6] who should lead off for the plaintiff? Select the person who knows the most about the facts and tells the story best. Hopefully, they are the same person.

No matter whom you select, the witness should be bulletproof on cross, or at least be able to withstand it very well. The best candidate often is an expert. Their experience on the stand increases the odds of a good start, and insulates against a disastrous one.

By the time the first witness steps down, the jury should know how the plaintiff was harmed, why the defendant is at fault, and if possible, the dollar amount of the damages—although that usually comes in with an expert later. Since the plaintiff is asking the jury to transfer money or property from the defendant to her, as many jurors as possible have to be convinced that the defendant owes it and that the plaintiff deserves it.

When no one person knows the entire story, you can use a series of witnesses to tell it. For continuity, let the jury know what is coming next—don't leave them guessing. "You told us that after the crane quit operating, you called in Mr. Johnson, the company's chief mechanic, to work on it, didn't you?" "He's waiting just outside the door to testify, isn't he?" That announcement creates a platform for Mr. Johnson's testimony, and helps weave the story together before he takes the stand.

Following the first witness, those remaining should testify in the order in which things actually happened, a human chronology. That way, the testimony and exhibits that follow will make better sense. It just confuses jurors to find out a plaintiff died on the operating table without knowing what he was doing there.

The rule of recency tells you to save a strong witness for last. Not only can a dramatic final few minutes inflame the passions of the jury, they can also undermine the effectiveness of the first witness for the defense, who follows. In a tort case where there are serious bodily injuries, that choice is not difficult. For instance, in a death case, a close survivor, such as the

---

6. See p. 253, "The first-witness effect."

widow, or an older child should go last. The emotional effect you want to create is almost guaranteed. Everyone is moved by that kind of emotion.

In plaintiff's commercial cases, however, you have to work harder to find the right person to go last. It should not be the damage expert (who should testify next to last). Instead, put someone on who can put a human face on the damage numbers. The CFO who knows how much the faulty equipment cost the company may also know some of the workers its failure forced him to lay off. "You've worked there 12 years. What's that like, having to tell people they don't have a job?" Even if he doesn't know them personally, laying people off is not easy. Just make certain that you've talked to him about this ahead of time. You don't want a bean-counting response about how tough life is in the big city.

2.   The defendant's disorder.

There is no real difference in the goals of plaintiffs and defendants putting on their case. Both parties should tell their story chronologically, succinctly, and convincingly. However, as a defendant, you generally don't get to choose the order in which you put on your witnesses. It is a harsh reality, but by the time the plaintiff rests, she may have called your best witnesses adverse. You can be left with no one to tell your story, at least no one the jury hasn't heard from already, and disliked.

Despite the difficulties, there are too many defense verdicts for things to be all that bleak—no matter how many witnesses you have left. In the first place, your witnesses may have done well when they were called adverse. Moreover, plaintiff's counsel may have failed to call all of your witnesses—either through inexperience or because he believes he has the case won. Ordinarily, jurors will be especially attentive to the first witness for the defense, even in tort cases, with highly charged facts arrayed against you. They will look to that witness to reassure them about the defendant's conduct. With both sides of the story told, watch the jurors' reactions. Their relief or consternation will be written all over their faces—a strong indication of how the case will come out.

Just as in a plaintiff's case, select the most likable, knowledgeable person you've got remaining in your lineup to go first. If you have enough witnesses left, leave someone for last who has a stake in the outcome of the case—not an expert. If the president of the company is a good guy, end with him. Let him explain how hard he and his employees worked to avoid the dispute that the jurors have heard about. Let him detail their efforts to satisfy the plaintiff's complaints, and how, despite everything they tried, it has all come to this. If the company has been harmed by the lawsuit, either through bad press or the cost of litigation, bring it out, but don't play the victim—especially when the plaintiff actually is one. If applicable, have the president testify to the recurring executive complaint about lawsuits—that they drain money from research and development, which for defendants like pharmaceutical companies is an accusation that means something to consumers on the jury.

Finally, with the right witness, you can pull the teeth out of some of the most emotional points of your opponent's closing argument—which follows soon. Given the advantage plaintiffs enjoy, going first and last, that should always be an objective with the defendant's last witness.

B. Just Before Your Client Takes the Stand

All the preparation and waiting may well have created tension between you and your client, even when your intent was just the opposite. It never hurts to calm things down with a last-minute show of support. Find a quiet spot in the courthouse. Ask your client if she truly believes in her case. When she answers "yes," tell her how honored you are to represent her and that you believe her case is just. Remind her to keep her head up, her voice firm, and let the jurors see and hear that same sense of conviction.

Remind her also that the two of you are there as a team. Ask her to correct you politely if you make a mistake during her direct. Warn her that if she appears irritated with your error, the jury will feel like it is eavesdropping on an argument. Both of you will lose credibility.

Emphasize that she should answer opposing counsel as directly and courteously as she does you—but to insist on the truth of her direct testimony. Assure her that if counsel leaves a false impression during cross, cuts her off, or in any way draws blood, you will fix the problem on redirect, if humanly possible. Warn her that if she is impeached, to stay calm. There's no need to cave in after that, making unnecessary admissions just to get off the stand. Explain that you sometimes have to take a hard blow at trial, and to keep on fighting back.

Finally, tell her that you trust her to tell her story well. Remind her how hard you worked to get this jury, that they like you, and that they are ready to believe what she has to say.

C. The First Days of Trial

As the plaintiff, you must tell a persuasive story. As the defendant, you must tear that story down and tell a more plausible one of your own, whenever possible. Often, the opportunity for either side to achieve these goals will be over by the time the first witness steps down from the stand. Jurors can decide that quickly.

1. The first-witness effect.

There are watershed events in the life of a trial, moments that have a significant impact on the outcome of the case, which is why the first witness is so important. If that witness falls apart on direct or cross, he can bring the case down with him. If he does well, he can win it.

In the *Westinghouse* case, the South Texas Nuclear Project's (STP's) first witness, the plant manager, was doing a great job on direct. Advertised in the plaintiff's opening as the man who knew more about the plant than "anyone else in the world," he was living up to his billing, explaining in a plainspoken way how the tubes in the generators were corroding, and threatening the life of the plant. However, toward the end of direct, counsel casually asked if the power plant was still doing *steam generator* business with Westinghouse. Counsel carefully crafted the question to elicit a "no" answer, which was literally the truth and opened no doors. But the witness blurted out, instead, "As soon as the lawsuit was filed, we quit doing business with Westinghouse altogether." As if that weren't clear enough, he added, "We couldn't trust them."

In fact, STP and Westinghouse had done a huge business since the filing of the suit, almost $175 million in four years. When we told that to our focus group "jurors," they were astonished. It was hard for any of them to believe that STP would do any business with a company it claimed defrauded it, much less $175-million worth. As one of them put it, "You don't do business with the devil." However, as we later learned, the companies had agreed not to introduce that evidence at trial—and the agreement was reduced to a joint motion in limine. However, *their* witness had "busted" the motion in limine, and we were ecstatic.

Before starting cross, I approached the bench to let the judge know I intended to go into the issue. When the plaintiff's lawyer argued that the witness's answer hadn't opened the door, the judge asked: "Where does that agreement say he can mislead this jury? I'm letting David go into it." So I did, holding the agreement in my hand:

Q: Now, you testified earlier that the plant quit doing business with Westinghouse after the suit was filed. Do you remember saying that?

A: Yes.

Q: That's not true, isn't it?

A: I thought we had an agreement.

The Court: Answer the question.

Q: Before you answer, let me hand you a copy of the agreement. Please look through it. Where does that agreement say you can mislead this jury? (I saw no reason to waste good material from a poorly attended bench conference.)

A: I didn't mislead the jury.

Q: You didn't mislead this jury? I want you to turn to the jury right now and tell them that you personally hired Westinghouse to clean and service the nuclear steam generators eight weeks *after* South Texas filed suit.

A: We had no choice.

Q: Excuse me. Perhaps it was the way I asked my question. Did you or did you not personally hire Westinghouse after the plant sued?

A: Well, we never did steam generator business with them again.

Q: I see. What you really meant when you said the plant quit doing business with Westinghouse altogether after the suit was filed, was that Westinghouse only serviced the steam generators one time after suit was filed. Have I got it right now?

A: Yes. That's correct.

Q: Surely you don't mean to imply to these men and women on the jury that the service contract was the only business STP did with Westinghouse after this suit was filed?

A: We didn't do any more business on the generators.

Q: Excuse me. Perhaps it was the way I asked my question. Did the South Texas Nuclear Project do any more business with Westinghouse at the plant, at all, after suit was filed?

A: Yes. We did quite a bit.

Q: "Quite a bit?" Let's explore what you mean by "quite a bit."

With that, I put up a chart showing that STP had bought $175 million in goods and services from Westinghouse in the four years since filing suit. Nothing much the witness said after that mattered. Testimony that disastrous would have hurt STP's chances at any time in the trial, but the plaintiff chose to put him on first—the standard-bearer for its cause. The agenda was no longer corrosion in the steam generator tubes, but the massive business STP had done with Westinghouse. STP, not Westinghouse, was now on trial.

What is the next move? As plaintiff, you have the greatest advantage. If your first witness did well, shorten the trial. If you can make your entire case by calling the defendant's best witness adverse, do it, and if that goes well, rest. If not, the advantage of the First Witness Effect can be squandered by the passage of time, unnecessary witnesses, and effective cross.

Of course, when you represent the defendant, as in *Westinghouse,* all you can do is cross-examine whomever the plaintiff throws up on the stand, and try to extend your lead. In this instance, the plant called a Dr. Gorman, a straightforward engineer and corrosion expert, whom STP considered the second in its duo of game-breaking witnesses. My colleague Quinn crossed him brilliantly—in a matter of a couple hours. Gorman's own publications illustrated that the risks of corrosion in nuclear steam generators were well-known at the time the contract was signed, contrary to STP's claim of having been misled about them. I especially liked it when Quinn proved engineers at the power plant subscribed to *Corrosion Magazine.* That was a nice touch.

Of course, when you settle confidentially you lose bragging rights, but the outcome of the trial was never in doubt. The only reason we didn't go to a jury was that Westinghouse's investment bankers would have pulled out of its pending purchase of CBS had we lost, a risk the company couldn't take. The plaintiffs had their moments in the months that followed, but the trial went against them from the very start.

2. Seamless transitions from opening arguments to the first witness.

By the time opening arguments are over, one side or the other is often far ahead, usually the result of especially compelling facts or a disparity between the lawyers' talents. "Ahead" is where you want to be at this point in every case you try. But life, as President Kennedy noted, is unfair. Following opening arguments in *Samsung v. Texas Instruments*, the one involving the most favored nation clause, I was light years behind.

Fresh from back-to-back trials, TI's lawyer was unprepared, but you would never have known it. He spoke from a notebook his associates put together, delivering an opening filled with pride in his client and contempt for mine. Exhibits scrolled in cadence to his arguments across a 60-inch monitor at his side. To prove how important the case was to TI, he dramatically introduced its board chairman sitting in the gallery. As he reached the end, he leveled the most serious of his many allegations against Samsung—that it had been sued by the Justice Department in 1986 for "dumping" microchips on the American market, along with several Japanese companies:

> In 1980, the worldwide semiconductor business was located primarily in the United States. Between 1980 and '85, Japanese companies and Samsung dumped DRAMs [memory chips] into the United States—that means to sell in the United States market at below their cost because of their own government subsidy or their labor expense. That caused all the American companies that dominated the industry to go out of business except Texas Instruments.
>
> In 1985, Texas Instruments increased its royalty amount—all these companies, Japanese and Samsung, had to come to Texas Instruments to sell in the United States because we owned the patent.

Not only had my client been part of a Far East conspiracy to overthrow American companies, TI was the instrument of vengeance against the foreign horde. There was, however, one problem with counsel's argument about dumping. It wasn't true; nor were several others.

While it is always powerful to tie what has happened in one phase of a trial to what happened before, there is no better time to do it than at the beginning, creating a seamless transition between an opponent's opening argument and the first witness. The key is to listen carefully to your opponent's opening for any misrepresentations or serious mistakes he makes and, depending on which side you represent, to make them the focal point of your direct or cross of the first witness. The next morning, I went over each mistake with Samsung's patent counsel:

> Q: Sir, do you recall that [counsel] accused some Japanese companies and Samsung of dumping DRAMS into the United States market?
> A: I remember that, yes.
> Q: Is that true or false?

As if on cue, which, actually, it was, he looked at the jury and replied, "That's false; that's not true. It never happened."

> Q: How could that be false? After all, TI's counsel said it.
> A: It's just not true. In 1985, the U.S. government accused the *Japanese* companies of dumping into the United States. Samsung did not even manufacture DRAMS until 1986—the year *after* the investigation. There was a major investigation with respect to the Japanese companies . . . but it did not involve Samsung.

When I passed the witness on a Friday afternoon, defense counsel, to his credit, spent time correcting his mistakes. Finally, he asked if there was anything else he should change, and when our witness said "no," the judge shut it down—leaving jurors with the lawyer's gaffes to contemplate over the weekend. The following Monday counsel did a little better, but it was too late. Three weeks later, with the jury waiting for closing arguments, the case settled.[7]

A postscript is in order: Under the terms of the confidential settlement, TI dismissed nine patent infringement suits it had filed against Samsung worldwide. Samsung's royalty payments were cut almost in half to a flat $1 billion over ten years. My client extracted many other concessions. It was a home run.

You may be wondering how I can discuss the terms of a confidential agreement. Before the ink was dry, my opponent had sent out a press release made to appear like a court order, announcing the first "billion-dollar royalty agreement in history." I searched in vain for any mention of Samsung's favorable terms, but, curiously, counsel forgot to include them. Still, you've got to hand it to the man. Even when you beat him, you can't beat him.

D. Make Objections That Matter

A lawyer shouldn't do something simply because she can—especially when it comes to making objections. You must choose the right moment, and make the right objection—or don't make an objection at all.

1. Objections are not the first option.

Jurors don't like objections. You think you are protecting the record. They think you are hiding something from them. Ironically, even when you are successful in objecting to particularly egregious questioning or testimony, the judge's instruction to disregard it sears into the jurors' minds exactly what you wanted them to ignore.

For those reasons, tell your witnesses that you are going to let them fend for themselves once you pass them for cross, at least for a while. You

---

7. It's not just plaintiff's lawyers who can benefit from an adversary's mistakes or misleading comments. Defense lawyers can respond immediately to them during their own opening argument, and, on cross, embarrass the first plaintiff's witness with counsel's mistakes.

want the jurors to see the witness respond to your opponent's most significant cross—on her own. The less you interfere, the more likely it is that the
jurors will identify with your witness—alone on the stand—responding
calmly and directly to everything the lawyer throws at her. If she stays
beneath him emotionally, playing the slightly bemused parent to the angry
lawyer/child, the jury will love it.

The same advice applies when opposing counsel has his own witness on
the stand, especially at first. The jury will think his story is killing you if
you are constantly on your feet. It's far better to sit relatively silent, even
letting in some objectionable testimony, particularly if you can impeach it
on cross. Besides, a verdict is rarely reversed on appeal because of an incorrect evidentiary ruling.

There are exceptions. If you have a *real chance* of stopping your opponent from developing testimony or introducing a document that is truly
harmful, object. I'm not just talking about the obvious situation, such as
where the evidence violates a motion in limine. Rather, object, also, when
that evidence *smacks* of a violation of the motion in limine. For instance, if
the judge has ruled out any mention of prior litigation between the plaintiff
and his brother, and his brother's name comes up in relation to something
else that's harmful, object, based on that ruling. In my experience, opposing
counsel, afraid of violating the judge's order, frequently will move on to
another subject. Too, some lawyers have a propensity to treat all objections
like an adverse ruling, abandoning their line of questioning with a comment like, "I'll move on, Your Honor," when "Your Honor" hasn't said a
word. Of course, when you know the judge will sustain an objection against
you, remedying the problem with your question before he rules is smart,
sparing you from being corrected in front of the jury. But that is different
from the lawyer who responds to objections as if the judge ordered him to
"move on." The very fact that he changes subjects conveys the impression
that you were right—and that he was doing something wrong.

2. Objections should make sense to the jury.

One of the tests of a well-made objection is whether jurors can
understand why you are making it. Passively objecting that a lawyer is
"leading" is like yelling "movie" in a crowded theater. The judge will roll his
eyes and the jurors will, too. Instead, objecting that counsel is "leading and
suggesting answers to the witness," lets jurors know what the lawyer is doing
wrong.

Although judges don't like "speaking" objections such as that one, trial
lawyers can't seem to make any other kind. Even after being cautioned,

caught up in the battle, lawyers still turn objections into miniarguments. When that happens, opposing counsel feels obligated to respond in kind, and on the argument goes. As a result, some courts won't allow lawyers to say anything more than "objection" and add a one- or two-word statement of the legal basis. In a case I tried recently, the judge allowed the lawyers to say only "objection." When an objection was sustained against me, I rarely knew what I had done wrong, so I'd ask the same question with different inflection and that seemed to make everyone happy.

One *possible* remedy is to object and then request permission to state your reasons. If you do so a few times, succinctly, the judge may loosen the reins.

3. Objections that matter.

To be effective, you must be discriminating. Some objections are basically worthless, such as the lame "leading" objection in the example above. Some are essential, such as when you object to a question or testimony that violates the motion in limine. However, what makes an objection matter is that it is a) sustained and, b) at a significant cost to your opponent's case. That's the lesson of the next two examples, objections for unresponsiveness and under the doctrine of optional completeness. While any well-timed objection can make a difference, I selected these two because, by their nature, when you are right in making them, they are deadly.

a.   Unresponsiveness.

Don't object right away when a witness is unresponsive. Give the jurors a chance to see how evasive he is. The last thing you want is an early admonition from the court that intimidates him into responsiveness. Instead, impeach the witness. Pin him down. Then, after it's clear to the jury that he won't give you a straight answer, object. The judge may issue only a mild rebuke at first, instructing the witness to "answer the questions." However, if the witness persists in being evasive, watch out. The judge may send the jury out even before you object, lecture the witness like a schoolboy, and threaten him with contempt. When the jury returns, the chastened witness will admit away the case.

b.   Doctrine of optional completeness.

Federal Rule 106 and its state court counterparts allow you to correct the record immediately when a "writing or recorded statement" is taken out of context, or when evidence is omitted, "which ought in fairness to be considered." What makes this objection so powerful is that if the judge sustains it, you make a case against your opponent just by lodging it. Telling the court that counsel is "misleading the jury," and then demonstrating precisely how he has done so, undermines his credibility.

For example, lawyers frequently make impeachment sound legitimate when it's not. By the tone of their voice, or by ever-so-slightly massaging the witness's prior statement, they can make what he said sound inconsistent. When you catch an opponent at it, make him pay. Indignantly tell the judge and jury that your client's testimony is being misquoted.

Hand the judge a copy of the deposition, to let her see for herself the part he's misquoted. Once you are given permission to proceed, turn to the jury and read the transcript yourself—*never* opposing counsel. Your tone of voice alone will convey the gravity of what he's done. His will obscure it. Moreover, if this is not the first time you've caught your opponent speeding, ask the court to admonish him—in front of the jury.

It's difficult for a lawyer to regain his composure once caught misrepresenting the record. It also shifts the momentum. You not only protect your witness from unjustified impeachment, you also take command of the courtroom by interrupting his cross.

4. When the judge gets mad.

If the judge gets mad at opposing counsel or his witness, *any* objection matters; in fact, it becomes a potential game-breaker. When it happens it's like having another member on your trial team, this one the most influential person in the courtroom. The black robe gives the judge a clergyman's moral authority. She appears to be fair and impartial (whether she is or not). Jurors search her words and facial expressions for clues for how to decide the case. They interpret a judge's anger as her verdict. Invariably, the jury follows suit. More than once, I've witnessed the overwhelming effect on jurors when judges have lost their temper, or barely disguised it, as they retired the jury to admonish a truculent witness. One judge's warning in particular ("I'm keeping my book on contempt right here, so I won't have to look for it when I sentence you to jail") so undid the witness that he actually gave away the case when the jury returned. In every case I've been in, when the judge has gotten mad at the other side, they never recovered.

Without your objection, however, the judge is unable to vent that anger, so you must be alert to the body language and circumstances that should trigger an objection from you. While it is difficult to predict what makes a judge mad, unless you've practiced in that court before, there are at least three circumstances that should: (1) when the lawyer has misled the court;

(2) when the witness won't give a straight answer; or (3) when either of them violates a prior ruling. As for telltale body language, some judges will all but invite the objection by looking at you; others will scowl until you get on your feet.

5. Motions for mistrials.

If any testimony is so unfairly prejudicial that an instruction won't cure it—the proverbial "skunk in the jury box" —you have the *option* of moving for a mistrial. That is a hard decision. You may be entitled to a mistrial, but you may not want it. You may be winning. The last thing you will want to do is start over again. But, if the improper evidence is bad enough to create reversible error, you almost have to make the motion to protect your record, just in case you lose.

When you move for a mistrial, always approach the bench, out of the earshot of the jurors. You don't want them to think that you would rather have another jury decide the case. If the judge won't let you do it at sidebar, cushion what you say in front of them. Let them know that you have no choice: "Your Honor, the law now requires me to make this motion for mistrial." If you really don't want the judge to grant it, signal him by saying something like, "I realize that you probably won't grant this motion, but the law requires me to make it." Ordinarily, the judge won't want a mistrial any more than you do. But, if he's mad enough at your opponent for whatever has happened, you run the risk that he will haul off and grant it. On the other hand, if he does, you wouldn't want to be in your opponent's shoes. The judge will even the score with each of his rulings the next time around.

E. Witnesses and the Judge

In some jurisdictions, judges are allowed to question witnesses and to comment on the testimony. That potential hovers like a funnel cloud over your most significant witnesses—especially your clients. Warn them of the possibility and teach them how to respond if it happens.

1. When the judge decides to cross-examine.

Unfortunately, if the judge questions your witness, it's almost always because she is skeptical about the testimony, not simply to clarify it. Rehearse your witness so that he won't come undone if it happens. While you're rehearsing his cross in that deserted courtroom, put a colleague on the bench. Have the "judge" occasionally jump in with questions the minute your witness gives a bad answer. Rehearse him until he is no longer nervous or defensive, or answers with a curt, "yeah," or nods his head. Only "Yes, Your Honor" and "No, Your Honor," in a calm voice, will do.

The witness needs to know that when a judge has chosen sides, she will hear in his responses what she wants to hear. Warn him that the judge may get mad no matter what he says, and that if he fights back, the situation can spin out of control. At those moments, he has to double his efforts to answer directly and politely, and to readily admit a mistake.

2. When the witness rules on objections.

I've heard more than one witness snap, "I *was* being responsive" or the like, following an objection. While I don't want to discourage spontaneity, it does seem bad form for the witness to rule. Judges are there for a reason, and deciding objections is one of them.

Instruct your witnesses that simply because a lawyer objects doesn't mean that he is right—that you have a chance to respond. Make sure she understands that some objections are aimed at upsetting her, and that she should avoid biting on that cheap top-water bait. Warn her that she must sit quietly when there's an objection, and stay out of the lawyers' fight. Her sole responsibility is to follow the arguments and listen carefully to the judge's rulings. Convince your witness that she must accept immediately whatever the judge decides, and that she should never argue with his decision. That happens, and it always ends up ugly for the witness. However, if she is unclear about how he ruled, she can politely ask him to repeat it, so that she doesn't violate it. But, once again, indicating that the judge made a mistake is a bad idea.

F. When Your Witness Craters on the Stand

From time to time in your life as a trial lawyer, your witness will simply crater on that stand. There are myriad reasons why, but none that will make things better. The witness may have gotten up on the wrong side of the bed or, as one of mine once did, swallowed enough Valium to relax Cincinnati.

When that happens, you have to know how to handle it. That is why it is incumbent on all of us to learn the story of Ron Waska, and pass it on from generation to generation. I had wandered into the back of a federal courtroom, where Waska, then an Assistant United States Attorney, was trying an interstate auto-theft case. As with most federal criminal prosecutors, little proof was required. All Waska had to show was: (1) a stolen car (2) was driven across state lines, and (3) the defendant was the driver.

With his star witness on the stand, Waska turned to the jury and, thumbs tucked under his suspenders, asked: "Did you see the defendant driving the car through Texarkana [a small town that straddles the Texas/Arkansas border]?" The witness looked carefully at the defendant, then back to Waska, repeated the exercise, and with a quizzical look on his face, finally answered, "No, sir. I sure didn't. Never seen him driving at all. In fact, I never seen him before today." One could hear the SNAP of Waska's suspenders in adjoining courtrooms, but no emotion creased his face. Without turning from the jury he said emphatically, "Exactly. Exactly my point."

There is a serious case to be made for reacting like Waska did, whenever you get an answer like that. Acting as though the answer doesn't concern you goes a long way toward convincing the jurors that there is nothing for them to be concerned about, either.

It's Never Too Late to Win—or Lose | 8

I.   THE IMPORTANCE OF CLOSING ARGUMENT

The sunset creates amazing colors over the ocean. But with nothing in your cooler except an empty six-pack, it will only annoy you—a reminder that you've been skunked. You're tempted to pack up and go home. Instead, you resist the urge to quit. You continue casting, until, miracle of miracles, you feel a mighty tug on your line, and suddenly the entire exercise seems worthwhile.

Once again, fishing imitates trials. By the time for closing arguments, you may think you are far behind. You may be far behind. But whether ahead or behind, you must not ease up. A lackluster performance is proof positive of everything your opponent has contended. This is not just a pep talk. Minds can be changed, for or against you, even at the end of a long trial. So forget about being ahead or behind, and keep trying to hook jurors. Deliver an argument so logical and compelling that it can persuade your toughest critics on the jury, be they one or 12.

In the early seventies, I represented a black kid who was accused of armed robbery. The jury convicted him, then, unexpectedly, gave him probation. Afterwards—I can still see this moment—a juror named Mrs. Rich told me that my closing argument had made a difference in the sentence.

What an encouraging thing to say to a young man just learning! And what a profound lesson to learn so early on: Even late in the game and with the odds against you, it's never too late to win, so don't give up. "Good trial lawyers," says a trial lawyer friend, "got no quit in 'em."

II.   THE GOALS OF CLOSING ARGUMENT

The trial doesn't end just because your argument has. You must arm your friends so that they can disarm your enemies during deliberations. Tell them how to answer *each* jury question, and *why.* Organize the evidence into an eloquent argument, laced with common sense and lofty ideals. Leave the jury resolute about voting for your client, certain that they are doing justice. That's not Utopian—that's what you came to accomplish.

III.   CONSIDERATIONS FOR CLOSING ARGUMENT

A.   *The Elements of Eloquence*

By "eloquence," I don't mean sounding like a finalist in a high school oratory contest. But your argument must be more than neatly stacked documents and bloodless rhetoric. By what you say, and how you say it, you must impart your conviction that your client's cause is just.

It is the failure to show that kind of commitment that kills many defense lawyers with juries. Restrained and aloof, they fail to convey that they care about their client and his case. Not that you can manufacture emotion. Insincerity doesn't fool anyone, especially jurors. But there is plenty of room in closing argument for genuine passion.

1. Passion.

In 1979, the Chief Justice of the Texas Supreme Court, Jack Pope, wrote an opinion affirming not only a verdict but the trial lawyer's tradition of passionate advocacy as well. At issue was a particularly unrestrained defense summation in a personal injury case, including the lawyer's contention that the plaintiff drove by a *"thousand* [legitimate] doctors between the Astrodome and Spring Branch, [clear across town], to hire the [quack] who testified." [Emphasis added.] Because of the argument, the intermediate appellate court reversed the defense verdict, a decision soon reversed again by the Supreme Court. In approving the argument, Justice Pope must have identified every known quote containing the word "thousand," to justify counsel's comments:

> Hyperbole has long been one of the figurative techniques of oral advocacy. Such arguments are part of our legal heritage and language. Shakespeare wrote about "a thousand blushing apparitions" and "a thousand innocent shames" in *Much Ado About Nothing.* In *The Tempest* he wrote, "Now would I give a thousand furlongs of sea for an acre of barren ground"; in *King Richard III,* "My conscience hath a thousand several tongues, and tongue brings in a several tale. . . ."; in *Hamlet,* "And by a sleep to say we end the heartache and the thousand natural shocks that flesh is heir to"; in *Hamlet* again, "To be honest, as this world goes, is to be one man picked out of ten thousand"; and in *Romeo and Juliet,* he has Juliet saying, "A thousand-times good-night!" This method has often been employed to make a point.

The good justice was really into it. In a detailed footnote, he added even more quotes in which the word "thousand" appeared, everything from Milton, in *Paradise Lost* ("Those thousand decencies that daily flow from her words and actions"), to Ed McMahon, talking to Karnack the Magnificent (Johnny Carson), on "The Tonight Show" ("A thousand welcomes to you").

All of which is to say, let fly. There is much you can do to win—and little you can do to create reversible error.[1] Liberated from the strictures of opening argument, there is no need for those formulations like, "What I am about to say is merely argument." It's not "merely" anything. It's your chance to tell the jury everything you've been thinking all the months and years that it took to get this far. On the other hand, there's never a place for melodrama. Modern juries are not impressed by yelling and crying. Restrained anger, indignation, and a thousand (!) other understated feelings are much more likely to move them.

2. Organization.

Organization isn't just about putting things in chronological order: It is an element of eloquence. To be moved by your argument, the jurors must be able to follow it. The very order in which you argue the evidence creates drama and meaning all its own. (See p. 281, "Arguing the evidence: Logos.")

3. Allusions.

Allusions work best in closing argument, when judges and jurors alike expect a bit of drama and flair from the lawyers. They add depth and meaning to your argument. As Robert Greenman writes in his book *Words That Make a Difference*,[2] "[W]ith a single word (Hercules) or phrase (a thumbs up)," allusions "double the impact of their message," and "create intimacy between writer and reader."[3] In trials, they have the same affect on lawyers and jurors, another way of breaking down barriers.

---

1. Beware of the arguments that are likely to result, some automatically, in incurable error: 1. Appeals to prejudice (including race, religion, sex, national origin, and geographic bias); 2. Highly prejudicial, inflammatory remarks ("The defendant is a liar—a perjurer"); 3. Personal attacks on opposing counsel (Little you could do is more unprofessional. On the other hand, never buddy up to opposing counsel during trial. Clients won't understand it and jurors will think it hypocritical); 4. Expressing personal opinions (about the credibility of witnesses or sufficiency of evidence); 5. Arguments outside the record; 6. References to income disparities between the parties (Plaintiffs: Why say it? It will be apparent); 7. Misstating the law (Even if accidental, it looks awful); 8. The golden rule (You can't ask jurors to put themselves in your client's shoes. You can ask them to treat both sides as they would want to be treated); 9. Repeated error (It is the cumulative effect of improper arguments that is most likely to result in reversible error). These arguments are anathema not only because they create reversible error. They also backfire: Jurors hate it when lawyers get down into the mud.

2. ROBERT GREENMAN, WORDS THAT MAKE A DIFFERENCE 402 (2002).

3. *Id.*

Choosing the right allusion is not difficult. It can come from any source—the Bible, history, baseball, an insight that you have about life (so long as you attribute it to your grandmother). If it fits your case, and means something to you, it will mean something to the jurors. In *Sakowitz,*[4] I paraphrased the lyrics from an old "Leadbelly" (Hudie Ledbetter) song about the Galveston hurricane of 1900. The jurors, chosen to include longtime area residents, knew all about the Galveston hurricane—they had grown up listening to stories about its devastation. That imagery captured our: defense, What happened to the Sakowitz stores was beyond Robert's control:

> "Leadbelly," the great blues singer, sang about the Galveston hurricane. He sang, "Wasn't that a mighty storm, Lord, that blew the children all away?" That's where we ought to start—because it was that same "mighty storm" that blew away the Sakowitz family's first store, down in Galveston, in 1900, almost a hundred years ago. And as you recall from the evidence, the entire family rallied around and moved north—up here to Houston—and began a tradition that lasted almost a century.
>
> And wasn't that another "mighty storm" that came in the '80s? The oil markets collapsed. Houston's real estate values went south. There has never been the number of bankruptcies in this country's history as there were in Houston, Texas. And when that bust blew Robert Sakowitz's business away, when it blew Lynn Wyatt's business away, when it blew Ann Sakowitz's business away—instead of rallying around him, the Wyatts turned on him. They abandoned him. They bad-mouthed him all over town. No one stepped up to the bar but Robert. He put millions of his own dollars into the business trying to save it. And his family was nowhere to be found. Nobody in the family stuck by him but his mother. And she hasn't stopped to this day.

Of course, it's easy to make a point with just the *right* allusion. Any trial lawyer with a double-digit IQ and a *Bartlett's Familiar Quotations* can do that. A bigger challenge is to find one that is totally *in*appropriate. Early in my career, I managed to meet that challenge.

In the mid '70's, I represented a couple of Virginians who were accused of making several unauthorized withdrawals from a variety of banking institutions in Dallas. The state had accumulated what I think most fair-minded people would call persuasive evidence, if you call apprehending the accused with the bank wrappers still around the cash, persuasive. As luck would have it, the night before closing arguments I was reading the *ABC's*

---

4. See p. 41, "Excerpts must be accurate"; and note 5, the Sakowitz family tree.

of Relativity by the British philosopher Bertrand Russell. (I am embarrassed just to mention it.) Russell's book raised profound questions about existence and perception, such as: "How do I know that the color brown I see is the same color brown that you see?" That was it! I would use old Bertie's reasoning about reality to demonstrate how hard it is to know something beyond a reasonable doubt. The next day, I started with the color of the prosecution's table, moved to the nature of the wood, and within minutes, had reduced the entire table and the evidence piled on it, down to subatomic particles. Well, boys and girls, Dallas jurors are beady-eyed generally, but the 24 eyes staring back at me that day were narrowed to disbelieving slits. In candor, it was actually 26 beady eyes, because the alternate hated me, too.

And so—since it's now the 21st century—my clients should be released any day. Frankly, I haven't encouraged them to visit.

4. A simple logic.

With all the evidence in, compare your strongest argument with your opponent's. In three or four sentences, demonstrate with simple logic that his case is absurd. Had *Westinghouse* not settled, we would have focused on the obvious flaws in STP's case:

> If the nuclear steam generators are in such horrible shape—ready to crumble from corrosion any minute now—why was the South Texas nuclear power plant the single-largest producer of electricity in the world last month? And how can it continue to be among the most profitable, productive plants on the face of the planet, month after month, if the generators are falling apart? That doesn't make any sense.

The more arguments along these lines that you can make—straightforward, easy to understand—the more likely you are to carry the jury along with you. Of course, simplifying complex issues does not mean omitting important details—only that you not get so immersed in them that you lose the jury. Besides, in commercial cases, if you haven't simplified the evidence long before closing, it will be too late.

5. A reminder: Action words.

In a previous chapter, I discussed the importance of choosing just the right words. (See p. 135, "Choose forceful words.") As with allusions, the right ones magnify whatever point you are trying to make. Remember: Your opponent doesn't *say* that your client did something. She *claims* it. Your opponent doesn't *agree* that he's partially responsible. Your opponent *admits* it. The defendant doesn't *avoid liability*. He's *incapable of accepting responsibility*. Your client didn't *die* at the intersection. She got *killed* there.

B. The Plaintiff's Huge Advantage

Customarily, the plaintiff argues first and last in closing, with the defendant's argument squeezed in between. While both sides get an equal amount of time, the opportunities are anything but equal, for a gloriously simple reason: Once the defendant finishes his argument, he can't respond. The plaintiff then makes her most compelling arguments—leaving the defendant with a churning stomach, and nothing to do, other than make the occasional limp objection.

C. Passion in Part Two

Plaintiffs are theoretically required to cover all their arguments during part one, so that the defendant has a fair opportunity to respond to each one. But that's not what happens. In almost every court I've ever been in, all the plaintiff's lawyer has to do is obliquely mention an issue during part one and the judge will allow her to make "related arguments" during part two.

Watch how this works. During part one, the plaintiff barely mentions the words "misappropriation of trade secrets" and "unlawful profits." During part two, they become "stealing" and "profiteering." The final argument in personal injury cases can be devastating, especially if an East Texas friend of mine named George Chandler is trying the case. During part one, he'll talk about the catastrophic accident. During part two, you will hear about the "19 words that paralyzed little boy will never say: 'Dad, let's go play catch.' 'May I have the next dance?' 'Mama, can I help?' 'Will you marry me?'" Every plaintiff's lawyer knows a variation on that theme. That argument may appear melodramatic on the written page, but, in the final moments of the trial, delivered in a calm, unemotional voice, it can move the most callous of jurors.

D. Overcoming the Plaintiff's Advantage

The question arises: If the plaintiff has such a huge advantage, what is the point of showing up if you're the defendant? They shoot horses, don't they? The reason is, there are ways out of the trap, that's why.

1. Turning the advantage against the plaintiff.

Ironically, the plaintiff's advantage—understating and omitting arguments during part one, preparing to leap all over you during part two—can create an equal advantage for the defense. When she omits or understates arguments, leap all over yourself. Bring up your weaknesses first. Embrace them, explain them, apologize for them—do whatever you have to do, but beat her to the punch. If you pull the teeth out of the best she's got, her words will ring hollow when she responds—and her retreat will be obvious if she doesn't respond at all.

There is another option when the plaintiff fails to make a complete opening: You can move the court to compel her to do so. If the lawyer's not nimble on her feet, her timing and organization may be thrown off by the unexpected order to open more fully, all the while using up a chunk of her time remaining for part two. She may also dent her credibility with the jurors: It looks bad when a lawyer has to be ordered to do the right thing.

There is a downside. By successfully objecting, you give counsel the opportunity to fill in the gaps she left in her argument, which you may be better off filling in yourself. It's a difficult decision, depending, I would think, on that "nimbleness" issue. If she's not quick on her feet, object. Your decision also depends on how critical it is for you to know what her argument is going to be. For instance, if she's argued for punitive damages without specifying the amount, then you almost have to object to flush out that answer. If it's none of the above, let it go, and make her best arguments yourself.

2. The defendant's one certain advantage.

Defense lawyers have one advantage they can depend on in every case. They can enlist jurors to make their arguments for them, once they've finished arguing. To be effective, you must be able to predict what your opponent is going to argue once you sit down. In the *Westinghouse* case, STP's closing arguments would have been obvious:

> Ladies and gentlemen, when I sit down, the plant's lawyer will try to tell you that the evidence of microscopic corrosion in the steam generators is a sure sign of disasters to come. He is going to claim that the plant needs new nuclear steam generators *now*—and that the South Texas Project shouldn't have to wait to get them until they fall apart. He will tell you that this is the plant's only day in court, that STP can't come back here again—after the damage is done. He will make that argument knowing that I don't have a chance to respond. So, when he stands up here and tells

you to award $800 million dollars to replace those nuclear steam genera-
tors, I want you to rebut those arguments for me—in your minds—as you
listen to him talk. You already know the answers. As that panelist said
months ago, when we selected this jury, "If it ain't broke, don't fix it."

And, if any of your fellow jurors brings up that argument during
deliberations, I want you to hold up your hand and say, "Wait a minute.
Remember what David [Berg] said. That plant is operating beautifully." I
want you to say to that juror: "We're not giving STP $800 million dollars
for new steam generators when the old ones don't need replacing."

When you anticipate what a lawyer is going to argue, you must be 100-
percent accurate about what you say, no matter how derisively you say it.
Otherwise, you'll regret mischaracterizing the argument the minute your
opponent tells the jury that you missed his point.

Once you have anticipated the arguments that you know are coming,
anticipate those that you can't predict:

And let me ask one more thing of you. If you hear STP's lawyer make any
argument you haven't heard before—whatever it might be—ask yourself
one question: Why now? Why wait until Berg sits down to bring that up
for the first time? Ladies and gentlemen, all these Westinghouse folks ever
asked for is a fair trial—and bringing up an argument when I have no
chance to answer it—that's anything but fair.

These arguments may be typical, but they are also very subtle. On the
surface, they appear to be no more than a plea for fairness, but on a deeper
level, they are an accusation of cowardice—that the plaintiff's lawyer didn't
have the courage to make his main arguments until you could no longer
respond. They are also an expression of trust, that when the plaintiff's
lawyer makes a particular argument, or some misguided soul on the jury
dares mention it, that the jurors will rebut it for you. It is a gilt-edged invitation to jurors to join the defense team.

3. Achilles' heels.

Plaintiffs lawyers spend so much time developing liability that they
often give short shrift to damages—scrambling around in the waning days
of discovery for an expert to pull it all together. Defense lawyers regard that
weakness as the Achilles' heel of many plaintiff's cases. It provides a safety
net for the defense—and a calming, analytical offset in closing to the plaintiffs emotional appeal:

If this case were about emotion, I would lose. The plaintiff clearly has
been hurt. He has lost his business. Everyone in this courtroom has to feel

for him. But to claim that the folks I represent cost him one dollar is totally wrong. You saw the deposit slips and bank statements. You saw the financial reports. In the year after my client was supposed to have stolen away the plaintiff's customers, he made less money than in each of the prior five years. Let's look at this logically: If my client "unjustly enriched" himself, as the plaintiff claims, where is all that money?

Defense lawyers also have an Achilles' heel—one of their own making. Emboldened by the hit they know they can put on the plaintiff's damages, they often fail to put on a damage model of their own, insisting while Rome burns that the plaintiff is not entitled to a single penny. The result is often a disaster. Even when the plaintiff's damages are weak, the jurors can get so mad at the defendant for his bad behavior, that they hit him with a big verdict, anyway. There's also the chance that the defense assessment of the plaintiff's damages is incorrect. In all but a slam-dunk case, it is wise to offer the jurors a simple, rational alternative—a smaller amount of money than the plaintiff has asked. You're not conceding that the plaintiff is due a single dollar—you're just buying some insurance for your client and creating arguments for yourself.

Pennzoil vs. Texaco, with its $11.1-billion verdict, is the prime example. That award, often held up as an example of a runaway jury system, actually was attributable to Texaco's failure to offer the jury any alternative to Pennzoil's huge damage claim. Think about what Texaco's lawyer might have been able to argue, armed with an alternative, especially in Houston, Texas, where it was tried, and which had just lived through a depression in the oil business:

> Pennzoil has never made profits of more than $100 million in a single year—and now Mr. Jamail wants you to award the company billions? Now, you may believe that our executives were too aggressive at times, maybe even overstepped their bounds in getting Getty Oil to sign with Texaco instead of Pennzoil, but business is business, and sometimes, especially in the oil business, it gets rough. But Jamail's demand for billions is outrageous—just old-fashioned greed.
>
> As I said, we don't believe Texaco owes Pennzoil anything, but if you disagree, then we would understand if you were to award Pennzoil its out-of-pocket expenses and some reasonable amount attributable to lost profits. But before you arrive at any amount of money, consider the testimony of our expert—that the price of oil can be back down to $8 a barrel in six months' time. You, of all people, don't need an expert to tell you that. In the last ten years, Houstonians lived through the worst depression in the oil business, ever. No one, certainly not Pennzoil's expert, can say with certainty how profitable Getty Oil is going to be in the future. As our expert told you, predicting profits more than six months down the line in the oil business is

pure speculation. And His Honor will tell you, you cannot base your decision on speculation.

So if you decide that Texaco is liable, let me suggest that the amount of money damages is a lot closer to $50 million than the $3 billion Mr. Jamail wants—much less the billions he's asking for in punitives. And let me add the obvious—$50 million is a huge amount of money.

If nothing else, the defense would have created a powerful argument for fairness in all things financial—something jurors are notoriously good about when given the chance. But those jurors weren't given any other option. In the aftermath of the verdict, Texaco's stock price heaved violently for several years, terrorizing stockholders, until the case was settled, for $3 billion.

There is a deeply psychological reason defense lawyers fail to offer alternative damage models: "Winning" is a relative term for them. When a large verdict would be a defense victory, it doesn't appear so to the public or to other lawyers. Only a "zero" verdict does. In retrospect, a $500-million verdict against Texaco would have been viewed as a huge loss, but the jury's $11.1-billion award makes it look awfully good in comparison. And by now, the entire affair would have been forgotten.

4. Tailor arguments to the leaders.

If you have kept an eye out during the trial, you should have a good idea who the leaders are on the jury, and which way they are leaning. Once you've identified them, there is no difference in the way you tailor your testimony than during opening, or for that matter, with a witness on the stand. (See p. 148, "Appeal to the leaders"; see also p. 237, "Tailor testimony (but rarely).")

In the Fleisher case,[5] the judge told us that a juror complained that another juror insisted on discussing the case during breaks in the trial. No one could stop her, not even by reminding her of the judge's admonitions not to discuss the case. After talking privately to the juror, the judge disqualified her. When she brought the jury in to tell them, several turned directly to one particular juror and smiled—a nonverbal high five (and a large clue). That told us he was the leader—and a candidate to become the foreman. Better yet, he was with us. It showed on his face every time a particular defense lawyer got on his feet. He did everything but swivel his chair

---

5. See p. 94, "Linkage and your themes."

around and look out the window. That was invaluable information about the strongest, most influential juror—and caused me to tailor a particular argument to him, as subtly as I could. A former trial lawyer with a defense firm in Wisconsin, he had moved to New York to become a music teacher at a public high school. That told me that he was empathic. I also knew, from things he said in voir dire, that he was happy to leave his defense-lawyer days behind him. I emphasized the indifference of the defense argument, that if those lawyers truly did not understand why "Fleisher was complaining" after three weeks of trial, then they weren't listening. I hoped the argument reminded him of the defense practice he'd left in Wisconsin. In fact, he did become our foreman, leading the charge, we were told by other jurors, to a $4.6-million verdict in our favor.

Sometimes, the news isn't so good about a juror, but bad information is equally valuable, telling you that there is someone that you must work hard to persuade. In Orlando, trying a fraud case, I got stuck for an hour on an elevator with a juror who insisted on talking about the trial. No matter how many times I told him I couldn't say anything, he kept on talking about it. When I reported the incident to the judge, suggesting the man's disqualification, the other side disagreed, and he stayed. He was their juror—and they knew it. The guy hated me.

Despite my attempt to tailor an argument to him—he was a commercial artist who ran his own company—he resisted my entreaties. In fact, he came very close to taking the jury along with him on every liability question—ending up in a minority of one on the jury's lone favorable verdict, a game-saver worth $52 million to my client. If I needed any more evidence of how he felt, when I walked into the jury room when it was all over, there was a decidedly unflattering caricature of me on the blackboard, and last I checked, there was only one artist on the jury.

I have only one additional piece of advice on the subject of tailoring your arguments—something that occurred to me while I watched an episode of MTV's "Real Life," where cameras follow young people just starting out. In this particular episode, a young woman was breaking up with her lover over the phone. She was really angry, repeatedly demanding, "Do you know the worst thing? Do you know the worst thing?" I thought she must be into Bob Dylan, because she answered her own question with a version of one of his most famous lyrics: "You just wasted my precious time." Fully expecting her follow-up to be the next line in Dylan's song, "But don't think twice, babe, it's all right"—she said instead, "Do you know what I could have done with those 14 days?"

Wow. Fourteen days. I wasted the first 25 years of my *life* and she's worried about two weeks? There isn't an adjective sufficient to describe the gap between that young woman and me. If I were trying to tailor an argument to her, or her contemporaries, I would have to have some help from my nieces, themselves young women just starting out. So, if you've got people on your panel whose age or experience is very different from your own, find someone close to their demographics, and get some advice about what arguments might matter most to them.

IV. DELIVERING A POWERFUL ARGUMENT

A. A Reminder about Cicero

The rules in this book for organizing opening and closing argument are derived from Cicero, the great Roman lawyer. (See p. 129, "Cicero Is Not Just a City Near Chicago.") He wrote that the most persuasive speeches include appeals to (1) the common ground between jurors and the client (ethos); (2) the jurors' intellect (logos); and (3) their passion (pathos). In brief, argument should resemble the three layers of an Oreo cookie, with the emotional appeals coming first and last, and the appeal to logic (which has an emotional appeal all its own) sandwiched in between.

In addition, there are components within each layer that organize argument further. Many of them, however, are movable parts that you can argue in the order that seems right for your close. For instance, you may want to start with your most dramatic facts, or move them to the end. Or, having created a powerful graphic summarizing the evidence, you might want to lead with it, rather than sandwich it in the middle.

As noted, plaintiff's lawyers enjoy greater latitude in argument because they go first and last, which creates the temptation to load up the strongest arguments in the second half. Even if a plaintiff's lawyer chooses to open briefly, she should always open fully, covering her own arguments before the defense lawyer makes them for her—turning up the volume on her emotions only slightly, to capture the jurors and pressure the opposition. Then, during part two, she can turn it up full blast.

1. The beginning: Ethos.

The first moments of closing are crucial. You must grab the jurors' attention immediately, reminding them forcefully why they should care. By what you say, and how you say it, you must remind them that you care, too.

a.   Start with the biggest theme.

In the end, civil suits are about money. But if that's all you make of your case, you won't connect with jurors. They believe that they are there to do more than just award dollars. They believe that they are there to do justice—and almost always, they do. You must help them figure out how to do just that.

Step back from the details of your case. Some deeper meaning had to have emerged from the testimony of witnesses and the conduct of the lawyers during trial. Not from the documents or the graphics—but from the *people* involved. That "big theme," whatever it might be, should come early in your argument, to get the jurors' attention, and to point the way to a just decision.

Maybe the Sakowitz trial is too easy an example, because it was about family, and family relationships are always compelling. But it makes the point. The lawsuit started out as a dispute over an estate and ended up, as estate disputes always do, destroying the family. That was the thought I tried to convey in the opening moments of my summation:

> You know, it never occurred to me until this very minute while I was sitting here listening to [opposing counsel] talk about greed and power and betrayal, that he had never once mentioned the greatest asset of all. The greatest asset that the Sakowitzes had was what? They had their family.

We knew from their body language that the jurors were angry at Douglas. The question I asked in opening—"Did he file this suit for sport or for spite?"—had been answered repeatedly, "both," by the evidence. Pointing first to Douglas, then to his father, and then to his mother, seated together inside the rail—I attempted to bring the trial full circle:

> And now this family has been torn apart by an utterly meaningless, spiteful lawsuit filed by that man, fueled by that man, and made possible by Lynn Sakowitz Wyatt.

There is no bigger theme than the sanctity of the family, and no greater tragedy than a family torn apart. Making that argument at the start of closing carried the jury with me to the end.

Compelling arguments aren't just about spoken words. They're also about the nonverbal messages you convey. The movie *The Verdict* suggests silence—not saying a single word—as one method of drawing jurors in immediately. In it, Paul Newman plays a lawyer whose client has been left in a vegetative state following surgery. The judge ("owned by the big boys downtown") makes one ruling after another in favor of the powerful defendants—two surgeons and a large hospital. One ruling in particular, in which the judge excludes a copy of an altered medical record, is enough to make you leap to your feet and start arguing in the theater.

In the final scene, the judge tells Newman to give his summation, but he doesn't respond. He sits at counsel table, staring, an anguished figure lost in thought. The judge repeats his order, but Newman ignores him. Finally, as the judge is losing his temper, Newman stands. Without having said a word, he's said a lot, conveying by his silence his contempt for the corrupt proceeding. By the time he speaks, the jurors are rapt, leaning forward to hear what he has to say.

Hollywood understands the power of silence. Like humor, it is even more powerful in the courtroom because it is so rare—and unexpected. So, when you begin your summation, rather than start with a meaningless, "Ladies and gentlemen of the jury, I want to thank you for your attention," pull a Paul Newman. It doesn't have to be silence. It can be a look, a gesture, a dramatic new graphic—whatever you decide. But from your very first words, remind the jurors that they are part of something important, something that matters, not only to your client and to you, but to them, as well.

b.   Remind them that they are your clients' jury.

Think of how you've felt when you've been singled out for praise. If it was significant, you probably can remember what was said, who said it, and the moment it happened. That's the theory of reminding jurors that your clients helped select them:

> You are John's jury. You are Fiona's jury. You saw the three of us during jury selection discussing who should be on this jury. They believed back then you would be fair. They believe that now.

That kind of recognition (begun during voir dire) creates friends—the kind you'll need during deliberations. It also reminds jurors that they aren't debating esoteric legal issues, but a life-changing decision affecting the very people who helped select them.

c.   Make your best case first.

You may be anxious to anticipate an argument about a bad fact in your case, or to respond to one that's already been made, but don't do it too quickly. Make your best case first. It calms the dialogue, clears the air, and prepares jurors to accept your explanation of whatever those bad facts are.

2. Arguing the evidence: Logos.

The order in which you argue the evidence takes on a life of its own, creating passion and commitment as the logic mounts. The added burden during closing argument is to weave all that well-organized evidence into the court's instructions and the jury questions.

a. Organize the evidence into arguments.

By carefully organizing critical evidence, you create a roadmap through your argument, eliminating the need to argue from your notes. You don't need notes, anyway. After all this time, the argument is inside of you. All you have to do is follow those neatly stacked exhibits, excerpts, and graphics—they'll take you where you need to go. Besides, there is something less than inspiring about a lawyer who dramatically argues, "There is no more important issue than this," and then shuffles through the pages on his Big Chief tablet, looking for the rest of the sentence. Then again, maybe I'm being judgmental. To some, it may be perfectly understandable that a lawyer forgot why his client came to court.

b. Answer the jury questions for them.

At some point you must tell the jurors how you want *each* question answered. It will be a lot easier to convince them if you've "talked the talk" from day one, asking questions and obtaining answers in the words and phrases that they will find in the judge's instructions. Then, it takes only a short leap for them to fill in the blanks exactly as you suggest.

However, since jurors aren't allowed to take notes during argument (what you say still isn't evidence), make those answers memorable. Create a chart on butcher paper. If there are five jury questions, number it 1 through 5 down the left-hand side. After you've filled in every answer, as you argued each question, the chart will look like this:

Figure 8.1
Chart of Jury Questions

1. *yes*
2. *no*
3. *yes*
4. *yes*
5. *$1.2 million*

That should be sufficient for the jurors to remember the answers you suggest; however, you don't have to stop with the chart. Create a mnemonic, or, if the glove doesn't fit, offer a rhyming scheme, such as the "No, No, Zero" I suggested for the answers in the Sakowitz case.

In many jurisdictions, you are not allowed to tell jurors the effect of their answers. That makes it critical to underscore the importance of answering each question the way you want. For instance, a neutral-sounding jury question about the date an injury occurred may not sound to a friendly juror like anything that she should argue about with your enemies during deliberations. However, the wrong answer knocks you out on the statute of limitations—or, if you are the defendant, the wrong answer keeps you in. When you tell the jurors how to answer that question, emphasize that it is "critical" to your case. Maybe some jurors will figure that out themselves, but you can't take the chance.

When you get to the dollar amount of damages, do the math for the jury, especially if the numbers are large. Go through it step by step. Use a calculator in front of them, so they can see that your conclusion is reliable. Fill in the blanks. Use a red marker so that the numbers will stick in their minds, or urge them to write it all down. (I know I said jurors were perceptive. I never said they were good at math.)

c. Explain the jury instructions.

Be careful not to misquote the law as you explain it. Don't even paraphrase it. Read the definitions verbatim from the charge, and let the jury and opposing counsel see that is what you are doing. Even if you make an innocent mistake, you leave yourself open to a humiliating objection that you misstated the law—the last thing you want said at any point in the trial, but especially at the end.

d. Too much detail is the death knell.

Some lawyers believe that you must repeat every argument and theme three times if you are to win. But by closing, saying something once is usually plenty to make your point. By then, jurors generally understand the evidence—especially in long trials. They interpret repetition as condescension—your vote of no confidence in them. Paring down the evidence delivers a punch, and a message: that you believe that they "got it," and if not, that they can figure it out. Thank the jurors all you want for their attentiveness, but what they really need to hear is an argument that assumes their intelligence.

Cases generally come down to just a handful of exhibits and some key testimony—no matter the thousands of pages produced. Be selective about the evidence you argue and make it stick. Pound home your best points from cross. List the significant exhibits by number on a sheet of butcher paper. Circulate a couple brief documents to the jury. If a document has a distinguishing feature, like a line drawn through it, or handwritten notes across the top, point it out. But never burden jurors with documents that they won't need to decide the case.

You should also use demonstratives sparingly. Each one should make an important point, and make it clearly. This is a time for straight talk, not high tech.

Some years ago, Harry Reasoner, former managing partner of Vinson Elkins, tried an antitrust case against several railroads. Each railroad president was deposed, and since none of them came to the trial, they appeared through video excerpts. Each president's memory was afflicted, oddly enough, in the same way. They couldn't remember anything clearly—especially about meetings they had with one another. For closing, Harry extracted excerpts from each of their videos, and merged them into a single 20-minute tape—a fugal chorus of "I don't know" and "I can't recall." The video, one of a handful of graphics in his close, was painful to watch, like those tobacco executives denying before Congress that cigarettes are addictive. The jury went out angry and came back quickly—with a verdict of $325 million.

Just being aware of the need to keep things simple helps make it happen. However, as an incentive, remember: When you get mired in detail, you don't just lose momentum—you lose the jury, too.

e.   Highlight misstatements and broken promises.

There is no case as easy to win as when the jurors distrust opposing counsel, and no greater source of that distrust than a lawyer's misleading statements. If your opponent failed to deliver on a significant promise that he made during opening, or has misstated the evidence at any time during the trial, get a transcript of what was said, and have it enlarged or project it on a screen. Make him squirm under the weight of his own words.

In *Sakowitz,* the plaintiff's lawyer told the jury during opening that he would bring the plaintiff's mother, Lynn Wyatt, as his first witness, to "set the record straight" about my client's alleged wrongdoing. Instead of bringing her live, he presented her testimony through a videotaped excerpt from her deposition. (See p. 41, "Excerpts must be accurate.") The tape, however, omitted any of her favorable testimony about her brother (my client), Robert Sakowitz—and there was plenty of it. Immediately after counsel played his excerpt, the judge allowed me to play ours—which included the omitted testimony. By the time our tape was over, the case was, too.

In a last-ditch attempt to undo the damage the tape had done, the plaintiff called Mrs. Wyatt live as his only rebuttal witness. During closing, I used her appearance as a springboard to remind jurors of the misleading tape:

> You know the problem—why they brought Mrs. Wyatt back? Because the videotape of Mrs. Wyatt's testimony, which he played the first day of this trial, was misleading . . . do you remember? [T]hey played the part . . . that had [Mrs. Wyatt] saying, "I didn't know anything about RTS Leasing [one of her brother Robert's private investments], nobody told me, I was unaware, didn't know anything about it." Then we played our videotape and, sure enough, Mrs. Wyatt admitted, not only that she knew about RTS Leasing—but that Robert himself had told her about it. It was in the minutes of the board of directors meetings.
>
> So it is clear, the real reason they brought her back down here is that her videotape is an absolute disaster for the plaintiff's case. Why else do you snip and edit in such a deceitful fashion? Why? There's no point in it. (Objection by counsel: sustained).
>
> I apologize to counsel, but I'll leave it to you to judge the accuracy of the plaintiff's videotape.

In a commercial case, counsel must never make a significant misstatement for another reason. When you represent a business rather than an individual, jurors are inclined to equate the lawyer's behavior with the client's. During opening argument in the Samsung case against Texas Instruments,[6] defense counsel made several significant misstatements. The case settled just before closing, but should the opportunity ever arise, I still have the blow-ups of what he said, which the jury would have been able to read them from their homes, much less the back row. It would have been an easy argument:

> Counsel told you the first day that Samsung dumped microchips on the American market, and was sued by the Justice Department, along with Japanese chipmakers. Take a moment to read his words. You learned quickly that was a false statement. In fact, counsel was forced to admit that he was wrong.

---

6. See p. 255, "Seamless transitions from opening arguments to the first witness."

What does that say about the defense of this case? It says "A," they didn't do their homework; "B," they wanted to enrage you against Samsung in the opening moments of trial; and "C," that the defendant's fraud has continued into this courtroom.

Linking counsel's failures to the party he represents—if your argument's not too personal—doesn't paint with too broad a brush. More than one juror has said to me, derisively, about an opposing counsel, "the company sure picked the right lawyer."

3. Finish strong: Pathos.

As you near the end of your closing, do not meander in search of a place to stop. Have in mind arguments calculated to stir the jurors to a great verdict. If the final moments aren't the time to strip the bark from the trees, to say what is in your heart, then when? But say just what needs to be said, and sit down.

a. Empower the jury.

There are several ways to tell the jury how powerful they are, like the time-honored "you are the sole judge of the facts." But standing alone, that comment is more obsequious and abstract than useful. They already know that they are powerful. It is up to you to tell them how to exercise their power—and why they should.

In *Sakowitz,* the opposing lawyer, a devout man, had described himself as a "Christian with a capital 'C,'" I was told, on an elevator carrying several jurors. So I knew what was coming. However, never underestimate an Old Testament lawyer with a New Testament wife. The night before closing argument we found a perfect quote. I knew I'd find a way to work it in:

> I may not be, as [opposing counsel] said, "a frustrated Baptist minister," but I know what the Bible says when it talks about wealth. It says that it is easier for a camel to get through the eye of a needle than a rich man to enter the Kingdom of God. The Wyatts may not know this, frankly. They have had entree all their lives to whatever they wanted. They have never suffered as Robert has. . . . There have been no "no's" in their lives. They have always gotten what they wanted.
>
> Only you can tell them "no." Only you for the first time in the history of their family can say, "You've gone too far this time. . . . You didn't bring us any facts. . . . You didn't know what you were talking about. You brought us snapshots. Mr. Sakowitz brought us history."

If they didn't know before, the jurors knew after that argument that they had the power to do something they had never done before. They could tell a bunch of rich people, "No."

Sometimes, jurors will be reluctant to use their power—especially when cases are highly publicized, fearful that their decision will leave them open to criticism from family and friends. Be aware of those outside influences— the "jurors" not seated on your panel. In the Westinghouse case, tried in a county dominated by the power plant and its employees, that would have been a significant problem. In such situations, help the jurors anticipate the heat they might face:

> Being the sole judge of the facts means your decision on how to vote, is yours alone. That is what your oath as a juror requires of you. To deliberate with other jurors, and then, to vote your own conscience. You don't have to answer to your neighbors, or even your husband or wife. Once you leave this courthouse, you don't owe an explanation to another living soul. You just have to be able to look at yourself in the mirror and say, "I did the right thing."

That argument is also similar to the one that you would make to hang a jury, should you ever decide to try. Although a rarity in civil cases, there are times when a defendant would be better off escaping with no verdict at all, just like a defendant in a criminal case. However, all it takes is one juror to hang a criminal jury, because, unlike civil cases, the verdict must be unanimous. Obviously, in civil trials, you'll have to convince more than one member of the jury to hang it. If that's ever an option, take that last argument— an appeal to the juror's conscience—a step further. Steel the jurors who favor your side against the pressure of those who don't:

> If your conscience tells you to vote "no" and everyone else says "yes," then stick to your guns. Deliberate and discuss the matter, but if you still feel the same way, vote "no" until hell freezes over. That is what you swore to do when you took your oath as a juror. You are not required to surrender your conscience.

In every case I know about, when a plaintiff's verdict is reversed, the defendant does better the second time around—usually settling the case for less than the jury awarded. I can't imagine that the same wouldn't be true if a civil jury hung—leaving the plaintiff with a delay until the next trial, and all the time and expense to face again.

b.   Empowering a particular juror.

During voir dire, you may have tried to influence the choice of the presiding juror by singling out favorable panelists. ("If your fellow jurors ask you to serve as foreman, would you accept?") During closing argument, you can suggest who that person should be, but do it as subtly as possible. If you show your hand, you will offend just about everybody—including your nominee.

Try burying your "nomination" in other comments. For instance, you can say that the jury has, "collectively, more than 500 years of experience, 32 children, and 12 different jobs. There is even a *lay minister* on this jury." Of course, you can't mention the juror by name, but singling him out with a passing reference may be enough to get that juror elected. Even if not, your mention may be enough to make a friend.

c.   Be reasonable, not dismissive.

As a defense lawyer, your candor about your client's responsibility (to the extent he is responsible) and your decency toward a badly damaged plaintiff buy you credibility with the jurors. Consider the argument defense counsel in the MoPac wrongful death case could have made, had he not chosen to blame the accident entirely on Mrs. Lemon:

> Would it have been safer to have automatic gates at the crossing? Without a doubt. But you have heard enough testimony to know that MoPac can't afford to signalize all 14,000 crossings in this state, and in fact, has no legal obligation to do so. That doesn't make Mrs. Lemon's death, or Missouri Pacific's part in it, any easier for anyone to bear.
>
> You heard what MoPac's district manager said on the stand: "If the company had reason to believe this was an especially dangerous crossing, it would have installed an automatic gate years ago." But there had been only one minor accident at this crossing in 53 years. Now, ladies and gentlemen, fairness, and the law as His Honor will instruct you, require you to consider all the facts surrounding this tragic accident. Was MoPac's crew responsible for her death? Yes, of course, to some extent. But the fact that there was no gate at the crossing does not make MoPac the only responsible party. Was Sharon Lemon also responsible? Of course. Does that make her anything less than the incredible wife and mother we have learned she was? Of course not. It makes her human—and every human being makes mistakes. Mrs. Lemon had been across that intersection by her husband's count at least 100 times at night. She should never have driven that fast across those tracks. She should never have tried to beat the train. For those reasons, when you come to question number 7, I am asking you, in fairness, to hold Mrs. Lemon 75-percent responsible.

When you make an argument that is reasonable, and not dismissive, what plaintiffs label "the defendant's long list of excuses" become solid defenses. If you are too defensive, blaming everything on the other party, when your client has real exposure, the jurors will be furious. Besides, if you think about it, that's the way life is most of the time—there's plenty of blame to go around. Which is why it's called *contributory* negligence, not a finding of *all your fault*.

d. Save the most dramatic argument for last.

If there's a rule for the last five minutes, it's to pull out all the stops. That's what I intended in the final moments of the *Sakowitz* argument—that and a little revenge. The plaintiff's lawyer could not have found a more hateful thing to say about Robert Sakowitz than that he had betrayed his father—and he said it often during trial. That was hard to hear, knowing how close the father and son had been. So, I decided to let "Mr. Bernard," as Robert's father was known by his employees, tell the jury how he felt—and how they should answer the questions. Because I slipped in and out of his character, I have included references where necessary to indicate whether it is Mr. Bernard, or me, talking:

> The answers to each of these jury questions, we feel, are very clear, but I would like to answer them in a little different way. Counsel has said that the only way that we could possibly find out what Bernard Sakowitz had to say was through his will. I don't think that's true . . . I almost feel Mr. Bernard's presence here in the courtroom. I believe I know what he would say if he were asked to answer these questions.

The first jury question was whether Robert breached his fiduciary duty by failing to disclose his private investments to the family:

> Douglas Wyatt would ask his grandfather, "What about all the self-dealing?" And Mr. Bernard would say, "Douglas, I encouraged Robert to go into personal real estate transactions. The board knew all about them."
> [Berg] Douglas, didn't you hear what your grandmother, Ann, said on the stand just yesterday—that she and your grandfather wanted Robert to have a nest egg outside of Sakowitz? Didn't you hear, didn't you read the board of directors' minutes? . . . Robert was on the record with his deal in Tulsa, with his deal in Dallas, with his deal in NASA, and the San Antonio transaction, too.

If that first question were answered "no," the jury would then skip to question 4, which asked if there had been gross misconduct or mismanagement of the estate. To prevail, the plaintiff had to prove either that Robert commingled his funds with Sakowitz, Inc.'s, or that there had been "imprudent expansion" of the stores:

Next issue, was there commingling? Douglas says "[R]obert put a million dollars into the business and later took it out and put it into [a private investment]." Mr. Bernard would say, "Wait a minute, wait a minute. . . ." And he would have to remind Douglas, as I will, of the testimony of Sakowitz, Inc.'s chief financial officer—Mr. Sachs. He sat on that stand and said, "We were always careful not to commingle. We kept Robert's funds segregated from the business's—including that million-dollar loan he made to the company." And Mr. Bernard would ask, "Douglas, why try to punish Robert for that?" . . . And Mr. Bernard would say, "Shame Douglas, shame. . . ."

[Berg] There was no commingling. It is a figment of Douglas's rather vivid imagination.

Douglas would then say to his grandfather, "But what about all this imprudent expansion?" To which, I think it would be very clear, Mr. Bernard would say, "Listen, Douglas, *I* started that—no wait a minute, I didn't start the expansion, your great-grandfather Tobias did. He had a store going in Houston before the one down in Galveston was destroyed. We had a store on Main Street, then we went to the Gulf Building, then we opened Post Oak, then we opened . . . Douglas, what are you talking about? All the expansion was approved of by the board of directors."

Then I paused for a long moment. . . .

And you know what else Mr. Bernard would say? He would say, "I raised that boy. I pushed the gavel to him [in a board meeting] when I resigned as CEO. I said to him, Robert, you have the family's trust and love, and I admire you and respect you." And he would say, "I love you son. You did exactly as you were supposed to do. You have never betrayed me. You have never for a moment, done anything but act in the interest of your mother and your family."

Then, he would put his arm around Robert's shoulder, and he would say, "So you lost the business—start another one." That's what Mr. Bernard would say.

I know that there were objections that could have been lodged, but the judge wasn't going to stop me without one. Moreover, given the voluminous board minutes reflecting his dad's votes, and his mother's testimony about how "they" felt, the judge may not have stopped me even with an objection. That made it possible for me to put the love of a father and son front and center in the crowded courtroom. That was not only important in persuading the jurors, but also, after the public battering he had taken, important to Robert, too. I had no doubt that every word I said was true.

With minutes remaining, I reminded the jurors once again of the first words I had spoken to them:

> I said at the start I didn't know whether this suit was filed for sport or for spite, but it's clear now that this has been a spiteful lawsuit—and that your time has been wasted. Please answer question 1—was there a breach of fiduciary duty?—No. Number 4, was there misconduct or mismanagement? Answer, no. Number 5, are there any damages? Answer, zero. To them all, please answer: *No, no, zero.*
>
> And if you do that, if you will do that, you will give Robert Sakowitz and his family something they richly deserve—another chance and peace of mind.

I ended as I had begun, standing behind Robert and his family seated at the table, making of the case the family affair it really was, making no distinction between the member who'd been sued—Robert—and the members who'd also been harmed—his mother and wife. There is no better time than the waning moments of a trial to embrace your clients once more, and to ask the jurors for their help in lifting the burden a lawsuit becomes.

V. WHEN YOU SIT DOWN

A. The Arguments You Forgot

The regrets begin the minute you sit down. Every argument that you meant to make but didn't comes rushing to your mind. You listen nervously to the plaintiff's close, making an occasional objection when he goes out of bounds. Then, with both sides finished, and the judge's instructions in hand, the jury files out. You search their faces for clues as they leave.

Throughout deliberations, you must remain near the courtroom in case the jury has a question, so that you can argue about the answer. More important, you must be in sight so that as the jurors come and go, they will see that you and your client are still there: a reminder of how much you care. Besides, you couldn't go back to work if you had to.

B. When the Buzzer Sounds

When the jury retires, you will want your clients to be able to say, "No matter how this comes out, I know that you did everything you could to win my case." More important, you will want that to be true. Even so, if you lose, there is little comfort in that compliment, nor much consolation in the cliché that "the lawyer doesn't make the facts." Unfortunately, trial lawyers write their personal history from their last verdict forward. The object of the exercise is to win.

Waiting on a verdict is always nerve-wracking, and *Sakowitz* was no different. However, after they returned from dinner—jurors aren't likely to miss a free meal—the buzzer sounded twice. They had a verdict. It took a while to round everyone up, maybe 20 minutes. Finally, the jurors filed back in. Even now, a decade later, I can see the reassuring looks on their faces as they walked to their seats, many of them smiling and laughing in our direction. I remember thinking what Haynes always says: "A laughing jury won't hurt you."

The room fell absolutely silent, save the judge's time-honored question: "Mr. Foreman, have your reached a verdict?" The lay minister rose, and replied, "We have, Your Honor." "And how do you say, Mr. Foreman?" "No," "No," "Zero," he answered to each question, and bedlam, as they say, broke out in the courtroom.

C. Justice Delayed: A Postscript

At dinner with my family and Robert's a few weeks after the verdict, I wondered aloud what was taking the judge so long to rule on Douglas Wyatt's motion for new trial. "You watch," Ann Sakowitz said, "he's going to grant a new trial." I assured Ann, somewhat testily, that wasn't going to happen; that there was no error in the record. But, a few weeks later, the judge set aside the verdict and granted a new trial.

I was outraged—and went to work to overturn his decision. Over the next few months, I discovered that the judge had a personal relationship with a family friend of the Wyatts, a one-time reporter, who told the *Houston Press* that she had talked with the judge about ghostwriting a book on his high-profile cases. I immediately noticed her for deposition, where she testified that the first person she contacted after receiving my subpoena was the judge. She testified that she had met privately with him in her home during the period of time the motion for new trial was pending, to discuss the book, and that the Sakowitz case was to be included in it. She also testified that during that same period of time, she had dinner alone with Douglas Wyatt, and, among other things, discussed the motion for new trial. There was more, but that was enough. I moved to recuse the judge, and to set aside his order granting a new trial, arguing that the book gave him a financial interest in the outcome of the case. The motion was denied, and the decision affirmed in the intermediate appellate court and the Texas

Supreme Court. Saying he felt vindicated by the rulings, the judge attacked me for creating a "sham issue," and resigned from the case, "to eliminate that sham issue."[7]

In a last-ditch attempt to reverse the ruling on the motion for new trial, I filed in federal court for a stay of the state court retrial, which, because of the federal anti-injunction statute, was unlikely to succeed. At the same time, convinced that Robert was walking into a trap, I encouraged him to get the case settled. However, without leverage and facing a new trial, he couldn't get it done. Then, four days before the retrial was scheduled to begin, Judge Melinda Harmon, a conservative jurist who would later gain fame presiding over the Enron class actions and the criminal case against Enron's accounting firm, Arthur Andersen, granted our injunction. *The Houston Chronicle* reported:

> Because of [Judge] Gregory's and [the former reporter's] relationship, Harmon wrote, "There is a substantial likelihood that Sakowitz can show at a hearing in an unbiased forum that Judge Gregory was disqualified from granting a motion for new trial."[8]

With Judge Harmon's ruling in hand, 18 months after the verdict, Robert got the case settled. The assets were divided and the estate dissolved.

---

7. *Judge decides to quit Wyatt-Sakowitz case,* Houston Chronicle, May 5, 1992, Business, at 1.

8. *Judge halts Wyatt-Sakowitz retrial,* Houston Chronicle, October 23, 1992, section A, at 31.

Epilogue

Years ago, I asked my son Gabe to do some research for me. I was interested in learning how our part of the profession, trial law, came to be. What he found was impressive. I was struck by how far back our roots go, especially the pre-Christian era in Athens and Rome, where jury trials began to take on the shape of what we do today. But, even more stunning, in 1500 B.C., 3,500 years ago, certain citizens of Abyssinia "spoke with the hand of another"—representing neighbors in boundary disputes before ruling councils. It is that, "speaking with the hand of another" that elevates what we do from a craft to a calling.

When John Steinbeck received the Nobel Prize for Literature, he said he "roared like a lion with pride in his profession." As I hope that this book makes clear, that is how I feel about ours. For one who began the practice when trial lawyers were among the most admired people in this nation, it has been especially difficult to watch our profession vilified. Yet, the ultimate victims are not we trial lawyers, but jury trials themselves. Swept up in the anti–trial lawyer hysteria that began in the 1990s, jury trials are diminished in the public's mind as vital to a free society.

It seems to me that the greatest challenge for the next generation of trial lawyers will be to win back the public's respect. So, each time you walk into a courtroom, walk in well-prepared, exquisitely skilled, and proud of what you do. Maybe the most effective way to convince the American people of the value of jury trials, and of what we do, is to convince them 12 at a time.

Index

About the Author

David Berg is a member of the Texas and New York State Bar Associations and the founding partner of Berg & Androphy, located in Houston and New York City. He is recognized in the 2003–2004 edition of *Best Lawyers in America* in three trial law specialties: business litigation, personal injury and civil litigation, and criminal defense. In 2002, *The Texas Lawyer* named Berg to the list of five "Top Notch" trial lawyers in plaintiff's civil litigation in Texas. In 1992, *The National Law Journal* included him in its annual list of the nation's top-ten civil trial lawyers and in 1993 listed him as a member of the nation's "Who's Who in White Collar Defense." *Texas Monthly* wrote that "Berg's style and courtroom victories put him in a league with Texas's legal legends," including Joe Jamail and Richard "Racehorse" Haynes.

Beginning his career as a civil rights lawyer, Berg has since tried virtually every kind of case, many of them featured in this book. Since 1991, he has tried civil cases almost exclusively.

Mr. Berg graduated from the University of Houston Law Center in 1967. He is a Fellow of the International Academy of Trial Lawyers. He has served as a Special Counsel for the Texas State Bar Commission on Lawyer Discipline, a pro bono group that prosecutes lawyer misconduct. He is a frequent CLE lecturer on trial skills.

Mr. Berg has published dozens of articles and essays on legal and general topics in such publications as *Litigation Magazine,* the *New York Times,* the *Los Angeles Times,* and *Newsweek.*

Mr. Berg is married, to Kathryn, and has three children—a daughter, Caitlin, and two trial lawyer sons, Geoff and Gabe. He is based in Houston and New York and has a national practice.